Spiritual Education in a Divided World

In this era of globalisation debate has turned to the vital need for a thorough understanding of its impact on the spirituality and health of the youth of today.

Spiritual Education in a Divided World recognises the urgent need for effective research in this area and takes an interdisciplinary approach to tackle some of the key questions.

The book is divided into distinct sections to aid a clear understanding of the topic

- Research and training issues with practical professional experiences and leading international experts, such as Zygmunt Bauman and Mary Grey.
- How globalised patterns of economics, conflict and consumerism are affecting the spirituality and imagination of children, young people and their families.
- Critical evaluations of practical responses from both research and professional experience.

Readers in professions across teaching, youth work, social work, chaplaincy, nursing, mental health, as well as those concerned with community economics and environmental issues, will find in this volume an exciting, diverse and coherent collection of essays which can offer wider perspectives on their work.

This book was previously published as a special issue of *The International Journal of Children's Spirituality*.

Dr Cathy Ota is Director of the Working With Others Research and Education Unit at the University of Brighton, UK. She is co-editor of the International Journal of Children's Spirituality.

Dr Mark Chater is curriculum adviser with responsibility for Religious Education and spiritual and moral development for the Qualifications and Curriculum Authority of the UK, and an Associate Research fellow of Bishop Grosseteste University College Lincoln, UK.

Spiritual Education in a Divided World

Social, Environmental & Pedagogical Perspectives
on the Spirituality of Children and Young People

Edited by
Cathy Ota & Mark Chater

Routledge
Taylor & Francis Group

LONDON AND NEW YORK

First published 2007 by Routledge
2 Park Square, Milton Park, Abingdon, Oxon, OX14 4RN

Routledge is an imprint of the Taylor & Francis Group

© 2007 Cathy Ota & Mark Chater

Typeset in by Plantin by Genesis Typesetting Ltd, Rochester, Kent
Printed and bound in Great Britain by MPG Ltd., Bodmin, Cornwall

British Library Cataloguing in Publication Data
A catalogue record for this book is available from the British Library

ISBN 10: 0-415-39191-1 (Hbk)
ISBN 13: 978-0-415-39191-7 (Hbk)

International Journal of Children's Spirituality

VOLUME 11   NUMBER 1   APRIL 2006

Special Issue: Spiritual education in a divided world: Social, environment and pedagogical perspectives on the spirituality of children and young people

Guest Editors: Cathy Ota and Mark Chater

CONTENTS

Preface

All but one of the articles in this Special Issue were contributions by scholars to the Fifth International Conference on Children's Spirituality, which took place at Bishop Grosseteste College, Lincoln, UK, in July 2004. This Fifth Conference in the series took place against a background of very serious social, economic and religious conflict in the world. Many of the papers at the Conference reflected this situation by addressing spirituality from diverse national, anti-consumerist and politically radical stances, in addition to a continuing interest in the nature and praxis of spirituality and spiritual pedagogy and a revived interest in addressing spirituality with integrity and truthfulness about contextual factors such as oppression, diversity and the power of markets.

We are privileged that Professor Zygmunt Bauman and Professor Mary Grey, who gave keynote addresses, have contributed to this issue. We are also grateful to the other chapter authors who contributed to the Conference: Joyce Mercer (USA), Ping Ho Wong (Hong Kong), Daniel Scott (Canada), Joyce Bellous (Canada), Jacqueline Watson (UK), Clive Erricker (UK), Cornelia Roux (South Africa), Marian de Souza (Australia) and Karen-Marie Yust (USA). We greatly appreciate the additional contributions of Raven LeFay (UK) and Helen Johnson (UK) who could not attend the Lincoln conference, but whose work adds important dimensions to the discussion.

The importance of this volume is that it brings together, for the first time, the work of a collection of scholars responding to the challenge of looking at spiritual education through social and economic eyes. As in previous issues, the diversity of disciplinary approaches, stances, questions and conclusions is among the strongest, most distinctive and exciting features. That challenge, we believe, takes two forms, made evident in the two sections of this issue. The first is to understand and name the various pressures impacting on spiritual education. We describe this task, in the title of the first section, as 'diagnosis', and we are pleased to note that the contributors use several disciplines—among them, sociology, theology, language and philosophy of education—to frame the debate. The second challenge is to draw conclusions about the paradigms of a politically aware spiritual education, one that reflects consciousness, that does not cease from critically examining its aims, uses of language and pedagogical approaches, all of which are inevitably value-laden. We describe this task, in the title of the second section, as 'praxis', and again we offer no single blueprint (for we believe there is none), but rather a collection of perspectives on practice from many national contexts, gathered with the hope that, through them, the professionals and academics working in this field will be stimulated to further engagement and learning in their practice of spiritual education in a dangerously divided world.

Cathy Ota
Mark Chater

Diagnosis

Introduction

Cathy Ota

If we wish to engage with and explore spiritual education we are also required to listen to and recognize the experiences of others around us. To understand and offer a spiritual education for children and young people we are compelled to acknowledge and work with their experiences and lives. One way of achieving this is to enter into dialogue with the children themselves; to talk and listen to what they are telling us about their relationships and what is important to them. Another avenue is to consider the broader context within which children and young people live and have these relationships. For every child and young person these relationships and experiences will be different; differences that also mark out social, cultural, religious and economic divisions. To engage with our children and young people, to be able to offer them any meaningful and relevant spiritual education (however we conceive it), we have to be aware and sensitive to the realities of these lives and divisions.

The contributions in this diagnostic section draw from a range of disciplinary and international contexts including sociology, theology, language, social theory and philosophy. Their voices expose and critique the spiritual manipulation of us all and, in particular, children. Zygmunt Bauman considers the globalized nature of our consumerist economy and its impact on children and their carers in creating a spiritual poverty. Also offering a critique of the global market-place and consumerism, Mary Grey highlights the different economic contexts of children's lives. She offers a Christian liberation theology for children as a way of rediscovering and re-enchanting childhood. Joyce Mercer also addresses the reality of the global consumerist economy regarding children and their parents, this time framing her observations and analysis within a specifically US perspective. She also identifies a commodification of spirituality itself within the US and calls for greater awareness of its problematic and constructive effects.

Raven LeFay brings a very different environmental and ecological voice to this diagnostic section. She examines and offers a critical analysis of how environmental issues within Western mainstream education serves the capitalist and colonial interests of corporations. In her challenge, she provides a vision for a radically different ecological education. Mark Chater also addresses education systems, focusing on discourses of violence that permeate all aspects of education language. In analysing this violence, he considers how spiritual education can critique, transform and create peaceful cultures in our schools and education curriculum. Finally, Helen Johnson reflects on political and social understandings of identity, citizenship and spiritual education that are also informed by her personal experiences within the UK, and specifically in London. She questions how schools and spiritual education can build a shared identity and social cohesion in the face of terrorist acts—the 'ultimate disregard' of the feelings and rights of others.

Citizenship, identity and understandings of relationality within a globalized, consumerist-driven market-place that frames and oppresses us is a recurring theme across each of these different contexts and voices. They expose the social, economic and spiritual costs to our children and us. In locating spirituality in a truly divided world we must consider our response and find ways for spiritual education to engage with these realities.

Children make you happier ... and poorer

Zygmunt Bauman*

Childhood and desire

Having children costs money—a lot of money. Having a child portends (for the mother, at least) a considerable loss of income and simultaneously a considerable growth of family expenditure. Unlike in times past, a child is a consumer pure and simple—it won't contribute to the family income. The charity Daycare Trust calculates that the average price of a nursery place in Britain for a child under 2 grew by the end of 2002 to £134 per week, as against the average British family income of £562 per week (Carvel, 2004). Hundreds of thousands of families are already condemned to the life of poverty. Hundreds of thousands more watch their plight and take note.

In our market-ruled society every need, desire or want has a price tag attached. Things are not to be had unless purchased, and purchasing them means that other needs and desires must wait. Children are not an exception—why should they be? On the contrary, they would leave more needs and desires waiting than almost all other purchases (and no one could tell how many and for how long). Having a child is presenting a hostage to fate or mortgaging your future, yet you have no inkling how large the repayment of your mortgage loan will be and how long it will take to repay.

*1 Lawnswood Gardens, Leeds LS16 6HF, UK. Email: Janzygbau@aol.com

The total price is not fixed, your obligations are not explained and there is no 'money-back guarantee', in case you are not fully satisfied with the product.

In a society of buyers and sellers such reasoning sounds credible. But it does not seem to be the whole truth. The reading public pays keen attention to popular theories about love, lust and children, embracing each theory with enthusiastic zeal. For example, an expert in addictive behaviour attributes 'falling in love' and 'being in love' to the excretion of oxytocin in the brain. This is a chemical that 'makes us enjoy sex' (Spicer, 2004). The brain has internal drug factories that cause chemical cocktails to be released, activating dopamine, which makes us ecstatically happy when we are with the person we love. The snag is that the drug is produced only for a limited time—as if it had been designed to keep the couple together for as long as it takes to have sex and then raise a baby to a safe level—about two years. Or again, a rehabilitation of lust, one of the seven deadly sins, has it that we should welcome its pleasures for their own sake (Honigsbaum, 2004) and not be ashamed.

The public response to these and other messages is a most important phenomenon in its own right—a puzzle that needs to be reflected on. There is only one explanation: since as a rule people tend to listen most eagerly to such messages as they want to hear, the public's attentive response can make sense only in so far as those statements fit closely with some explicit or half-conscious wishes. I suggest that the messages (and plenty of similar examples exist) receive such grateful acceptance because of their promise to mitigate and placate the spiritual torments many people nowadays go through, and which they try to shake off or stifle in vain. 'In vain' because the distress is genuine and will not go away without an effort most people feel too inept to make or reluctant to take.

One kind of distress is a side-effect of living in a consumer society, in which the roads are many and scattered but all lead through shops. Any life pursuit, and most significantly the pursuit of dignity, self-esteem and happiness, requires market mediation; and the world in which such pursuits are inscribed is made of commodities—objects judged, appreciated or rejected by the satisfaction they bring to the world's customers. If objects fail on their promise, if the satisfaction is not complete or not as big as expected, the customers return to the shop and expect their money back. The offending objects—not living up to their promise, too awkward for trouble-free use or squeezed dry of the pleasures they were capable of giving—are disposed of. One does not swear oaths of loyalty to things whose sole purpose is to satisfy a need, desire or want. Risks cannot be avoided, but the dangers seem less once commitment is denied. This is a comforting thought, but it is also pregnant with distress when those 'things' for consumption are other human beings. When it comes to humans, commitment is hard to avoid, even if unwritten and not duly endorsed. Every encounter leaves behind a sediment of human bond, and that sediment thickens in time, enriched by memory. Interaction has no natural end; ends can only be artificially contrived, and it is far from obvious who decides when that end has arrived, since (to apply consumerist concepts) in human interaction both sides are, simultaneously, consumers and consumed, and the sovereignty of the consumer can be claimed by both. Established bonds may be broken, and further interaction refused, but not without the bitter after-taste and a feeling of guilt. It is difficult to double-cross moral conscience.

This distress might be avoidable in a world less liquid than ours—a world changing less rapidly, one in which objects of desire do not change so swiftly or lose their allure so tragically, and a world in which human life does not seem to be split into a series of self-contained episodes and meanings. But no such world is available—and overwhelming odds militate against the exemption of human bonds from the rule of consumerist cognitive and behavioural patterns.

Indeed, the more liquid the world, the greater is our need for firm, reliable ties of friendship and mutual trust. Friends, after all, are people on whose understanding and helping hand we can count in case we stumble and fall, and in the world we inhabit even the fastest runners and most sprightly skaters are not insured against that eventuality. On the other hand, that same liquid world privileges those who travel light; if the changed circumstances require us to move fast, long-term commitments are difficult to untie and may prove a cumbersome burden. There is no good choice, then. You cannot eat your cake and have it—but this is precisely what the world in which you try to compose your life presses you to do.

Childhood and the market

Into such a world children are born, in such a world they grow, and into such a world they are expected to seek admission. Children watch us and learn. They take to heart what we adults do. After all, we are the authority. We represent the world. Jean-François Lyotard, the acknowledged spiritual father of the postmodern turn in our perception of the human world, insisted that it is the lot of children to represent humanity most fully: 'shorn of speech, incapable of standing upright, hesitating over the objects of its interest, not able to calculate its advantages, not sensitive to common reason, the child is eminently the human because its distress heralds and promises the things possible' (Lyotard, 1991, pp. 2–7). This was not Lyotard's discovery; he merely restated a modern preoccupation with the gap yawning between the imagination and innocence of children and the mundane routine and corruption of most adult life, and with the careless way in which the spiritual powers and creative potential of children are thoughtlessly squandered. He went on to comment sadly that all the efforts of society, all the socializing pressures, bodily and mental, whether by design or default, are aimed at streamlining a process called maturation, that is of leaving childhood, with its all-too-human qualities, behind. As if the logic of human society were to run away from humanity.

Society shows little hospitality to those 'not sensitive to common reason', and is downright hostile to those 'not able to calculate [their] own advantage'. Society does not take lightly to an infinity of possibilities; what else is any social order about, if not the cutting down of the number of possibilities, and stifling all the rest? The essence of all socialization is a lesson in realism: to the newborn, its newcomers, society offers admission on condition that they accept the right of reality to draw the line. The line separates some possibilities now regarded as power-assisted probabilities from all the others, authoritatively decried as being misbegotten, vain or downright antisocial.

Since the early modern discovery of childhood as a separate and unique stage of human life, society has eulogized children for qualities (such as free play and a spirit of amity) sorely missing in adults. But at the same time, children have been viewed with deep suspicion: after all, the life of adults requires that free play is either shunned altogether or relegated to leisure time, at all other times replaced by discipline and routine; and the spirit of amity is securely constrained in the straitjacket of contractual rights and duties. Children are not to be trusted and left without vigilant supervision; 'raw childhood' needs to be processed and so 'detoxified'—purified of its natural ingredients that society would not wish or be able to ingest. In practice if not in theory, childhood is not treated as a haven or shelter, but as a simulacrum of adult life.

The kind of end-product which this processing is intended to achieve depends on the capacity in which members of society are called to service. For a better part of modern history, the part marked by massive industrial plants and conscript armies, society has shaped and groomed its male members to work and soldiering: obedience and conformity, and endurance of drudgery and monotonous routine have been the virtues cultivated. Fantasy, passion, a spirit of rebellion and reluctance to fall in line were the vices to be exterminated. It was the body of the would-be worker or soldier that counted; it was the spirit that had to be silenced, and once silenced, could be left out of account as of no consequence. A society of producers and soldiers focused its reprocessing of childhood on the management of bodies, making them fit to inhabit their natural habitat: factory floor and battlefield.

The era of the producers' society, in the prosperous West at least, is over; we live now in the society of consumers. The natural habitat is the market, the virtue to be cultivated the compulsive and addictive urge to buy. The mortal sin that needs to be exterminated, or punished by exile or banishment, is indifference to market-managed seduction or lack of resources. Accordingly, a society of consumers focuses its reprocessing of childhood on the management of spirits, to make them fit for their natural habitat, the shopping mall. Never mind the bodies—drilling them is old hat, for the 'great novelty' is the conquest and redeployment of the soul (Dufour, 2003, p. 10), betokening nothing less than 'battles over the nature of the person' (Cook, 2004, p. 149).

In a book with the tell-it-all title *What kids buy: the psychology of marketing to the kids,* Dan Acuff (1997) presented a comprehensive strategy for invading and conquering, then managing the 'kid market'—heretofore, fallow or barely cultivated land and with well-nigh infinite profit-making potential. He explains to future invaders how to create, develop and market products and programmes targeted at young people from birth through to the teen years. Acuff, and probably most of his readers, believe that by converting children to the spirit and practice of consumerism they perform a moral task, just as the pioneers of capitalist industry two centuries ago believed themselves to be moral missionaries while filling their mines and mills with child labour. Those pioneers kept children's wages so low that their long hours at work became a necessity to be obeyed as long as they lived. Today's moral missionaries, the marketing practitioners, try instead to generate in children a state of perpetual dissatisfaction by stimulating desire for the new and redefining what preceded it as useless junk—the ultimate purpose being to reproduce the cycle of perpetual desire in which consumer capitalist childhood is embedded (Bauman, 2003).

The moral act of marketing to children has itself been re-branded, re-founding children's sacredness not as romantic innocence, but as possessing a knowing and choosing self:

> The world of peer evaluations of children based on goods, media characters and product knowledge … is increasingly coming to stand for the norm to which children and parents must conform if they are to have a 'healthy' social life. (Cook, 2004, p. 150)

The commanding role of commodity markets in raising, educating and forming children—the 'commodification of childhood' (Schor, 2003, p. 7)—is rapidly expanding and self-replicating. Children are viewed by their parents as knowledgeable about currently binding and passé fashions, and are increasingly consulted by parents when a shopping decision is to be made. And children increasingly have direct autonomous purchasing power from the primary school age (McNeal, 1999). Consumerism conditions or trains the child (Schor, 2005). It has destabilised older, more institutional identity formations such as family, church and school, and so created a vacuum that it then hurries to fill (Davis, 2003). Major selling brands deliberately take on the role of emotional connection points that allow wearers, for instance, a sense of meaning, or even foster a religious loyalty (Kunde, 2000).

Conclusion: sequestered spirituality

In this context, the child's soul is besieged by the pressures of an expansive and invasive market, stripped of its normal familial and social defences and made more vulnerable by the reversal of authority and command structures. Children's homeless and free-floating needs are harnessed to the 'great brands'; human loyalty is replaced by brand loyalty in shaping the life expectations and skills of the consumers.

There is ample research evidence showing that 'insecurity—both financial and emotional—lies at the heart of consumerist cravings' (de Angelis, 2004). There is a need for psychology to shift its focus from individual behaviour to the social settings in which a child becomes a compulsive shopper or consumer. Children are the victims of corporate culture, and should not bear the whole blame.

Spirituality may be a child's birth gift, but it has been sequestered by the consumer markets and then redeployed to lubricate the wheels of a consumer economy. Childhood, as Kiku Adatto has suggested, has become merely a preparatory stage for the selling of the self, as children are trained to see all relationships, including friendship and family, through the prism of marketing-generated perceptions and evaluations.

Notes on contributor

Zygmunt Bauman is Emeritus Professor of Sociology at the University of Leeds. Born in Poland in 1925, he has held academic posts in the Universities of Warsaw, Tel

Aviv and Leeds, as well as numerous faculty memberships and honours from universities in Europe and North America. He has written on postmodernity, moral values in society, the holocaust, freedom, globalization and class. From his many published works, those which most closely touch on the themes discussed here include *Intimations of postmodernity* (1992), *Postmodern ethics* (1995), *Postmodernity and its discontents* (1997), *Globalisation: the human consequences* (1998), *Liquid modernity* (2000), *Liquid love: on the frailty of human bonds* (2003), and *Wasted lives: modernity and its outcasts* (2003).

References

Acuff, D. (1997) *What kids buy: the psychology of marketing to the kids* (London, Free Press).

De Angelis, T. (2004) *Consumerism and its discontents.* Available online at: http://www.apa.org?moniotor/jun04/discontents (accessed 14 July 2005).

Bauman, Z. (2003) *Wasted lives: modernity and its outcasts* (Oxford, Blackwell).

Cook, D. (2004) Beyond either/or, *Journal of Consumer Culture,* 4, 147–153.

Davis, J. (2003) The commodification of self, *Hedgehog Review,* 5(2), 44 ff. Available online at: http://www.viginia.edu/iasc/hedgehog (accessed 14 July 2005).

Dufour, D.-R. (2003) *L'art de réduire les têtes: sur la nouvelle servitude de l'homme libéré à l'ère du capitalisme total* (Paris, Denoel).

Carvel, J. (2004) Childcare rises to 25% of income, *Guardian,* 26 January.

Honigsbaum, M. (2004) Don't you want me, baby? *Observer Magazine,* 8 February.

Kunde, J. (2000) *Corporate religion* (London, Pearson).

Langer, B. (2004) The business of branded enchantment, *Journal of Consumer Culture,* 4, 251–277.

Lyotard, J.-F. (1991) *The inhuman: reflections on our time* (Cambridge, Polity Press).

McNeal, J. (1999) *The kids market: myths and realities* (New York, Paramount Market).

Schor, J. (2003) The commodification of childhood: tales from the advertising front lines, *The Hedgehog Review,* 5(2). Available online at: http://www.virginia.edu/iasc/hedgehog (accessed 14 July 2005).

Schor, J. (2005) *Born to buy: the commercialised child and the new consumer culture* (Riverside, NJ, Simon & Schuster).

Spicer, K. (2004) Love is the drug, *Observer Magazine,* 9 May.

The disenchantment and re-enchantment of childhood in an age of globalization

Mary Grey*

Globalisation: the new religion

Here, I am not concerned with the dominating form of globalization as unregulated global capitalism. The word itself evokes a certain glamour. Heather Eaton wrote:

> Ideologically, it appeals to a sense of adventure, entrepreneurship and superiority; with inviting expressions about global prospects for business, such as 'gateways to the world, go global, track global competition, spread global wings, crossing international borders, and becoming master of one's domain. (Eaton, 2000, pp. 42–3)

Anthony Giddens highlights the excitement conveyed through being in control of the new global arena. He alludes to the new knowledge economy, with financial markets at its leading edge: 'Financial markets today are stunning in their scope,

---

*West Mill, Fullerton Road, Wherwell, Hampshire SP11 7JS, UK.
Email: marygrey@rivertest.fslife.co.uk

their instantaneous nature, and their enormous turnover' (Hutton & Giddens, 2000, p. 1). This is a world in which transformations happen at the level of everyday life, and in which all borders can come down, although old inequalities persist and new threats arise (Hutton & Giddens, 2000, pp. 3–4).

What is important for spirituality is that the focus on new centres of power, such as transnational corporations, the World Bank, IMF and WTO, has meant that the notion of what 'life' means has shrunk to the business model of life:

> Implicit in that business is the greatest possible model of life; far superior to governments, nationalities, cultures ... There is no talk of differentiated and diverse cultures of people, of ethnicity or gender, of animals and land, of national or international regulation or indeed that there is any genuine limitation to this frontier of capital exchange. This 'globe' of which they speak is an utter abstraction with no accountability to anything but economics. (Eaton, 2000, p. 43)

It is also a drastically shrunken notion of economics, made possible by the separation of money from real commodities, manufactured goods and agriculture. All this has led to the overwhelming suffering of poor countries the world over but especially the Two-thirds World, and specifically through the continuing debt crisis, with a direct impact on our theme.

But one project has always and continues to dominate the phenomenon of globalization with an almost bewitching effect: that the contemporary crisis is, at heart, a spiritual one is manifested by the fact that global capitalism in its idolatry of money is a religious phenomenon, *a crisis of the spirit dressed up as economics.* Through the pursuit of money it has hijacked our imaginations and desires, a Disneyfication on a massive scale. We have become addicts. There is no space where we can stand outside, at least, that is what we are led to think. We are *be-wildered*,[1] captive in a wilderness where old values appear derisory and archaic.

The magic of global capitalism has succeeded in spinning an all-encompassing web, a corporate enslavement to money, sex, alcohol, drugs and shopping, or a concoction of all of these. Inside this web we—and now especially children—are indeed bewitched, and robbed of heart, health and wholeness. This addiction has all the trappings of religion. *Tesco ergo sum* is one expression of the recent, all-pervasive, claim to self-definition. Shopping-malls encourage even openly a spirituality of shopping.

But in psycho-spiritual terms, what is destructive is that this addiction has hi-jacked our imaginations, cheapened and vulgarized aspirations of fulfilment, mutuality and intimacy. It has substituted yearning for the infinite and experience of the sacred, for an insatiable, endless grasping for some new consumer good. This global economic system absolutely depends on adults never being satisfied with the new car or TV, and children being desperate for the right trainers, designer T-shirt, mobile phone and latest Barbie doll: for, to maintain itself, globalization must continue to feed us with insatiable desires for the next brand. This is a:

> deep cultural pathology ... When the power of ecstasy is subverted into destructive channels, then, as in the Roman world, we are in a disastrous situation. (Wilshire, 2000, p. 25)

We have become sleep-walkers, hypnotized, walking round in a semi-trance, living in the collective market-driven dream, characterized by erotic dysfunction (McIntosh, 2001, p.107). Mammon is a control freak:

> He must get richer, exponentially ... or else collapse into a crater-like bankruptcy of the sou ... He must keep sucking all attention to himself because he requires total spiritual presence - worship. (McIntosh, 2001, pp. 107–8)

Harvey Cox describes how the discourse of Mammon is comparable in scope—if not profundity—to the *Summa* of Aquinas, or the works of Karl Barth. At the apex of the system is the market as god, a market with divine attributes, we are assured, even if not visible to us, with its own liturgies, sacraments, priests and seers of its mysteries. Even the domain of spirituality is not immune from the market, since previously unmarketable states of grace, such as serenity are now appearing in its catalogues. What was once only to be acquired through ascetic disciplines like prayer and fasting are now commodified through aromatherapy or 'a weekend workshop in a Caribbean resort with a sensitive psychological consultant replacing the crotchety retreat master' (Cox, 1999, p. 8).

Children and the market: childhood's disenchantment

Children are adversely affected by the market in two ways: as victims and as consumers. Because of the market's relentless pursuit of profit, children in many countries play a vital role as cheap labour. In fact, 250 million children worldwide are involved in labour, many of them in dangerous and exploitative conditions. In agricultural areas it is expected that children will help in the fields, will take care of sheep, goats and younger siblings (affecting girls especially) and who will inevitably miss out on schooling.

Whether we refer to the street children of Latin America; children exploited through pornography, trafficking and prostitution; children abused or bringing up their siblings in Aids-stricken Africa; children as refugees and asylum-seekers, and denied education because of the need to work, the global problems are horrific. A quick look at the websites of, for example, Christian Aid or Save the Children, conveys the impression of brave attempts to remedy a situation spiralling out of control.

This story illustrates the crisis: a young East African woman, China Keitetsi, (now 27), was born in a village near the south-western border, where she was cruelly treated by both her father and stepmother and ran away from home at the age of 9. But she was found by look-out soldiers of the National Resistance Army, the guerrilla army of Yoweri Musuveni, now Uganda's president, and forced, along with other children, as young as 6, to be a soldier. The children were given guns and told that the guns were their mothers. To lose or damage a gun carried penalties of beating, being rolled in mud an, ultimately, the firing squad (Keitetsi, 2004). The army was her home until she was 19 years old, when she escaped. Abused by officers and forced to have sex— China now has two children—the girls were forced by day to act like boys, but their roles were reversed at night. Many children did not survive, either they died in skirmishes or took their own lives. And there are an estimated 300,000 child soldiers across the world.

This story points to the diverse and often tragic realities of children's lives across the globe. Poverty, gender, wars, environmental disasters, caste and social position, and lack of legal protection, all determine the contours of a child's world. And now market forces, competition and profit are forcing half the world's children into degrading work and the other half into consuming the products.

Children and the market: children as consumers

Let us step to the other side of the picture and, specifically, the brave new world of cyber-space:

> A child clicks an icon on her computer and is immediately transported to a richly graphic, brightly-coloured, interactive children's playground on the World Wide Web. Bathed in psychedelic colours of hot pink, lime green, and lemon yellow, the site's home page serenades with whimsical tunes and beckons with vibrant flashing signs. 'Bug your buddies with creepy-crawly e-cards made by you', says one. 'Zap your friends with Wacky DigSig cards made by Fruit Gushers and Fruit Roll-ups', urges another. One click on 'play', another on 'buzz', and the child is invited to display her own artwork in 'Kids' Gallery', or 'hang-out' with the site's web characters, Devin, Jessie and Zach. (Montgomery, 2002, p. 189)

It is unquestionable that these interactive features have an enormous and rich potential for education. My concern here is their vulnerability to commercial pressures and what affect this has on children's worlds and spiritualities. In the USA a growing number of children have access to their own personal media devices:

> Among children aged 6–17, for example, 86% have access to a VCR (23% in their own rooms); 70% have a videogame system at home (32% in their own rooms). 50% have a TV in their own room; 40% have their own portable cassette or CD player; and 35% have their own stereo system. (Montgomery, 2002, p. 191)

But research also shows that time spent in front of the TV is declining, whereas time spent in front of the computer is shooting up: 'In 1998, according to Jupiter Communications, approximately 8.6 million children and 8.4 million teenagers were online … expected to grow to a combined 38.5 million by 2002' (Montgomery, 2002, p. 191).

Sociological and demographic factors (including divorce) have combined to produce a situation where children's spending power has increased so that children under 12 now control or influence the spending of almost $500 billion. A new kind of marketing, called interactive and relational, has become interwoven with children's online culture. Despite some legal attempts to curb the pressures on children, the potential of engaging and compelling one-to-one marketing is growing. It is not just that advertising is woven into children's content area, but that in many cases *the product is the content*. Barbi.com would be a good example, where a personalized Barbie can be made and purchased for a particular child. Commercial sites now deliberately home in on a child's developmental needs, for example, the need to belong.

> The belonging (affiliation) need, which causes us to seek cooperative relations, is very strong in children ... Also children are looking for order in their lives. There are so many things to encounter that some order is necessary to cope with them all. A trusting relationship in which satisfying acquisitions can always be expected helps to give order to an increasingly complex life. (McNeal, 1999, pp. 92–3)

It is not only belonging that is vulnerable to commercial pressures. Increasingly storytelling is being targeted: 'narrative strands' within a programme will lead viewers to a 'buying opportunity' and then return them to the story after a purchase (Montgomery, 2002, p. 199).

One website offers replicas of furniture, clothing, cars and producers from such popular teen shows as *Charmed* and *Seventh Heaven*. Viewers go to the website, click on a photo of the house used in the show, a room and then on an item within it. If, for example, the item is a rug, the customer is immediately hot-linked to the retailer's website where the rug can be purchased. The fact that this is steadily growing means that if the Internet is to succeed in offering a rich and diverse educational environment for children, legal safeguards, policies to curtail marketing abuses and commercially free sites, and a debate as to what quality programmes for children should contain, are all urgent. (Of course it has to be admitted, and as John Hull has described, that if the market co-opts the language of developmental psychology and hijacks spirituality, some developmental psychologists have also co-opted the language of the market: Hull, 1992, p. 109.)

The effect of interactive marketing on children has here only been seen from a Western perspective; but there is evidence that in other parts of the world a dependency culture is fostered by the advertising strategies of global corporations. Wole Soyinka speaks of African children lured or coerced into an incurable dependency by which they dare not be seen without a Walkman, and eventually consume themselves to death. The children in marginal cultures in Africa are left: 'at the mercy of the McDonaldised, standardised or routinised information, education, games and other entertainment burgers served in the interests of profit by the global corporate media' (Nyamnjoh, 2002, p. 46). To discover the answers to these dilemmas, let us listen to the voices of children themselves.

What do children really want?

I have shown that children, like adults, can be caught in the market's all-encompassing, addictive web of shopping for fashions, toys and fast food. In its merciless targeting of young people, who are comparatively powerless, in its deliberate Disneyfication of human yearnings and the cult of celebrity to persuade young people how they should look, and what they should buy and eat, childhood itself has been disenchanted and its very existence threatened.

If children themselves were given a chance to say what they really want, what would they say? My first example comes from an initiative of European children—Scottish, German, Norwegian and Danish—who came together to form the International Children's Parliament. These children identified the most important areas that they cared about as being: identity and belonging; feeling safe and being cared for; free-dom; caring for the environment; and having a say. The achievement of these children was to design – imaginatively and creatively - an eco-city in Belfast called Castlevale. The values witnessed to in the project were, for example, cooperative learning by doing, and support for environmental education.

The second, even more ambitious, example is OXFAM's Youth Parliament, involving 145 partners in 61 countries. These young people, largely from poor cultures, highlighted issues more related to sheer survival, like access to water and the violence inflicted on their sense of security (the European children had highlighted 'feeling safe and being cared for', above). They were concerned about the lack of education, about the vulnerability of young people in agriculture, about the traffick-ing of young girls and denial of human rights. Both groups wanted to be listened to.

So any authentic attempt to address the re-enchantment of childhood has to begin from a real-life context. It cannot ignore the children of sectarian Belfast or the child soldiers of Africa, or refuse to separate basic human rights from the longings and dreams that are an inseparable part of childhood. I have experienced often in Rajasthan, in my work for the NGO, Wells for India project, that poor communities are desperate for basic necessities like water, yet sometimes Westerners presume that this would preclude deeper, more spiritual longings. Nothing could be a worse distor-tion: I have seen people continually hungry, practising both great generosity and hospitality—deeply religious values. I have seen them dreaming of lives of dignity and longing for their children to have a better life, and children capable of great fun, curi-osity and a sense of adventure.

The once and future child

The first necessity for the re-enchantment of childhood is that we adults return to our senses, to a different set of values, freed from the market's many-faced addic-tions of drink, drugs, sex and shopping, or a spicy cocktail of all of these. What is essential is to turn again to the earth, to recover the lost connections; our alienation has made us refuse limits to growth, and led us to exploit resources like oil and water, even to the extremes of fighting wars (Grey, 2003). The market's language of desire must be replaced by reflecting what we really long for, like satisfying relation-ships and intimacy, meaningful communities where our values are shared, with working conditions that do not create an unbearable level of stress, enough income to cover basic and leisure needs, and planning for the future. Embracing all this is a desire to maintain and hand on to our children an earth that offers genuine possibil-ities of flourishing.

Secondly, this must also involve us in a Liberation Theology for children. Elsewhere I have called for a new revelation of the Spirit for our times, as the green face of God, the Wild Bird that leads us into the mystery of God (Grey, 2003). If dis-connection with the earth leads to addiction, reconnecting with nature in its many forms—including its wildness/wilderness—is a part of the way forward, not self-indul-gently, but as earthing the dream of new creation. The Spirit as Wild Bird invites us to healing, to a re-enchantment of this world. This is not an invitation to exchange reality for Magic Kingdoms, but to become embodied kinships of women, men, children and earth creatures in a re-imagined and transformed world of sustainable earth communities of healing and hope.

Can the once-and-future child lead the way? What should be the characteristics of childhood (not eliminated by the market, poverty, war or despair)? Surely curiosity, play, joy in the present, a sense of adventure, belief in magic, a sense of the sacred, a love of secret spaces and belief in a special relationship with birds and animals come to mind? If adults can create the conditions and safe spaces for children to experience childhood (and not be forced into becoming soldiers, as described above), we ourselves might be shown the way back to a relationship with the earth.

Safe spaces where children seek refuge can be a means of escape, and for nurturing inner experiences and imagination. But they can also be places for relating to nature in a special way that can be picked up as part of a child's life journey. William Horwood described his loneliness as a boy at boarding-school. His way of coping was to explore, during a break on Saturday mornings, the extensive woodlands in which the school was situated:

> I would wander alone in these woods, for they made me feel safe, and took me out of the loneliness of being with others who did not want me. I did not know it but my dream was that somewhere in those woods I would find a friend. (Horwood, 2000, p. 143)

Through finding a friend, his childhood became re-enchanted. His friend was a paralysed boy in a wheelchair, with whom he could communicate only by eye contact and smiles over the wall at the edge of the woods:

> Though I saw the boy but once a week, in imagination he became my constant companion. My explorations of the wood, of nature, of the advancing seasons, of rabbits, were all with him ... When I went home for exeats and holidays, he came with me in spirit, and tramped along the shingle beaches near my home with me. (Horwood, 2000, pp.150–1)

This friendship had extraordinary consequences. Horwood believes all childhood stories have a mythic dimension and loosely follow what he calls the Campbell–Vogler pattern of the Hero's Journey. This has three phases: the call, then initiation or descent into darkness and, finally, return or homecoming. I agree, provided that we factor in social circumstances (which he does not), and gender sensitivity. Even a cursory glance at mythic patterns shows a proclivity to make the masculine journey the model, something that even Tolkien does not avoid.

The point of this example is that later in life, William Horwood had a baby daughter, Rachel, born with cerebral palsy, and unable to cope with the situation, he walked away from his family. Eventually he returned to the institution where his boyhood friend had lived and found his grave in a woodland cemetery. His name was Arthur Edward, who became the hero of Horwood's novel, *Skallagrigg* (2001). The novel was his way to healing and an expression of his love for his daughter, Rachel. But the book did not sell half as well as his successful previous and later novels. He admits that 'one of the tragedies of modern capitalist culture is that its institutions are more interested in *product* than story' (Horwood, 2000, p. 156).

This gives a clue to the process of re-enchantment. Horwood found a path to healing by telling a story, but the story depended on his re-evoking his relationship to nature as a sacred place, and how this had led him to a special companion. Re-telling Arthur's story, and re-creating Arthur as a mythic figure, enabled a homecoming to the person that Horwood now is. Horwood cited the words of his grandfather, Henry Wheeler Robinson, a scripture scholar, in explanation: 'We see a miracle of transformation wrought in the meaning of things by the attitude of individual spirits and we dare to believe in an ultimate transformation of the meaning of it all by the Spirit of God' (Horwood, 2000, p. 156). Is this not the revelation of the Spirit as the green face of God? I now explore how such a revelation can enable the re-enchantment of childhood, despite the pressures of global capitalism.

The Holy Spirit and the re-enchantment of childhood

What is happening now, though superficially appearing to be a crisis of economics, is actually a deeper crisis, of spirit and of soul that has caused massive broken-heartedness. This spiritual crisis demands a spiritual answer. But why link the human spirit and the Holy Spirit, or use the word 'spirit' to describe human nature? The word 'spirit' touches levels of truth and depth about us, and bores deeper than the superficial level at which we mostly exist, aiming for the truth of human personhood.

'Spirit' is used in thousands of ways: we are 'generous' or 'mean' spirited, in 'low' or 'high' spirits. If someone's spirit is broken or crushed, this means possibly the end of hope. At times the poetic spirit may keep alive emotions and aesthetic sensibilities alive in a more dynamic way than theology ever could. Yet the world of 'spirit' never touches us merely as individuals: through 'spirit' we find *kindred* spirits, (soul-friends?), connect with the 'group spirit', the 'spirit of the age', or *Zeitgeist*, an animating spirit rippling through society that may derive from ancient sources. We also connect—this is especially true for children—with the spirit world and the spirits of the ancestors, with ancient cultures where the spirit world includes the spirits of trees, spirits inhabiting rivers and wells, and with the spirit world of angels and wicked spirits.

In Christian theology the Holy Spirit coexists in the Trinity with the Father and Son, as the 'communing dimension'. Feminist theology attempts to rise beyond the patriarchal imagery, sometimes imaging the Trinity in non-sexist ways as 'Creator', 'Redeemer' and 'Sustainer'. Seeking the dimensions of the interface between 'spirit' and the wider understanding of human and non-human beyond the limits of Christian discourse, and especially as related to children, I use *spirit* here in a widened sense, as Jürgen Moltmann does, as the power of life and space for living, and as a means of splicing the false dichotomies of God or freedom (Moltmann, 1992). Spirit is vitality and energy and is the great awakener to widened visions of truth. The Spirit enables the power to discover cracks in culture and to give birth to alternative cultural expressions, appealing to the disenchanted, as well as to the disenfranchised (Grey, 2000, pp. 58–78.) Perhaps we stand now at the fault-line of this globalized culture, with signs of cracks or chasms in the global dream being sold to us.

How, then, could the Spirit enable the process of the re-enchantment of childhood? First, the language of the spirit seems to find its home at the edges between the personal and non-personal. Wind, breath and fire are all images with a symbolic appeal to a humanity sunk in apathy, yet they are linked too with the non-human. A renewed theology of the Spirit re-awakens the power of imagining a different reality, something that happens naturally with children—witness the phenomenal success of the Harry Potter stories, and the attraction of the Kingdom of Narnia. In children's books and imaginations, both adults and humans lose their dominating role: talking animals are part of the fascinating discovery of the diversity of all life-forms, for whose well-being human beings have responsibility. Children have a unique role in caring for animals, as this nourishes their own sense of growing identity, even providing safe spaces against the cruel world of adults.

Secondly, the spirit is the depth principle of life and here is the first link with God's creative spirit. Can the Divine creative Spirit rekindle the longings and desires of humankind in a way that provides an alternative to the desires stimulated by global capitalism? The Spirit as depth challenges cultures that live to superficiality, to virtual reality instead of embodied relationships. Children's needs are very simple. When adults awaken from this market-driven dream, there is hope that children's voices will be heard.

The Hebrew word for spirit, *ruah*, brings the sense of elemental, creative, formless energy, the energy of connection breathing life into all creatures (Gen. 1:1). This breath of life emerges from chaos and formless void, the *tehom*, or watery chaos/womb and the moist, watery depths. Perhaps, as feminist theologians and some scientists are beginning to suggest, the watery chaos has not so much to be left behind in favour of dryness, separation and order (as the doctrine of *creatio ex nihilo* demands) but to be seen as the creative ground of fruitful interrelating (Betcher, 1993; Keller, 2000). Children need order and structure, but their need for messy, creative play, reawakens us to the often swept-aside creative potential of relating to nature.

The Spirit's role of drawing us into new and deeper forms of interconnectedness is not new: the late John Taylor saw the Spirit as spirit of mutuality, as a dynamic life-force drawing people together (Taylor, 1972). Taylor calls these experiences *annunciations* and understood them as taking place between people. I call them *epiphanies* of the Spirit whose field force of mutuality discloses new epiphanies of connection between the human and the non-human. Children often re-awaken these lost connections for us not only in their capacity to *be* in the present (to recall adults to the intensity of experience hidden in the simplest of activities), but in the way connecting is naturally extended to caring for all life forms.

The Spirit is also understood as the spirit of beauty, an ancient and often forgotten meaning. Beauty, in its numerous manifestations, is linked with the holy and the truthful, and it possesses a unique power to move hearts. The Spirit is *heart-warming*, especially in its awakening responses of wonder in ordinary daily life. This is linked with the Spirit active in the waiting and the attentiveness and the *waiting-on-God* stance of prophetic people, like Simone Weil, requiring listening to and hearing the speech of silenced voices. Paying attention refers as much to the rhythms of nature and the seasons as to political events and human interaction. The Spirit also leads us into the unknown, something that appeals to the childhood quest. Who is not haunted by the words of Frodo in Tolkien's *Lord of the Rings*, now a successful epic film: 'I will take the ring, though I do not know the way'?

The childhood quest is the forerunner of the lifelong journey, and embodies a special quality of courage and idealism, maybe honed and sharpened later (as was William Horwood's). That the world needs to return to the quest is certainly manifested in a global flocking to the cinema to watch the above-mentioned epic. Here cosmic good and evil are ranged against each other, overwhelming evil being symbolized by the power of the Ring to corrupt. Frodo was almost lost, but in the end was led, like Jesus and Moses, to face and confront the destructive powers. The Spirit leads us to respect otherness and difference—even the wretched Gollum was given an opportunity to turn towards the good. Here too the world of adulthood was disenchanted by corporate greed, redemption being offered through the courage of innocent children. But in the end worlds became re-connected, with talking animals and trees, and the final defeat of evil by the power of good. It is reminiscent of the Messianic promise of the Kingdom where finally:

> The wolf shall dwell with the lamb,
> And the leopard with the kid,
> The calf and the lion and the fatling together,
> *And a little child shall lead them.* (Isa. 11: 6)

Conclusion

I have suggested that global capitalism has disconnected humanity from a just relationship with the earth and encouraged the politics of greed and the idolatry of money. As such it has been responsible for the disenchantment of childhood, as children become either victims or consumers. The re-enchantment of childhood depends on adults breaking out and living by a different dream. This entails the establishing of legal, global safeguards for children, and the development of a different spirituality where children are freed to be children again. I offered a theology of Spirit where children themselves are even leading the way.

Calling on the Spirit as the green face of God highlights the need to recover the lost connections with the earth. The spiritual themes of wildness, creativity and embodiment are at home with ecofeminism and ecological theology alike, forming the basis of a liberation theology for children. The prophetic Spirit as green face of God speaks forth a language linking human and non-human, revealing the false logic on which this split is built. May the Spirit of truth lead us into a truth that builds just practices, enabling a flourishing of all life-forms and the re-enchantment of childhood.

Notes on contributor

Mary Grey is Emeritus Professor of Theology at the University of Wales in Lampeter, Honorary Fellow at Sarum College, Salisbury, and Professorial Research Fellow at St Mary's College, Strawberry Hill, Twickenham, UK. Her areas of interest include feminist liberation theology and spiritualities, Ecofeminist theology and the relationship between social justice and theology. She is founder trustee of the Wells for India project. She is the author of *Prophecy and mysticism: the heart of the postmodern church* (1997); *The outrageous pursuit of hope: prophetic dreams for the 21st century* (2000); *Sacred longings: ecofeminist theology and globalisation* (2003) and, with Rabbi Dan Cohn Sherbok, *Pursuing the dream: a Jewish-Christian conversation* (2005), among many other works.

Note

1. I owe this use of 'bewildered' to Thomas Culinan, OSB, from a meditation at the Conference on 'Globalization and the Gospel of Social Justice', Ushaw College, Durham, July 2001.

References

Betcher, S. (1993) Into the watery depths, *Living Pulpit*, April–June, 22–23.

Cox, H. (1999) *The market as God: living in the new dispensation.* Available online at: http://www.theatlantic.com/issues/99mar (acccessed 25 Novemebr 2005).

Eaton, H. (2000) Ecofeminism and globalisation, *Feminist Theology*, 24, 21–43.

Grey, M. (2001) *The outrageous pursuit of hope* (New York, Crossroad Herder).

Grey, M. (2003) *Sacred longings: ecofeminist theology and globalisation* (London, SCM).

Horwood, W. (2000) The novel and the safe journey of healing, in: P. Fiddes (Ed.) *The novel, spirituality and modern culture* (Cardiff, University of Wales Press), 143–157.

Horwood, W. (2001) *Skallagrigg* (Harmondsworth, Penguin).

Hull, J. (92) Human development and capitalist society, in: J. Fowler, K.-E. Nipkow & F. S   er (Eds) *Stages of faith and religious development* (London, SCM), 209–223.

Hutt   & Giddens, A. (Eds) (2000) *On the edge: living with global capitalism* (London,   . Cape).

Kei   2004) Child soldier, *Big Issue*, 7–13 June.

Kel   !000) The lost chaos of creation, *Living Pulpit*, April–June, 4–5.

M   A. (2001) *Soil and soul: people versus corporate power* (London, Aurum Press).

M   (1999) *The kids market: myths and realities* (Ithaca, NJ, Paramount Market).

N   , J. (1992) *The spirit of life: a universal affirmation* (London, SCM).

N   ery, K. (2002) Digital kids: the new on-line children's consumer culture, in: C. von   zen & U. Carlsson (Eds) *Children, young people and media globalisation* (Göteborg, Nordicom/Unesco), 189–208.

Nyamnjoh, F. (2002) Children, media and globalisation, in: C. von Feilitzen & U. Carlsson (Eds) *Children, young people and media globalisation* (Göteborg, Nordicom/Unesco), 43–52.

Taylor, J. (1972) *The go-between God: the Holy Spirit and Christian mission* (London, SCM).

Wilshire, B. (2000) *Wild hunger: the primal roots of modern addiction* (Lanham, MD, Rowman & Littlefield).

Capitalizing on children's spirituality: parental anxiety, children as consumers, and the marketing of spirituality

Joyce Ann Mercer*

there is a big emphasis on christian spiri

Children's spirituality is big business these days, particularly in the context of US consumerism. Anyone skeptical of this claim need only make a quick check of Internet bookseller Amazon.com to relieve any doubts. The Internet retailer lists over 46,000 titles for purchase under the category of 'children's spirituality'. While book and video sales in many other categories have dropped or remained flat during the recent global economic slowdown, sales pertaining to children's spirituality and religion appear to be on the rise. The popular US series created by Phil Vischer known as 'Veggie Tales' is only one example of the current commerce in children's spirituality.

Yet who would have thought that a line of videos, books, toys and music for children starring a bunch of talking vegetables who tell moralistic versions of Bible stories would move from evangelical Christian bookstores in the USA to mainstream retail markets in America and internationally? In its first ten years, the company making

*105 Seminary Road, San Anselmo, CA, 94960 usa. Email: jmercer@sfts.edu

'Veggie Tales' products sold over 25 million videos. The latest 'Veggie Tales' movie grossed $24 million in US box-offices and sold more than three million copies on DVD (Smietana, 2004). In addition to such products for which children constitute the direct marketing target, the number of workshops and conferences for parents, educators, health care practitioners and academicians concerned with children's spirituality multiply every year. Without a doubt, children's spirituality is big business at the outset of the twenty-first century.

In this article, I explore the shape of children's spirituality in the contemporary context of globalized consumer capitalism. I do so from my social location as a researcher-scholar, theological educator and practitioner of Christianity in North America. I also write as a mother and an activist whose experiences with marginalized women and children in North America and in various parts of Asia make me deeply concerned with the cultivation of spiritual practices that can be liberatory for children both locally and in other parts of the globe.

In a globalized market economy, the consumptive practices of First World US families and children increasingly depend upon the labour of families and children of the Two-Thirds world. Beginning with a succinct discussion of the commodification of children in the current economic context of late globalized capitalism, I will then explore the commodification of children's spirituality through products marketed for the enhancement and growth of children's spiritual lives. The article concludes with a brief analysis of the impact of such marketing upon contemporary children and their spiritual/religious lives.

Children's spirituality: defining and commodifying the intangible

Children's spirituality is more easily described and observed than defined. For purposes of this article, I am using the term 'children's spirituality' to refer to that aspect of children's lives connecting them to a wider sense of meaning-making, to relationships with others and to relationships with the sacred/transcendent. Children's spirituality references the lived experiences of children with a network of significant others and with the sacred. It concerns the narrative and symbolic means by which children make sense of their worlds. For many children, spirituality takes shape through the worldview and practices of a particular religious tradition. While, at present, there exists a lively debate among adults concerning the distinctions and commonalities between spirituality and religion, such distinctions are far less salient for children (Barnes *et al.*, 2000; McEvoy, 2003). In this article, therefore, I will use the terms religion and spirituality with considerable fluidity, recognizing that for some children spirituality and religion are synonymous, while for others they are not.

One might be tempted to think that anything as difficult to define and intangible as children's spirituality would resist commodification. Commodification is the process by which a thing or quality becomes objectified as an item available for exchange, acquisition and consumption. And yet, children's spirituality appears to be the *marchandise de jour* for the new century. Obviously, no one wrests something that is 'children's spirituality' from the lives of children and puts it out for sale on store shelves. However, every day countless numbers of parents, educators and others buy music, books, videos and attend workshops, classes and self-help programmes all supposedly aimed at the enhancement of children's spiritual lives. Such products have a market because of the implicit promise that buying them will supply something currently lacking in the lives of children.

How has children's spirituality come to be one among many items for sale? To respond to that question, we need to look at the larger situation of consumer capitalism that is the context in which children's spirituality becomes commodified. While I focus on the U.S. as the context best known to me, writings by European cultural critics such as Zygmunt Bauman (1998) and others convince me of the relevance of the marketing of children's spirituality in other contexts as well. Space limitations only allow the briefest sketch, but more detailed accounts may be found in Harvey (1990, 2001), Stephens (1995), Stearns (2001) and my own longer accounts of the construction of children as consumers (Mercer, 2004, 2005).

New consumption-focused forms of capitalism and the market for children's spirituality

Cultural theorists who track shifts in forms of commerce note that early forms of free market capitalism focused attention on the creation of a new kind of labour market that moved away from 'craft' to mass production. As this early capitalist economy of the late nineteenth and early twentieth centuries developed with new manufacturing techniques such as assembly lines, workers sacrificed their direct relationships to the products of their labour in favour of a new kind of manufacturing process that could produce goods for consumption on a mass scale.

The reward for taking on this often boring, 'alienated' labour was to be found in their access to a higher standard of living through the ability to buy these mass-produced goods that previously would have been luxury items. Households shifted from centers of production to centres of consumption. Children in middle-class and more affluent homes moved from being economic contributors in household economies to being economically useless as producers, but of inestimable social value to families and to market forces as consumers (Zelizer, 1985).

A further economic shift began around 1970, moving towards present market forms often referred to as late or globalized capitalism. This shift is characterized by features such as 'just in time' production, made possible by computers and the global Internet. It involves 'outsourcing' of manufacturing to minimize labour and fixed capital costs. It favours a more flexible labour force—i.e. instead of a stable workforce with mutual loyalty between employer and worker, most workers are 'term hires' who may be laid off easily when production needs or finances change. Similarly, late globalized capitalism is marked by flexible production facilities with equipment that either is easily retooled or inexpensive enough to abandon when fickle consumer preferences shift demands to new types of products.

Along with such flexibility, the role of finance and money markets take on increasing significance, equaling or surpassing the production of goods as the mainstay of the economy. Finally, late capitalism flourishes through a globalized mass marketing strategy based upon multimedia advertising. The market forces of this globalized form of capitalism strongly depend upon maintaining high levels of consumption and the creation of ever-new forms of consumer activity through the stimulation of new desires in consumers, and through a focus upon marketing intangibles such as travel, entertainment and other experiences as opposed to the marketing of tangible commodities. Such a focus broadens the scope of consumer activity.

Consumerism refers to a way of life structured around practices of consumption. These practices are not limited to the moment of purchasing a desired object. They also include processes of cultivating and acquiring desires for consumer goods as happens through viewing advertising images throughout each day; the processes of thinking about, anticipating and planning for a purchase; shopping and buying; using the object; and its disposal. In a consumerist society, the activity of consumption dominates everyday life. It is a source of identity and status, and provides people with a sense of creative power for which the act of choice making is key.

In North America, talk show hosts extol the virtues of 'retail therapy' for beating boredom or depression. Where the slogan 'shop till you drop' draws more smiles of recognition than grimaces of distaste, clearly the act of consumption itself operates as a fetish. Fetishes are objects vested with magical powers to satiate yearnings and desires. The USA and Europe both constitute economic and social contexts in which persons, by and large, organize their lives in relation to consumption, fetishizing not only commodities for exchange, but the act of consumption itself, making these contexts unarguably consumerist societies.

In a time of the decline of social institutions mediating identity, status, and belonging—such as church, affiliation with a single company for career-long employment, and place-based families—consumption also has become a primary way in which persons achieve and mark their status and identity. In the USA brands displayed on clothing create a certain level of 'instant affiliation' among youth on a basketball court who otherwise are strangers to each other. Displays of consumption through the wearing of expensive brands mark a person's social class and status. And in the case of parent–child relationships, consumption on behalf of children by parents/caregivers becomes an important marker of identity and status for parents. A child in designer infant wear both establishes and communicates that the child is of great value to the parents, and that the parents fall into the identity category of doting if not 'good' parents by virtue of how they clothe the child. In this way, children through display of consumption become sources of social capital for their families.

Children play an important role in a society based upon consumer practices, as they now constitute one of the most influential among all market niche groups to which advertisers attend. James McNeal is a professor and researcher of marketing whose career has focused on children. He sees children as a marketing niche of such extreme value that producers-sellers cannot afford to ignore them. McNeal's (1999) well-known formula holds that children actually constitute three markets in one. First, they spend some $35.6 billion of their own dollars every year. Second, they directly influence the spending of another $187 billion by their parents and indirectly influence another $100 billion in parental purchases when parents take children's wishes into account as they make purchases for themselves. Third, children constitute an important future market, among whom profitable brand loyalties may be developed at extremely early ages.

Children's key role in accelerated consumption

Why are children so important as a target group for advertising? If market forces can construct children's identities around practices of consumption, and simultaneously, can use children as motivators and legitimators of the consumptive practices of their adult caregivers, then the market has a ready-made means to achieve the high levels of consumption necessary to sustain profits. As briefly alluded to in the summary of changes marking forms of capitalism, above, in the latter half of the twentieth century the US economy shifted to less stable, more flexible forms of capital accumulation, labour, and marketing (Harvey, 1990). In order to keep up production and, therefore, profits in societies like the US that are thoroughly saturated in commodities, producers and sellers have had to find ways to accelerate consumption.

One obvious way of doing this is to make durable goods less durable, requiring more frequent replacement. What parent has not lamented the rapidity with which new toys made with plastic parts break and must be replaced? Given the high costs of labour and the relatively lower costs of mass-produced goods, generally it is cheaper to purchase a new item than to have the old one repaired, a dynamic that further accelerates consumption in favour of market interests.

Another means of accelerating consumption to sustain the high levels of mass production on which markets depend involves mobilizing the concept of fashion not only in relation to apparel, but for other consumable goods as well. The latest model of computers, for instance, are marketed not only on the basis of their newer performance features, but also as they appear in the latest aesthetic colour scheme of platinum that makes the previous era's white consoles seem hopelessly dated and unappealing. The appeal of constant novelty and change represented in ever more sleek design and colour accelerates consumption far more rapidly than would the actual need to replace a product that has worn out.

In addition to such processes that manipulate commodity durability and aesthetics, however, marketers now attempt to accelerate consumption by creating increasingly narrow age groups to whom they target specific products, and whose occupants of today will need the new products of a more advanced age group tomorrow. 'Growing out' of an age-defined group necessitates replacement of products associated with the former group by new goods that mark one's status of belonging to the new group (Cook, 2000a, 2000b). The invention of the 'toddler bed' in the 1990s is a clear example, before which Western children went from crib or even family bed to their own bed without the need for purchase of yet another intermediate piece of furniture. Suddenly, in order to be good parents in tune with the developmental needs of their children, toddlers 'needed' their own specially sized and styled beds. The role of advertising in stimulating desires for new consumer goods thus rides on the coattails of contemporary parental anxieties not to shortchange their children's growth, to create a new market in children's furniture.

It is not difficult to see how such a strategy of accelerated consumption participates in organizing children into age-segregated niches and constructs them as consumers by marketing directly to them, as well as through them to their parents. The stimulation of desire for new commodities by advertising blurs the line between needs and wishes, while capitalizing on the anxieties of parents to make sure their children have the maximum opportunities for development in the midst of the culture of competition driving American lives. In the case of children, the push for parents to cultivate in their children the early development of every capacity from toileting hygiene, to feeding and reading makes apparent the degree to which even our seemingly most basic needs involve a high degree of social construction driven by market interests.

In this economy, for instance, savvy American parents who are *truly* concerned for their children do not simply provide them with a variety of nutritious baby foods in jars, with smiling, round-cheeked babies on the labels, as did a previous generation of parents. These contemporary parents actively encourage and help their children develop their capacities for more mature eating by purchasing and offering them increasingly advanced, 'graduated' baby foods (there is a line of baby foods marketed under the name of 'graduates'), labelled with a numeric order indicating the child's level of advancement in eating.

An additional strategy used by marketers for accelerating consumption colludes with certain postmodern cultural propensities often expressed in terms of the search for constant novelty, spectacle and an intensification of ordinary experience. This strategy involves a turn from the manufacture of consumable goods to the selling of novel experiences or events through travel and entertainment. Advertisers, for example, persuade parents that theme-park destinations not only provide the excitement and entertainment that will keep children from being bored, but also will be a way for parents to 'create lasting memories!' (an advertising slogan frequently employed), by providing their children with one or another intense experience of pleasure. Parents, ever-more convinced that an important part of demonstrating their identities as good parents is to keep their children entertained, become ready consumers of such experiences.

In the current economy of late globalized capitalism, then, children occupy a key place in the acceleration of consumption. The market for children's spirituality emerges as a part of this wider set of social practices within which market interests in accelerated consumption tap into an ethos in which parents are accustomed to securing the well-being and development of their children through acts of consumption.

The commodification of everything, including children's spirituality

In a sense, the commodification of children's spirituality through the development of products for purchase hinges upon certain slippages in boundaries formerly separating children from market interests. Social theorists such as Zygmunt Bauman (1998, 2000) and David Harvey (1990) note the hegemonic impact of consumer practices on the everyday lives of people, asserting that consumerism, in effect, colonizes all of life and transforms virtually everything into a process of consumption or commodity exchange. This colonization is particularly noticeable in the case of children, who in previous times held a protected status as a vulnerable group of innocents deemed in need of protective isolation from the tarnishing influences of money and market (Zelizer, 1985; Mercer, 2005). Accordingly, children's spaces, such as playgrounds and schools, were also considered off-limits to those who might promote market interests at the expense of susceptible children.

Over time, however, such boundaries began to erode as the entertainment industry began to develop a lucrative market in children's recreation and entertainment, first, through television, and later, through the transformation of children's play spaces from public common park spaces to privately manufactured entertainment spaces of children's theme parks and fast-food restaurant playgrounds (McKendrick *et al.*, 2000). Particularly after the advent of children's television programming in the 1950s and early 1960s, children began to constitute an important marketing niche for advertisers. Now, formerly protected childhood spaces such as playgrounds and classrooms, abound with advertisements and product logos. And, like adults, children's bodies become walking advertisements as they wear clothing emblazoned with company names in large bold letters reading 'Baby Gap', 'Nike' or 'Guess'.

Sometimes this insinuation of the market into children's spaces is quite direct and upfront, such as the infiltration of movie and toy ads on to children's breakfast tables through cereal packaging. At other times, it is more covert, as happens when a major computer company donates computers for public school classrooms and thereby obtains the right to display its logo and other brand publicity throughout the school. Whether overt or covert, both processes are examples of how consumerism effectively colonizes formerly protected spaces of childhood in ways that appear normal or 'natural' enough so as to go unnoticed much of the time (cf. Kasturi, 2002; Schor, 2003).

Having effectively colonized children's educational and play spaces, and thoroughly commodified their experiences through the production of specialized 'necessity' products for children, the globalized capitalist market is now in the position of, again, needing new avenues for maintaining and expanding levels of mass consumption that can support market interests. The marketing of children's spirituality represents one of the newer and most recently mined sites for colonization of children and childhood by market forces. In a social context such as the USA, parents have been 'schooled' by practices of consumption to view consumerism as a primary means of providing for the needs of children. Consequently, the purchase and use of commodities marketed as enhancing children's spirituality, instilling values and virtues, or teaching a basic catalogue of religious stories containing timeless truths, undoubtedly appears as a natural (and necessary) act on consumption on behalf of one's children.

When my twins were born nine years ago, in addition to the many practical gifts we received of items such as diaper supplies and baby clothes, we also were gifted with various presents that I would now classify as examples of the commodification of children's spirituality. Among these was a CD containing 'child spirit music to encourage spiritual qualities of gentleness and peacefulness in your baby' (my babies were rarely either gentle or peaceful in spite of hours spent with this music). We received books designed to 'speak to the inner spirit of your child with their timeless, uplifting stories'. Some of these books still stand on the childrens' bookshelves, alongside copies of 'baby's first Bible' and other items of a more specifically religious nature. We even received a few 'Veggie Tales' music tapes and videos. I do not in any way mean to disparage the goodwill behind such gifts, offered in celebration by people who know that religious and spiritual practice are central in our family life. Rather, I simply wish to point out that the existence of these types of products only takes place in a context in which people believe that children's spirituality can be enhanced and encouraged through the use of certain consumer goods. There is a market for 'child spirit music' only in a situation in which a gap exists (or is perceived) between the spirituality envisioned as important in children's experiences and adult capacities to foster its formation that requires commodity purchase to remedy.

To summarize the mechanism by which the commodification of children's spirituality takes place, the context for such a process is the consumerist economy of late capitalism requiring accelerated consumption to sustain profits. Market forces take advantage of the society's pedagogy of consumption in which parents and other adults over time become well schooled into an ideology that they can secure the growth and well-being of their children through the purchase of consumer goods. In the face of a growing public discourse on spirituality, parents, educators and others concerned with children's well-being consider it an important aspect of children's lives. Market forces insinuate themselves into this space of perceived need, creating new products and stimulating desires for these new products that play upon parental anxieties for their children's development. In many instances, these commodified forms of children's spirituality become fetishized, promising to turn children into value-filled, happy, whole and spiritually well-developed children through the purchase and use of such products.

Some implications of commodified spirituality

I will conclude with some brief comments about the impact of this commodification process on the spiritual lives of children. Some scholars of media and culture may herald the process I have just summarized as a zone of creativity in the development of a genuine 'children's culture' (cf. Jenkins, 1998). They perhaps would view the construction of videos such as 'Veggie Tales' and of children's books that give entertaining access to stories with sound moral lessons as a forward step: such media seem to take seriously children's needs and interests instead of expecting them to deal with adult-oriented forms of religious and spiritual expression. While I remain sceptical of the idea that there is much authentic children's culture or youth culture that is not market generated (see Docherty, 2001), I am willing to grant that there are some positive values in the commodity market associated with children's spirituality.

At the same time, however, I see several critical issues emerging in the processes by which the commodification of children's spirituality impacts their everyday lived spiritualities. First, commodifying anything for mass-market distribution requires making a thing 'generic' enough to appeal to a mass-market buying public. That necessarily means leaving out certain sharper, more nuanced, features in the name of mass appeal. As Vincent Miller (2004) points out in his excellent treatment of how consumer practices shape religious beliefs in the USA, when beliefs are bought and sold at discount department stores in America, the form they can take is necessarily restricted by the need to appeal to the broadest possible audience, to the most bland and generic qualities. For example, the sharp edges of the prophetic tradition in Jewish and Christian religious life would severely limit mass appeal of stories from these traditions, with their persistent critique of power. Consequently, these stories rarely show up in the mass-marketed cannon of spirituality available for purchase.

In order to appeal to a mass-consumer buying public, then, products such as 'Veggie Tales' videos tend to reduce the spiritual traditions they portray to a generic moral lesson (usually, in the case of 'Veggie Tales', on the theme of obedience as one of the highest virtues). Left out are stories of prophets speaking truth to power, as well as more nuanced spiritual visions that issue in socially transformative practices of justice. Both of these are significant in Jewish and Christian religious and spiritual traditions, but the features of mass-consumer marketing preclude their inclusion in the forms spiritual stories can take when on sale. Only certain kinds of stories are being told in these commodifications. The impact on children's spirituality concerns the reduction of internally diverse and complex spiritual traditions to narrow moralisms or only a select type of narrative and symbol (Warren, 1997; Lakoff, 2003). The ability of children to find in such spirituality the kinds of complex narrative and symbolic resources they need for dealing with ambiguity and increasing levels of complexity is similarly restricted.

Second, the context in which consumer products find their use matters considerably for the meanings these products possess and shape (see Warren, 1997, pp. 138–40). Commodified products for the enhancement of children's spirituality generally are purchased for an individual child, and used in the private space of that child's home. Such a context necessarily reinforces internalizations of spirituality as an individual, privatized affair rather than as a practice and worldview developed and sustained within a wider community. The commodifications of children's spirituality that focus on behavioural virtues such as obedience or listening to authority (whether divine or parental) shape a vision of spiritual life as the adoption of middle-class behavioural norms by children rather than as the adoption of alternative visions of new possibilities for well-being and wholeness (Bendroth, 2002; Mercer, 2005). These individualistic engagements with spiritual commodities thus have a domesticating effect on spiritual life and practice.

Third, a key feature of the definition of children's spirituality identified at the beginning of this article concerns children's relationships with a human community of significance and care, with the non-human creation and with sources of transcendence and/or the sacred. Commodified forms of spirituality risk reducing relationships to their use value, and of constructing human relationships as disposable. After all, the worth of any consumer good is measured by its usefulness, whether that refers to pleasure obtained in acquiring it or in some pragmatic good accrued from its use.

When one is finished using a commodity, it may be disposed of. Human relationships with other people, with non-human creation and with God or the sacred, on the other hand, involve many elements that cannot be reduced to utilitarian values. And the treatment of human relationships as disposable goes against the definitional grain of most spiritual visions of human flourishing.

And finally, as sales of products related to children's spirituality increasingly move into the US export market, persons concerned about the negative impact of globalization on local cultures (including local religious and spiritual expressions) will do well to consider the impact of marketing such narrow, US consumer-generated notions of children's spirituality in forms easily taken as normative (video, audio recordings, print media). Rich, local religious and spiritual practices currently being passed on to children outside the USA stand at risk of being replaced by practices of watching animated cartoon characters engage in slapstick humour while promoting spirituality in the lowest common denominator.

Few if any people are in a position to 'opt out' of participating in the current globalized capitalist economy with its commodifications of spirituality, including the spiritualities of children. We therefore have an imperative to become more aware of, and more skilled at reading, the processes by which such commodification takes place and its potential effects (both constructive and problematic) in the lives of children, both in the USA and beyond.

Notes on contributor

Joyce Ann Mercer teaches practical theology and education at the Graduate Theological Union and San Francisco Theological Seminary, California, USA. She is the author of *Welcoming Children: A Practical Theology of Childhood* (Chalice Press, 2005).

References

Barnes, L. L. *et al.* (2000) Spirituality, religion, and pediatrics: intersecting worlds of healing, *Pediatrics*, 104(9), 899–908.

Bauman, Z. (1998) *Work, consumerism, and the new poor* (Buckingham and Philadelphia, PA, Open University Press).

Bauman, Z. (2000) *Liquid modernity* (Cambridge, Polity Press).

Bendroth, M. L. (2002) Growing up Protestant: parents, children, and mainline churches (New Brunswick, NJ, Rutgers University Press).

Cook, D. T. (2000a) The other 'child study': figuring children as consumers in market research, 1910s–1990s, *Sociological Quarterly*, 41(3), 487–507.

Cook, D. T. (2000b) The rise of 'the toddler' as subject and as merchandising category in the 1930s, in: M. Gottdiener (Ed.) *New forms of consumption: consumers, culture, and commodification* (New York, Rowman & Littlefield), 111–129.

Docherty, N. *et al.* (2001) *The merchants of cool* (Boston, MA, WGBH Educational Foundation/PBS Video).

Harvey, D. (1990) *The condition of postmodernity: an enquiry into the origins of cultural change* (Cambridge, MA, Blackwell).

Harvey, D. (2001) *Spaces of capital: toward a critical geography* (New York, Routledge).

Jenkins, H. (Ed.) (1998) *The children's culture reader* (New York, New York University Press).

Kasturi, S. (2002) Constructing childhood in a corporate world: cultural studies, childhood and Disney, in: G. S. Cannella & J. L. Kincheloe (Eds) *Kidworld: childhood studies, global perspectives and education* (New York, Peter Lang), 39–58.

Lakoff, G. & Johnson, M. (2003) *Metaphors we live by* (Chicago, University of Chicago Press).

McEvoy, M. (2003) Culture and spirituality as integrated concepts in pediatric care, *American Journal of Maternal/Child Nursing*, 28(1), 39–43.

McKendrick, J. H. *et al.* (2000) Kid customerquest; Commercialization of playspace and the commodification of childhood, *Childhood*, 7(3), 295–314.

McNeal, J. U. (1999) *The kids market: myths and realities* (Ithaca, NY, Paramount Market Publishing).

Mercer, J. A. (2004) The child as consumer: a North American problem of ambivalence concerning the spirituality of childhood in late capitalist consumer culture, *Sewanee Theological Review*, 48(1), 65–84.

Mercer, J. A. (2005) *Welcoming children: a practical theology of childhood* (St Louis, MO, Chalice).

Miller, V. J. (2004) *Consuming religion: Christian faith and practice in a consumer culture* (New York and London, Continuum).

Schor, J. B. (2003) The commodification of childhood: tales from the advertising front lines, *Hedgehog Review*, 5(2), 7–23.

Smietana, B. (2004) Running out of miracles: big idea creator Phil Vischer had his dream crumble, but he's no longer s-scared, *Christianity Today*, 48(5), 44–48.

Stearns, P. N. (2001) *Consumerism in world history: the global transformation of desire* (London and New York, Routledge).

Stephens, S. (1995) Children and the politics of culture in 'late capitalism', in: S. Stephens (Ed.) *Children and the politics of culture* (Princeton, NJ, Princeton University Press), 3–48.

Warren, M. (1997) *Seeing through the media: a religious view of communications and cultural analysis* (Harrisburg, PA, Trinity Press International).

Zelizer, V. A. (1985) *Pricing the priceless child: the changing social value of children* (Princeton, NJ, Princeton University Press).

An ecological critique of education

Raven LeFay*

The ecological crisis

We live in troubled and turbulent times. A hurricane is raging from the mouth of industrial culture, rending the fabric of life's web, undermining the earth's ecological systems, eradicating species, billowing pollution, depleting resources and crushing communities, and sparking war, terrorism, racism, disease and poverty, and leaving an uninhabitable wasteland in its wake. Our current trajectory of capitalism and consumerism is leading straight down the road to oblivion. Despite the obvious signs of environmental and cultural decline, the crisis is intensifying. In 1993 the Union of Concerned Scientists (http://www.ucsusa.org) released the following statement as a caution to humanity:

> Human beings and the natural world are on a collision course ... If not checked, many of our current practices may so alter the living world that it will be unable to sustain life in the manner that we know. Fundamental changes are urgent if we are to avoid the collision our present course will bring about...Our massive tampering with the world's interdependent web of life—coupled with the environmental damage inflicted by deforestation, species loss, and climate change—could trigger widespread adverse effects, including unpredictable collapses of critical biological systems whose interactions and dynamics we only imperfectly understand ... No more than one or a few decades remain before the

*Treveglos Farm, Zennor, St Ives, Cornwall, TR26 3BY, UK. Email: raven.lefay@virgin.net

chance to avert the threats we now confront will be lost and the prospects for humanity immeasurably diminished ... [We] senior members of the world's scientific community ... hereby warn all humanity of what lies ahead. A great change in our stewardship of the earth and the life on it is required, if vast human misery is to be avoided and our global home on this planet is not to be irretrievably mutilated. (Gerber, 2001, p. 12)

This statement was issued more than ten years ago, and yet still humanity plunges into the abyss. How much time is left before the eradication of all life-supporting systems? The big picture does not look good: 137 species disappear every day; 6 billion pounds of toxic insecticides, herbicides, fungicides and other biocides are pumped into the environment every year (Global Toxics Initiative, 2003); the temperature of the planet is expected to rise by 10 degF during this century (Earth Trends, 2003); and world population growth (currently at 6.8 billion) is expected to reach a staggering 10 billion by the year 2050 (Population Action International, 2003).

A new learning paradigm

In the face of such overwhelming bad news, it is easy to give up hope of making any difference. Yet, if even some of the above prognoses are accurate, we cannot afford to sink into a state of powerlessness and depression. Our response must be urgent, yet also informed and careful. A key problem in forming our response is the nature of the thought processes that must save us. The dominance of Enlightenment-based ratio-nality has led into this predicament, by constructing a world we can manipulate, exploit and control, a place where we are both separate from and superior to nature (Plumwood, 2002). And if reason and rationality (the foundation of Western culture) have brought us into these dire straits, how can we hope that the same thinking will get us out?

What is needed is an intuitive, passionate and embodied response, a radical shift in the dominant Western worldview, a quantum leap in consciousness that will shake us from our cultural malaise and inspire us to take action and build practical solutions for sustainable living. The key to this transformation lies in education. Not the same education that got us into this mess, but a new paradigm for learning as a transforma-tive process, leading to a deep awareness of our interdependent place within the dynamic web of life, and a re-enchantment of the world as a powerful mystery. Education can and must be redefined and transformed to become itself a transforma-tive process, such that we learn to see the world holistically and act to protect, respect and restore the Earth, our living home.

The industrial education system

A critique of mainstream education cannot be separated from a critique of the indus-trial culture: the two are inextricably linked. Both emerged from the shift in worldview that took place around 500 years ago, during the period known as the Scientific Revolution. Before this time, an organic worldview held sway in the Western mind, one where the world was perceived as inherently alive and female, and possessed a soul, the *anima mundi*. But during the sixteenth and seventeenth centuries this organic worldview was replaced with a mechanistic one, marking a transition in epistemological power from religion to science, and a shift from a metaphysical to a physical cosmology. The new mechanistic paradigm has come to permeate every facet of Western civilisation, shaping our consciousness and giving birth to all our institutions, including those of education (Tarnas, 1991; Capra, 1996).

A few Western men laid down the mechanistic worldview—Copernicus, Descartes, Galileo, Bacon and Newton—scientists and philosophers who helped to build a culture based on order, certainty and control. The world was described as a machine. It could be broken down into isolated, independent, indivisible and inert parts that could be studied separately and objectively to reveal the universal laws of nature. The fabric of the cosmos was seen to be fundamentally mechanical and reducible to mathematics—it could be quantified, predicted, manipulated and ultimately controlled for the interests of Western man (Merchant, 1980; Shiva, 1995, 2003).

Analytical thinking (either/or logic) emerged with mechanism as the dominant mode of inquiry, with dualism its conceptual underpinning. The world was decisively split into mutually exclusive categories of object/subject, science/superstition, mind/matter, self/other, man/nature, quantities/qualities, reason/intuition, facts/values, matter/spirit and civilized/primitive, and one set of categories was valued over the other (Plumwood, 2002). These divisions formed structural power relations in the psyche of Western culture that legitimated the intellectual and physical colonization of non-Western cultures and local folk cultures (Plumwood, 2002). Western science firmly established itself globally as the only valid epistemology; all other ways of knowing were undermined as primitive, inferior and unscientific, an assumption that has strong ties with colonialism (Shiva, 1993).

Dualism justified the exploitation and domination of nature; it laid the foundation for the ecological crisis (Merchant, 1980). Nature was perceived to be separate from man, a wild and unruly force that—like women with which it was equated—had to be tamed, subdued and conquered, and bent to man's will for the purpose of creating a 'civilized' world. Furthermore, since the Earth was conceived as dead matter, it could not respond to the ruthless raping of its resources, and a mechanistic, reductionist approach could not bring to light the connection between human action and ecological consequence. The interdependent relationships between the world and humanity became invisible to a limited consciousness that had learned to see the world as a machine. What we do to the Earth we do not do to ourselves.

As the world was being split into smaller and smaller incoherent and independent parts, so was knowledge fragmented into increasingly specialized disciplines. Each discipline consisted of objective, undeniable universal facts that could be transmitted from teacher to student. All subjects were steeped in the scientific method: empirical, rational, reductionist, atomistic, linear and analytical. Subjects considered unscientific (the arts, crafts, humanities) became classed as inferior and accorded a lower place in the social and economic hierarchy. Mechanism, the limited worldview emanating from the minds of a few powerful men, managed to infuse the consciousness of an entire culture, giving shape to a monoculture education system that taught one universal lesson: life is a machine. As mechanicism shaped education, so did education become the primary means of disseminating the mechanistic worldview, creating a monumental positive feedback loop that continues to this day, to reinforce mechanicism and perpetuate the model of mechanistic education.

Undermining common knowledge

While the roots of the modern education system are locked deep in the conceptual bedrock of mechanicism, the actual structure was not laid down firmly until the Industrial Revolution. It was at this time that education as an institution emerged to serve the interests of government and business. The new industrial society required a large workforce of obedient, loyal and dependable people that would be content with work that was repetitive, dull and underpaid. These workers could not be allowed to think for themselves, or else they might come to question the power structures that exploited their labour for the benefit of an elite few. The compulsory education system was thus put in place as the factory for producing a compliant workforce that would turn the wheels of industry.

Education evolved as a process of 'hammering in' and 'moulding' a person, a purposeful design of beating people into the shape of passive workers and consumers in a mechanistic world. It was the tool for programming specific knowledge into the minds of the people, so that they became the cogs that ran the engines of society. People were atomized and isolated, conceptualized as individual automatons that could be neatly slotted into their place in the industrial machine. Through education people learned the primary lessons: to produce, to consume and to submit to an external control. In essence, people themselves became the product, manipulated in the same way that the earth was being exploited: as resources mined in the service of industry.

Prior to the rise of capitalism, common people learned trades from their families and within local communities in the tradition of apprenticeship education. Usually the eldest son was apprenticed to the father in the family business, and the other sons found apprentice positions within the local villages. Daughters were apprenticed with their mother to learn cooking, childrearing, healing, sewing and other household skills. The emergence of the industrial culture and large-scale urbanization combined to weaken these family and community bonds, or break them altogether. In cases where women had previously held power in their communities, with knowledge of traditional medicine and healing modalities, these forms of knowledge were devalued until their wisdom was destroyed, defamed or appropriated by the rising Western male scientific authority (Merchant, 1980). And while the poorer classes of women were allowed to work in industrial factories, it was only in the most menial of positions for the lowest of pay, much less than that given to their male counterparts. A developing and eventually compulsory schooling system stripped people of their traditional knowledge and skills, divided them from each other and their local community, and trained them to become the subdued workforce of the industrial machine.

Modern education and the corporate takeover

Although the contemporary education system has expanded and undergone many changes in structure, it still bears the stamp of its industrial invention. We are still taught not to think for ourselves, not to question the assumptions or political structures of Western culture and not to ponder on whether our institutions might be organized in a more sane and sustainable way. We are still being filled with facts that have no bearing on our experience of real life, that do not help us to understand who we are, or what our ecological impact might be, or whether we have a future on Earth at all. Instead, the core lessons being taught in our schools today are individualism, consumerism, careerism and anthropocentrism. And along with this we are programmed with an unerring faith in the dazzling achievements of technological advancement and the intrinsic value of economic progress.

John Taylor Gatto, an ex-teacher from the USA and a leading voice in the deconstruction of the modern education system, claims that there are seven invisible lessons (1991) being universally taught in the Western curriculum. This research is based on work within the US public education system, but his arguments are equally applicable to the UK National Curriculum, as follows:

1. *Confusion*—a lack of coherence, disconnected facts with no natural sequence or order to classify material or make meaning from it.
2. *Class position*— everyone has their place in class, a number that classifies their intelligence and stays with them throughout life.
3. *Indifference*— the system of bell ringing, ensuring that each student learns that nothing is ever completed of any significance. Students cannot become too involved or interested in any subject since they must move on to the next class and subject when the bell rings.
4. *Emotional dependency*— using a system of reward and punishment, students are kept in a position of powerlessness and are at the mercy of the authority of the schoolteachers.
5. *Intellectual dependency*— students learn to turn to 'experts' to tell them what to do in their lives, rather than finding their own inner wisdom.
6. *Provisional self-esteem*—report cards, grades and tests ensure that students' self-respect depends on the opinions of experts. Self-confident students do not conform easily to the system.
7. *One can't hide*—students are constantly watched and surveyed since they must be kept under tight control. Homework ensures that surveillance takes place outside of school hours. The student has no privacy and learns that no one can be trusted.

Gatto argues that these lessons constitute a 'hidden curriculum' that is essential to maintaining the capitalist consumer culture. By the time we leave school, we are programmed so thoroughly with these seven teachings that most of us unquestioningly take our place in society. Well-schooled people cannot think critically, cannot argue effectively and are unable to act from their own free will. According to social critic Ivan Illich, this is a deliberate strategy by the power holders in the industrial culture, since:

> People who submit to the standard of others for the measure of their own personal growth soon apply the same ruler to themselves. They no longer have to be put into their place, but put themselves into their own assigned slots, squeeze themselves into the niche which they have been taught to seek, and, in the very process, put their fellows into their places, too, until everybody and everything fits. (Illich, 1971, p. 45)

In the past 20 years, education has moved ever more into the realms of commercialization, and become what is now known as the 'education industry', with a fast-growing trend towards privatization, corporate sponsorship, and the selling of skills and knowledge products that demonstrate the market-driven values of the knowledge economy. Students are now consumers, parents are customers, and teachers are employees all servicing the needs of a burgeoning education business. In the USA the industry is estimated to be worth between $630 and $680 billion a year (Light, 1998) and in the UK education has an estimated value of £25 billion a year (Monbiot, 2002). Overall, the global education industry is worth trillions.

Because of this economic power, the education sector has attracted the attention of some very big global players. Working quietly behind the public's back, the Organization for Economic and Cooperative Development (OCD), the World Trade Organization and the World Bank have been enforcing structural changes in education policy to allow big business full market penetration of the education industry. These changes in the education system work in parallel with the economic 'structural adjustment policies' that the OECD, World Bank and other international agencies have laid down to push forward their neoliberal agenda of 'free trade'. This globalization of education is part of a wider economic strategy by powerful transnational corporations to ensure open, unregulated access to the world's markets, at the expense of social and environmental health. Unfortunately, the globalization of education remains largely unchallenged primarily because very few people realize it is even happening or what its long-term implications might be. But, more importantly, it remains unchallenged because it is being heavily presented (by government and business) as a key strategy for maintaining economic growth and competitive advantage in the new knowledge culture of the twenty-first century.

The high incidence of economic and social problems reported in the modern education system has created opportunities for global capital. The need for radical educational reform has become an urgent priority, and big business has exploited this need. The question of why our education systems might be failing, and how this may have roots in its historical development, are not being addressed. Instead we are witnessing a silent corporate takeover. The educational agenda has slipped deeper into the pockets of business leaders with production, profit and control on their mind. According to educational consultant, Stephen Sterling, the changes that are now taking place in education include:

> centralisation of control over the curriculum; weakening of local authority support and control; weakening of networking and collaboration between teachers and between educational institutions; encouragement of traditional teaching methods; heavy systems of inspection; competition between institutions to gain pupils/students and resources; precise control over teacher education; and turning heads and principals into managers. The

analogy with the factory is telling: young people and qualifications are produced; there are precise goals and targets; the curriculum provides directives for each stage of production; and teachers are technicians and therefore substitutable. (Sterling, 2001, p. 40)

Taking over the education industry is a corporate dream. Quick to perceive the benefits of getting a foothold in the system, corporations have produced materials, training, activities and events that ruthlessly promote their goods and services, and spread the ideology of capitalism. Exploiting the lack of government funding, corporations prey on failing educational organizations by dangling carrots of corporate sponsorship and privatization. By giving vast amounts of money to an education organization, or even buying them out completely, corporations can promise these institutions a competitive edge in the market economy, while gaining exclusive access to a pool of passive consumers. Corporations that have unprecedented control over the learning environment are free to mould the minds of students in insidious and unchallenged ways. The sooner they can grab the minds of the people the better, since young minds are more impressionable and will give brand loyalty for life (Beder, 1997).

Already students are bombarded with corporate marketing messages at all levels of the education system. The situation is much worse in the USA and Australia, but the corporate takeover of education is also happening in the UK and Europe. For example, the European Union has decreed that every publicly run school in Europe must be twinned with a corporation by 2010 (Sterling, 2001, p. 40). The most blatant example of corporate marketing in education is the appearance of logos and advertisements in books, videos, cafeterias, student buses, sports facilities, toilets, student bars and even on posters in corridors (Light, 1998). In her book *No logo*, Naomi Klein explores this corporate attack on education, and points out that corporations are no longer content with simple logo branding, but are now 'fighting for their brands to become not the add-on but the subject of education, not an elective but the core curriculum' (Klein, 1999, p. 89).

The US Consumers Union published a report in 1995 which found that: 'thousands of corporations were targeting school children or their teachers with marketing activities ranging from teaching videos, to guidebooks, and posters to contests, product giveaways and coupons' (Klein, 1999, p. 93). These companies publicly claim that they are providing invaluable educational resources, providing a necessary service to impoverished schools, when their real strategy is clearly to capture market share.

Greening education

Corporate messages have become deeply embedded in learning materials, with the most perverse examples being found in the popular sector of environmental education. There has been a growing public awareness that the industrial way of life is seriously threatening the environment, and this, in turn, is threatening the world of business. Public relations companies have realized that environmental education in schools can lead to activist children who then influence their parent's consumer behaviour. Most children care deeply about nature; corporations, recognizing this, are inundating schools with propaganda thinly disguised as teaching materials in an effort to teach children to passively accept the corporate view on environmental issues. As we shall see, some of this material claims to adopt a 'green' stance, while much of it claims objectivity. Most teachers, students and parents do not even realize that this is going on.

In 2001, Scottish Enterprise gave 20,000 copies of a magazine called *Biotechnology and you* to schools. Published by Monsanto, Novartis, Pfizer and Rhone-Poulenc, this magazine openly attacks organic farming, suggests that genetically modified crops are good for us, and further claims Monsanto's best-selling herbicide is 'less toxic to us than table salt' (Monbiot, 2002). The American Nuclear Society distributes *Let's colour and do activities with the atoms family*, in which they state, 'Anything we produce has some leftovers that are either "recycled" or disposed of—whether we're making electricity from coal or nuclear, or making scrambled eggs!' (Beder, 1997, p. 169). There is no analysis of the problems of radioactive waste, only the benefits are proclaimed. International Paper Corporation publishes *Conserving American's forests*, which explains how beneficial clear-cutting is for wildlife and people. Georgia-Pacific, one of the largest paper product manufacturers heavily investing in the clear-cutting of old growth forests in Indonesia, publishes materials that justify their unsustainable harvesting practices through claiming their work promotes wildlife, because:

> When no one harvests, trees grow old and are more likely to be killed by disease, rot, and the elements. Very old trees will not support many kinds of wildlife because the forest floor is too shaded to grow the ground plants animals need. (Beder, 1997, p. 170)

Mobil distributes the free video *Polystyrene, plastics and the environment*, which describes plastic as the ideal product to manufacture, recycle and dump; and General Motors distributes the video *I need the earth and the earth needs me*, to every school in the USA, proclaiming the benefits of oil recycling but without mention of the need to reduce transportation (Korten, 1995, p. 156, and 1999). The tactic employed by these corporations is deception by omission, and their overriding message is that 'chemicals and technology solve our problems, over-consumption is [our] birthright, and what's good for business is good for everybody' (Selkraig, 1998, p. 63).

Some corporations are clearly concerned that environmental education could expose their working practices, and might ultimately undermine their profit margins. They have teamed up with free market advocates, scientists, lawyers, misguided parents and religious zealots to form powerful global anti-environmental education coalitions. Jo Kwong is a member of one of these industry front groups known as the Environmental Education Working Group. He summarizes the main claims against environmental education as follows:

- It is based on emotionalism, myths, and misinformation;
- It is issue-driven rather than information-driven;
- It fails to teach children about basic economics or basic decision-making processes, relying instead on mindless slogans;
- It fails to take advantage of lessons from nature, instead preaches socially or politically correct lessons;

- It is unabashedly devoted to activism and politics, rather than knowledge and understanding;
- It teaches an anti-anthropocentric philosophy—man is an intrusion on the earth and, at times, an evil (Simmons, 1996).

These statements comprise a direct attack on environmental education and are being made by well-funded, industry-led prestigious organizations.

Conclusion: a new vision for education

What is needed to address these difficult times is a new vision for education. The existing education system has co-evolved within the context of the industrial culture, and has been subject to corporate takeover. As such, it is fundamentally flawed, and any reform to existing institutions would be redundant and ineffective. Instead, we need to design and build new learning organizations that have grown from the soil of a holistic, ecological worldview, moving us away from the metaphor of the machine towards embracing the metaphor of the whole, living organism.

The ecological worldview has been emerging over the last century from the fields of ecology, living systems theory, chaos and complexity theory, Gaia theory, eco-psychology, holistic health, ecological design, ecological economics and the sustainability movement. It is a worldview where the Earth is perceived as a whole living being: a vast, complex network of interdependent relationships, wherein everything is connected with everything else. The realization of the integrated wholeness of life is the hallmark of the ecological paradigm: humans are not separate from nature; we are nature. What we do to the Earth we do to ourselves. In some ways, this is a reflection of the perennial wisdom of indigenous cultures and Eastern philosophies, but the ecological worldview is not advocating any romantic return to the pre-industrial age; rather, it proposes an evolution towards a different way of living that is informed by the knowledge of the new living, global sciences.

The principles and patterns of organization that ecosystems have developed over millions of years to sustain the web of life provide the foundation for the creation of a sustainable human culture. If we are to make the shift to an ecological worldview, then the principles of ecology must become the principles of education. That is, the education system must be radically redesigned using ecological principles at every level: curriculum, pedagogy, philosophy, organization, management and architecture, and in its relationships with the wider community and environment (see LeFay, 2003). It is not enough to teach ecology as a 'subject' in a still fragmented and industrially orientated 'curriculum'; education systems must embody ecological principles in their total design. We must learn to create educational communities that model ecological communities, to devise educational structures and processes that are patterned on ecological principles, that mirror the web of life. Using ecological thinking, education systems can be designed to become themselves a dynamic teaching tool for ecological living and literacy (Orr, 1992, 1994).

We are in the midst of a great crisis, a final call to either step into a new way of being in the world or stay where we are. The fate of the Earth is intimately bound with the fate of humanity. Education has the power to answer our plight. The dominant form of education that has evolved from within the mechanistic framework has been responsible for a restricted consciousness that has all but killed our capacity for creativity, holistic thinking and critical debate. A new paradigm of education that enables us to participate fully and responsibly in the world, and is not sponsored or influenced by corporations and consumerism, will be driven by a process of genuine inquiry that seeks to understand the web of life and our place within it. An ecological education such as this would be a powerful force; it would have the potential to facilitate rapid change on a global scale, giving shape to a new consciousness and culture. Ultimately a new ecological education could transform our world and move us towards the realization of a truly sacred and sustainable culture.

Notes on contributor

Raven LeFay holds a BA in 'Culture, Ecology and Sustainable Community: Environmental Arts and Education' from New College of California, USA, and an MSc in 'Holistic Science: Ecological Education' from Schumacher College, in Devon, UK, a community-based living and learning programme for international ecological studies. She recently spent four months living and teaching sustainability in India, during the University of New Hampshire Faculty on the 'Living Routes Ecovillage Education' programme. She currently lives in West Penwith, Cornwall, UK, where she is an active member of local community and sustainability groups, and runs an organic dairy farm with her partner.

References

Beder, S. (1997) *Global spin: the corporate assault on environmentalism* (Dartington, Devon, Green Books).
Capra, F. (1997) *The web of life: a new understanding of living systems* (New York, Doubleday).
Earth Trends, World Resources Institute (2003) *Climate protection in a disparate world*. Available online at: http://www.earthtrends.wri.org/conditions_trends/feature_select_action.cfm?theme =3 (accessed 1 June 2003).
Gatto, J. T. (1991) *Dumbing us down: the hidden curriculum of compulsory education* (Gabriola Island, BC, Canada, New Society Publishers).
Illich, I. (1971) *Deschooling society* (Harmondsworth, Penguin).
Korten, D. (1995) *When corporations rule the world* (San Francisco, CA, Berrett-Koehler).
Korten, D. (1999) *The post-corporate world: life after capitalism* (San Francisco, CA, Berrett-Koehler).
Klein, N. (1999) *No logo* (New York, Picador).
LeFay, R. (2003) *Ecological education: restoring the ground of learning*, Unpublished thesis, Schumacher College, UK.
Light, J. (1998) *The education industry: the corporate takeover of public schools, Corpwatch*. Available online at: http://www.corpwatch.org/issues/PID.jsp?articleid=889 (accessed 1 July 2003).
Merchant, C. (1980) *The death of nature* (New York, Harper & Row).
Monbiot, G. (2002) The corporate takeover of childhood, *Guardian*. Available online at: http://www.monbiot.com/dsp_article.cfm?article_id=481 (accessed 1 July 2003).

Orr, D. (1992) *Ecological literacy: education and the transition to a postmodern world* (Albany, NY, State University of New York Press).

Orr, D. (1994) *Earth in mind: on education, the environment and the human prospect* (Washington, DC, Island Press).

Plumwood, V. (2002) *Environmental culture: the ecological crisis of reason* (London, Routledge).

Population Action International: Environment (2003) Population issues: environment. Available online at: http://www.populationaction.org/issues/environment/index.htm (accessed 1 July 2003).

Selkraig, B. (1998) *Reading, 'riting and ravaging: the three Rs, brought to you by corporate America and the far right* (San Francisco, CA, Sierra Club Magazine).

Shiva, V. (1993) *Monocultures of the mind* (London, Zed Books).

Shiva, V. (2003) *Challenging globalisation: alternative models: lecture notes and discussions.* Ms, Schumacher College, UK.

Simmons, B. (1996) *March/April issue newsletter of national environmental education advancement project: the EE advocate* (Stevens Point, WI, College of Natural Resources).

Sterling, S. (2001) *Sustainable education: re-visioning learning and change* (Dartington, Devon, Green Books).

Tarnas, R. (1991) *The passion of the western mind: understanding the ideas that have shaped our world view* (New York, Ballantine Books).

Just another brick in the wall: education as violence to the spirit

Mark Chater*

Education as inherently violent: discourse analysis

Discourses create worlds, and webs of discourse can create quite coherent nets of meaning. Discourse analysis reveals the connotations of these nets of meaning. It is always a subjective process; my interpretation may differ from yours. But the interpretation has, at least, the potential to resonate because of the common use of the words and phrases discussed (they are picked out in italics in this section) and because of the strong suggestiveness of their use. Occasional metaphors of violence may add up to little more than unfortunate turns of phrase, but I shall show that the present discourse far exceeds that. When leaders and policy-makers in education make frequent use of metaphors of attack, mechanized warfare and military occupation, this adds up to a convincing unconscious demonstration of aggression towards education, and is cause for concern.

*Bishop Grosseteste College, Lincoln LN1 3DY, UK. Email: m.f.t.vhater@bgc.ac.uk

Systems of accountability in education may in themselves be described as violent when imposed without consultation. In the UK, the overwhelming power of account-ability systems leaves no place for professionals to hide from the threat of criticism, of enforced changes to pedagogy, assessment or policy, of special measures or closure. The power to ensure what is called *compliance* implies violence against practices which are not approved. Educational systems require compliance with standards of quality and other specific regulations. To do otherwise is to be deemed *non-compliant* (OFSTED, 2002, p. 101 ff.), and to suffer penalties as a direct result. Some will object that calling compliance a violent word is an overreaction; that it is merely a civil service term in regular use to describe the meeting of minimum standards. But subju-gated people are also compliant, and are made so by superior force. Policy-makers or their agencies create measures that will lead to *modifying the behaviour* of the educa-tion system to achieve what they want (Hodgson & Spours, 1999, p. 137).

Compliance spawns a more casual quotidian discourse of compulsion: What do we have to do?; How do they want us to implement it?; or They will make us change, and similar phrases, are heard—not ironically (although sometimes resentfully) uttered by highly educated and qualified professionals. These levels of compulsion are checked by processes of *monitoring*. This word achieved 500 hits in the British government's educational standards website (DfES, 2005b). Monitoring has become so prevalent that many professionals have forgotten its sinister origins in surveillance. Significantly, there is never a discourse that describes any person or role as a monitor; the act of watching, tracking, checking and reporting is committed by a *monitoring system*, releasing it from any culpability for personal intrusion but heightening the sense of relentlessness. Whereas a human monitor might sleep occasionally, monitor-ing systems never close their eyes. Monitoring leads either to satisfaction or to denun-ciation. It reveals when disobedience or deviation occur. It leaves no place to hide and creates no forum in which to debate. Monitoring is the embodiment of coldness, mercilessness, totalitarianism and the absence of trust. The public *naming and sham-ing* of failure was a characteristic tactic of early New Labour and other national systems (Thrupp, 1998).

Particular agencies will occasionally organize campaigns of intense monitoring of types or categories of educational provision; schools will similarly instigate phases of scrutiny. These *surveys* are conducted like a military exercise, suggestive of an occu-pying power, gazing, checking and in the process dominating a territory. Often, an entire education *sector* will be *surveyed*, thus again, reinforcing a consciousness of occupation, delineation, masterful ownership and imposed identity that comes from colonial discourse. One Chief Inspector of Schools thought it constructive to announce that inspections would no longer be like a *searchlight*, but more like a *laser* (Slater, 2004).

Under this accountability, pedagogy itself becomes an activity of violence. People entering a school, university or profession in one year are a *cohort*; one sees them marching together, trained to move steadily through the system, reliably and obedi-ently and even with pride. Or else they are an *intake*, this being an image from mech-anized industry. A *pupil intake* is raw material entering the mouth of the machine, to be shaped to its master's specifications. It is wheat for the thresher, or coal for the sorter. It is an object; the violence of crushing, breaking or categorization is done to it. Perhaps it is good taste, or perhaps a fear of obviousness, that prevents the discourse from mention of pupil output.

The pedagogical machine, once powered, grinds all. Awkward or resistant materials are *isolated*; leaders promise to *stamp out* or *bear down on* them; teachers and managers are asked to *drive up* standards, which may imply making the machine go faster, or grind smaller. Policy-makers boast of being *tough on* standards, of *rooting out* failure (Learner, 2001). The machine itself is also held in judgement, as its *components* or *units* may be interchangeable or replaceable. Pedagogical systems are operational, and educational managers are those charged with the operating. Both in the examination of the language and in the experience of working with managers, it is hard to avoid the suggestion of the factory floor and the vast machine with its deafening clatter; of the shifts marking the apathetic coming and going of functionaries; of the promoted operative watching for malfunctions; or of the occasional casualty.

If our study of metaphors has led us from the field of war to the mass-producing mechanized factory, military purposes are still in mind. All the time, new educational initiatives are being *rolled out*. The *roll-out* is carefully timed and announced with a flourish. I am not clear about the connotations of this phrase, but I am suspicious of its possibilities. It could suggest the factory product tumbling mightily from the end of the machine; a new pedagogy, training framework or other initiative, designed and manufactured, now ready for transport to the places where it must be used. Freire (1972, p. 53) described as inherently violent the system of dichotomization by which education was manufactured in one place and used in another. Or it could make us think of the armoured personnel carriers, jeeps and tanks that roll from the belly of the cargo plane, down its ramp, across the tarmac and out to the occupied city or sector. Their purpose is to subjugate a people and make them want what the occupying force has. Illich (1971) made the point that schooling sets out to make the young want the society as it presently is.

That the machine is inherently violent, and makes violent things, is suggested in many other pedagogical terms. To summarize points quickly on paper is to use *bullet points*. Bullets are fast; they do their work directly, and are the substitute for extended discussion. When Goering became weary of culture, he reached for his revolver; when policy-makers want no more discussion, they reach for their bullet points. That teaching is defined by *aims*, and learning by *objectives*, is a less pungent reminder that a model of pedagogy is derived from the military strategists. That any form of developmental progress and learning is defined by *targets* reinforces the sense of violent threat. That any changes, interventions and training must have *impact*, and that success is described as *delivery*, sometimes *frontline delivery*, tell us very clearly that a penetrative, destructive process is being conceptualized.

The words confirm each other's purposes. The discourse of mechanized warfare, and of machine production for warlike ends, is inescapable. The violent language is deployed against managers, teachers and learners, and they are made to direct it against each other.

Another vocabulary, in opposition to metaphors of violence, is in use to describe the expectations of teachers' and learners' behaviour in relation to the system. While they may be violent towards each other, they must be prevented from rising up and using the discourse of violence against the war machine as a whole. A gentle language of irenic and communitarian metaphors is imposed on the profession as an expected way to behave. The British government's education department has a good example with its three principal aims, using the verbs *give*, *enable*, and *encourage* (DfES, 2005a). Other key examples are *collaboration*, *teamwork*, *cluster*, *consultation*, *knowledge*, *ecology* and *helpfulness*.

In education systems, being *helpful* means giving more powerful people what they want in order to help them run the system smoothly. To be helpful means to bow the knee to compulsion and to do so gracefully, with every semblance of professional normality. Helpfulness is the coinage that shows the system is not violent, does not do harm and cannot legitimately be criticized. All is well. Helpfulness is the pleasant surrender; it is the agreement that one person will be humiliated and the other will do the humiliating; it is the information that the interrogator wants, followed by the offer of the cigarette.

To a lesser extent, this language is also imposed on pupils and parents through terms such as *entitlement, responsibility, opportunity* and *choice*. The hidden rule in this seems to be that managers and policy-makers may use violent language towards teachers and pupils, and teachers may use it towards each other and pupils, but teachers may not direct the violent images at managers, leaders or the system, or at any descriptions of their work together: these images must remain peaceful and passive. Managers and leaders may invade; teachers may act as adjuncts to the invasion, but in reality they are, like pupils, the invaded, the emasculated.

That schools are violent places has been emotionally and artistically projected in Pink Floyd's rock album, *The Wall*, its title suggestive of repression and its soundtrack offering blurred, impressionistic and disturbing snapshots of shouting teachers and kangaroo courts. Even when no physical violence is committed, it is recognized that systematic violence exists and is inflicted, finally, on the young:

> We don't need no education
> We don't need no thought control
> No dark sarcasm in the classroom
> Teacher leave them kids alone
> Hey! Teacher! Leave them kids alone ...
>
> All in all you're just a
> 'Nother brick in the wall. (Pink Floyd, 1979)

Like an occupied and subjugated people, teachers and learners are harried and confined. Neither their physical space nor their time is their own. Like teachers, managers cannot control change processes in their work, and feel robbed of their time (Secretan, 1997, pp. 103–4). The violence of permanent, rapid and thoughtless states of change makes time seem 'cut into episodes—each with a beginning and an end but without prehistory or future' (Bauman, 1997, pp. 8–9). The language imposed on them, and which they internalize, both reveals and conceals a violence that is not physical. The violence is to ideas, forms of knowledge, methods of teaching, attitudes to learning and, through all this, to the emotional and spiritual core of human beings.

How serious a problem is violent discourse?

If the imagery of an education system is suggestive of violence, but effective learning is taking place and people are not being physically or psychologically harmed, what does the language matter? Even if some pedagogical acts are violent in the sense that they bring rapid change or impact destructively on assumptions, is this necessarily undesirable? Even if some damage to persons is caused by education systems that compel and by accountability systems that criticize, what is the objection so long as standards are being raised and the excluded are being brought in to levels of provision that were once closed to them?

Some violent forms of discourse may not always be a problem and may be either morally neutral or benign. The routine use by teachers and other education professionals of terms such as *objective* and *target* need not be objectionable. While some educators (Holmes, 2000, 2001) argue that objectives or learning outcomes are a confinement of what should be free enquiry, it is equally rational to assume them to be about the discipline of focusing on specific learning. The discipline and restriction is violent, but may be normative and harmless when contextualized in an environment of care for learners' and teachers' basic needs.

A second level of violent imagery exists in *delivery*, *impact*, *cohort* and other terms. These are inherently problematic because they describe processes of bringing people and learning together in ways that dictate the role of the learner as passive victim, and because other terms could be used with equal effect. For instance, teachers express their work as delivering the curriculum and evaluating the impact of teaching (something similar to load–aim–fire–alter aim). Instead, teachers could see it as bringing the pupils to knowledge and skills, accompanying them on a journey, helping them to discover and develop wisdom or skills. These are metaphors of mutual activity, not active/passive dichotomies, and of life, not death. Even so, those violent metaphors may not always be inappropriate in situations where high amounts of energetic, directive teaching are required, or where coaching and training are relevant.

Ultimate terms of violence exist in *compliance* and *monitoring*. These are the most damaging images because they exist not in classrooms, but in the system as a whole, from where they spread attitudes of passivity, resentment and anxiety. In the UK, Michael Barber, formerly an education policy-maker, was promoted to head the Delivery Unit (*sic*) in the office of the Prime Minister. He refined the strategy of centralized drives towards targets, imposed on education, health and other professions, enforced by budgetary and other penalties, and policed by quality agencies. As a prominent exponent of centralized compliance culture, he has admitted its tendency to undermine collaborative ethos among professionals, but threatens that the alternative is disintegration of the public service altogether (Fullan, 2003, p. 4). However, the destructive and distorting effects of this violence are documented by, among others, Rabbi Julia Neuberger (Carvel, 2002).

So some forms of violent culture in education may not matter, while others do. But violence is a continuum, and somewhere along it there exists a point of discomfort for each educator, beyond which he or she cannot go, according to their own ethical standards. Each educator's point of discomfort will be at a different length along the continuum. For some it may be compulsory schooling *per se*, or for others, the compulsive nature of the curriculum (Erricker, 2002). Competitiveness in all its forms, both academic and sporting, may represent the point, especially since its gendered nature constructs, and then exacerbates, some forms of violence under a deterministic 'boys will be boys' argument (Hutchinson, 1996). Others may take issue with the policing and monitoring roles of the watchdogs (Learner, 2001; Slater, 2004). Such school management practices as authoritarian administrative structures and procedures, inappropriate discipline and power to exclude may be the point of discomfort (Epp, 1996), or the managerialist culture that some see as having penetrated schools (Thrupp & Wilmott, 2003). But there is a necessity to reach and agree a natural or artificial point at which to separate the acceptable from the unacceptable. Harber (2004) sees violence as implicit and cultural, as well as sometimes physical; his argument uses social and cultural studies, and media references, to show that schools not only initiate violence, but reproduce and perpetuate it in the wider society (p. 3). The implicit factory idiom (and, by implication, war idiom and business/service idiom) breed alienation (p. 37), while the compulsory and authoritarian structure and daily management routine of schools breed attitudes of servility. The 'false consensus … that we all agree on the basic goals of education' (p. 14), as outlined in National Curriculum documents and legislation, give the impression that everyone is compliant, that monitoring is inoffensive and that resistance is irrelevant, useless or frivolous. This portrayal of covert and overt cultural violence, while episodic at times, demonstrates that violence is tolerated because there is no consensus discourse for exposing and confronting it.

Some important equipment for building an understanding of the proper limits of violent discourses and processes in our education systems exists in the work of a community of Jesuit academics who, themselves, suffered violent death as a direct result of their educational work. The six slain academics of the University of Central America were killed in specific and extreme circumstances of political repression, and in a reaction against their work for human rights (Sobrino, 1990). The extreme nature of their deaths has both rendered them iconic and distracted from the importance of their work (Chater, 2005). They realized that their academic work was pursued in the context of a university structure that served capitalism, and in immediate contexts of tragic conflict. Their vision of a higher education for justice was therefore 'contaminated', 'tainted' and suffered from 'cultural penetration' (Martin-Baro, 1974, p. 222). They argued that when education starts in this compromised way it will fail to take account of concrete reality. It will proceed from false premises and will, as Freire (1972) predicted, be prefabricated, bringing no relevant analysis to current issues.

Cultural penetration, in itself a violent act, is achieved structurally by means of the desk work of civil servants or other bureaucrats, who have control of funding, discourse or opportunities for promotion. Thus a technocratic, elitist normality is imposed, usually without a shot being fired. Everything is reduced to the technical, everything is subject to professional treatment and distinct social or economic divisions are enshrined.

We can extend this already fruitful notion of cultural penetration to include the enforcement of cultural norms through compulsory universal education and centralized or business control of the curriculum. The critiques of Bellah (1996), Bottery (2000) and Klein (2001) have begun to raise these concerns in the Western context. There is little ethical gain if schools absorb the socially excluded, only to commit cultural violence by imposing a curriculum and a set of covert values that have not been changed by their presence. Violence is also implied by the continuing fragmentation of knowledge into specialisms, the rising difficulties in establishing effective use of interdisciplinary approaches among students and the limited success of theories of the secular reintegration of knowledge (Wilson, 1998). Schools and universities themselves are caught in an increasingly urgent debate about their purpose as liberal and humanitarian or economically instrumental (Bouillon & Radnitsky, 1991)—the former occupying prime place in official rhetoric, while the latter is the dominant model in practice (Bottery, 2000).

How should spiritual education respond? Spiritual and pedagogical correctives to violence

We have established that violent discourses and processes exist, that at least some of them are damaging and that a shared understanding is needed if they are to be countered effectively. The developing tradition of spiritual education, or spirituality in education, ought to offer an alternative to violence and a creative response to it, but no clear method has appeared. In part this is because we often do not know whether we are talking about spiritual education as a radical alternative to established compulsory systems, or about spirituality in education as an entryist construct, quietly enriching the experience of pupils and adding notes of questioning where possible. While many agree that spirituality is explicitly critical of violence, and that spiritual education is implicitly critical of official education systems, no substantial strategic consensus exists beyond this.

Schooling systems are open to spiritual criticism for their determinism, technicist thinking, economic goals and, sometimes, elitist outcomes. Education is seen as imposing a normalizing process, turning human beings into objects and doing violence to their spirit:

> Normalizing education must lull to sleep that dimension of Being that enhances the living creative power ... Normalizing education ensures ... that you will not look for transcendence other than the one that puts you to sleep as a normalized disciple of the given order. (Gur-Ze'ev, 2004, p. 226)

Even spiritual education can be accused of complicity with this violence, if it serves to camouflage the violent essence of education (Gur-Ze'ev, 2004, p. 224) or if it cannot operate as an effective counter-educational cause (p. 232). The ambiguity of spirituality is highlighted by John Hull, who has understood both its power to criticize the violence of acquisitiveness (Hull, 1996, 2001) and its capacity to serve economically fuelled developmental enterprises (Hull, 1992).

Normalization and cultural penetration are violent acts that call spiritual educators to a response of the utmost courage. Almost daily, spiritual educators need this courage as they confront dilemmas on whether to find peaceful areas within the wider school and educational aims, where they can be left alone to promote spirituality, or to confront or subvert the structures because otherwise they will never be left alone. Having chosen one response or the other, they need courage again to enact it. The response of the Jesuit academics was to develop the concept of cultural creation as antidote to penetration (Ellacuria, 1975; Sobrino, 1990). As an educational idea, cultural creation meant that not only theory, but also practice, should change; that transformation must affect not only the definitions of excellence, but also, and crucially, the curriculum itself. Thus, they believed, could the moral climate of a university or school be justifiable. Cultural creation had to begin by being strongly critical of negative practice, and it owed a great deal to the theological assumptions of its practitioners (Chater, 2005). Some aspects of school democracy are known to promote more peaceful schools (Harber, 2004), while some models of school leadership promote non-violent and sustainable cultures characterized, for example, by activism, vigilance, patience in waiting for results, endurance, social justice and the sustaining of others in community (Hargreaves, 2005).

Conclusion

It must, then, be the urgent task of educators, leaders and policy-makers to rediscover a spirituality strong enough to resist the penetrative assault of normalizing forces. This will, in turn, have fruit in the emergence of a shared professional language that eschews violent or mechanical metaphors, and in a set of school structures and processes that avoid borrowing from the idioms of war, heavy industry or the service economy. When this begins to happen, schools themselves will become more pleasant, less controlling and less violent places, and incidents of physical violence (a real problem globally, not discussed here) may also decrease. The urgency is not only for those committed to spirituality, but also for that much larger group who wish to see the continuation of a healthy, coherent and inclusive public education service in their country. As with many successful revolutions, this change must begin from the grass roots. Professionals in education could begin it by simply compiling a list of the words they will no longer use and the structures or idioms to which they will no longer be accountable.

Notes on contributor

Dr Mark Chater is Reader in Education and Tutor in Theology and Education at Bishop Grosseteste College, Lincoln, UK. He has 20 years' experience as a teacher and manager in schools and initial teacher training. His interests are in teachers' values, health and spirituality, and in school ethos, leadership and management. He is convener of international conferences on children's spirituality, religious education, change and choice in education, and homophobia in schools. He is an associate editor of the *International Journal of Children's Spirituality.*

References

Bauman, Z. (1997) Alone again: ethics after certainty, in: G. Mulgan (Ed.) *Life after politics* (London, Fontana).

Bellah, R. *et al.* (1996) *Habits of the heart: individualism and commitment in American life* (Berkeley, CA, University of California Press).

Bottery, M. (2000) *Education, policy and ethics* (London, Continuum).

Boullon, H. & Radnitzky, G. (Eds) (1991) *Universities in the service of truth and utility* (New York, P. Lang).

Carvel, J. (2002) Labour initiatives 'overwhelm' NHS, *Guardian*, 12 April, p. 8.

Chater, M. (2005) Where the truth is told: the example of the University of Central America, *Prologue*, 4, 43–55.

Department for Education and Skills (2005a) *Our aims.* Available online at: http://www.dfes.gov.uk (accessed 23 June 2005).

Department for Education and Skills (2005b) *The standards site.* Available online at: http://www.standards.dfes.gov.uk (accessed 23 June 2005).

Ellacuria, I. (1975) Is a different kind of university possible? in: J. Hassett & H. Lacey (Eds) *Towards a society that serves its people: the intellectual contribution of El Salvador's murdered Jesuits* (Washington, DC, Georgetown University Press).

Epp, J. (1996) *Systemic violence: how schools hurt children* (London, Routledge Falmer).

Erricker, C. (2002) *When learning becomes your enemy* (Nottingham, Educational Heretics Press).

Freire, P. (1972) *Pedagogy of the oppressed* (Harmondsworth, Penguin).

Fullan, M. (2003) *The moral imperative of school leadership* (Thousand Oaks, CA, Corwin Press).

Gur-Ze'ev, I. (2004) Contra spiritual education, in: H. Alexander (Ed.) *Spirituality and ethics in education: philosophical, theological and radical perspectives* (Brighton, Sussex Academic Press).

Harber, C. (2004) *Schooling as violence: how schools harm pupils and societies* (London, Routledge).

Hargreaves, A. (2005) Sustainable leadership, in: B. Davies (Ed.) *The essentials of school leadership* (London, Paul Chapman).

Hodgson, A. & Spours, K. (1999) *New Labour's educational agenda* (London, Kogan Page).

Holmes, L. (2000) *Is learning a 'contaminated concept'?* Available online at: http://www.re-skill.org.uk/papers (accessed 25 June 2005).

Holmes, L. (2001) *Decontaminating the concepts of learning and competence.* Available online at: http://www.re-skill.org.uk/papers (accessed 25 June 2005).

Hull, J. (1992) Human development and capitalist society, in: J. Fowler, K. E. Npikow & F. Sschweitzer (Eds) *Stages of faith and religious development: implications for church, education and society* (London, SCM).

Hull, J. (1996) The ambiguity of spiritual values, in: M. Halstead & M. Taylor (Eds) *Values in education and education in values* (London, Routledge Falmer).

Hull, J. (2001) Competition and spiritual development, *International Journal of Children's Spirituality*, 6(3), 263–276.

Hutchinson, F. (1996) *Educating beyond violent futures* (London, Routledge).

Illich, I. 1971 *Deschooling society* (New York, Harper & Row).

Klein, N. (2001) *No logo* (London, Harper Collins).

Learner, S. (2001) Soft-touch style but tough on standards, *Times Educational Supplement*, 14 September 2001. Available online at: http://www.tes.co.uk/search/story (accessed 25 June 2005).

Martin-Baro, I. (1991) Developing a critical consciousness through the university curriculum, in: J. Hassett & H. Lacey (Eds) *Towards a society that serves its people: the intellectual contribution of El Salvador's murdered Jesuits* (Washington, DC, Georgetown University Press).

Office for Standard in Education (2002) *Handbook for the inspection of initial teacher training 2002– 2008* (London, OFSTED).

Secretan, L. (1997) *Reclaiming higher ground: building organisations that inspire excellence* (New York, McGraw-Hill).

Slater, J. (2004) Two-day warning of laser inspections, *Times Educational Supplement*, 13 February 2004. Available online at: http://www.tes.co.uk/search/story (accessed 25 June 2005).

Sobrino, J. (Ed.) (1990) *Companions of Jesus* (Maryknoll, NY, Orbis Books).

Thrupp, M. (1998) Exploring the politics of blame: school inspection and its contestation in New Zealand and England, *Comparative Education*, 34(2), 195–209.

Thrupp, M. & Wilmott, R. (2003) *Educational management in managerialist times: beyond the textual apologists* (Buckingham, Open University Press).

Wilson, E. (1998) *Consilience: the unity of knowledge* (London, Little, Brown).

Difference, explanation, certainty and terror: a view from a Londoner about the formation of children's spirituality as relational consciousness

Helen Johnson*

A starting-point

Beginning of July 2005: there can't be any better place to be on such a gloriously sunny day than down on the South Bank, looking across to Westminster Bridge and the Houses of Parliament. But there speaks a Londoner! The walk by the river, between meetings, has put me behind schedule so I'm literally running late as I rush, huffing and puffing, into the tube carriage. Responding to my discomfort, a young man kindly offers me his seat. A couple of weeks ago, when this happened for the very first time, I was embarrassed and politely refused. This time I wise-up, or own up to the passage of time, and gratefully

*Correspondence Address: School of Education, Kingston University, Kingston Hill, Kingston-upon-Thames, KT2 7LB, UK. Email: H.M.Johnson@kingston.ac.uk

accept. So there we all are, the usual London crowd of black, brown and white, old and young, and who knows what. We don't engage in casual conversation—this isn't Glasgow, another city with significance for me, where it is regarded as normal, being not stand-offish, to chat with strangers—but we sit in our seats, in our own separate lives, sharing the same public space, the common journey, albeit for a few minutes. Well-versed in London mores, we relate to each through a respectful distance and in the circumstances that we find ourselves—many feet under the River Thames in a small metal carriage—we behave reasonably.

It is seemingly self-evident to say that it is a fundamental human response to seek to examine and understand the experiences to which we are exposed. We will use these experiences as a source of our own learning and means by which other more formal learning in schools and colleges can be integrated. From that never-completed process of knowledge accumulation and understanding, we attempt to derive some wisdom and purpose. It is in this way that we will attempt to make our lives meaning-ful, despite the inevitability of death that otherwise might make them seem absurd. As much as we seek objectivity and 'extraordinary disinvolvement' (referred to by Daniel Scott in this issue) that intensifies our empathy with others and, at the same time, sharpens our skilled observation of their behaviour, you and I are *human* instru-ments. We may share, for example, a body of social science literature but we use and interpret it through our own personal prism of experience and identity.

Even locating this prism may be easier said than done. Zygmunt Bauman (2003) has influentially discussed a modern society, which is liquid and where individuals have 'no bonds'. In this, nothing is unquestionable or to be dutifully accepted without analysis. Thus, the process of self-definition is perpetual, without respite. Such a view to the educated and contemporary city-dweller in the world cities of, say, London, New York and Toronto, who is well-tutored or at least aware at the level of fashion of the works of, for instance, Foucault, Lyotard *et al.*, this might seem obvious, if not just a little passé. Whatever our intellectual position, relativism (and perhaps secular-ism) underpin a liberal society, and materialism might ensure that it is comfortable for some, at least.

The omnipresent childhood

But, whatever the intellectual position *we adopt as adults*, it is possible to say few, if any of us, leave the past behind, move completely from one paradigm to another or completely forget our place or country of origin, in geographical and, more profoundly, in emotional terms. Our personalities and identities, however trans-formed, are based, in part, on previous experiences and interpretations that we take with us for some form of certainty and concomitant ontological security, as a refer-ence point. The questions are perhaps: why we make the choice of particular experi-ences over others? Why they are significant? Why we do integrate them into our sense of self, into the creation of our own identity and use them to justify how we behave or commit certain acts? Rebecca Nye's work, with David Hay (1998), on children's spirituality can help us approach some of the answers—and importantly, show how early we all become conscious of the transcendental, things and people *beyond ourselves*. From many hours of conversations with small children, these influential researchers have identified 'certain categories of ordinary human experience' (Hay, 1998, p. 107) that even small children have spontaneously identified as significant. These categories are 'awareness of the here-and-now, 'awareness of mystery' and 'awareness of value' (Hay, 1998, p. 107). These 'awarenesses' comprise 'a relational consciousness', with which 'the child relate(s) to things, other people, him/herself and God' (Hay, 1998, p. 108).

In such a relational consciousness you and I may share something. For example, we may both be Londoners. However, the likelihood, the certainty, is that we will also experience difference (and so comparison, explicit or implicit): for example, that we were born somewhere else or have different ethnic identities. We may have different career trajectories, have varying degrees of financial security and expectations about the future and our place and status in society—and that we have dissimilar political beliefs and religious backgrounds. So it is clear that nothing can be assumed or 'taken for granted'. So this chapter accepts that in this explanation and meaning giving we are always dependent on definitions and interpretations. It will be argued, however, that it is necessary to make the effort to explore some of the current and fashionable generalizations about the nature of identity and the multicultural society upon which we base our shared lives in the city or journeys on the tube. This is especially true, at a macro level, when our working definitions and understanding—what might be called our comfortable liberal grey areas or 'fog'—are violently and brutally challenged by terrorists. At a micro-level, at the point of service delivery, in the form of some educational interaction and exchange, be it in the school classroom or university lecture hall, these issues have practical and educational—*real*—significance. The issue of young people's identity in a contemporary society is highly significant, for, of course, it impinges on, for example:

- How educational professionals work with pupils and students who lack a sense of self-esteem or direction in life;
- How schools attempt to deliver a curriculum, that has cultural value yet recognizes subcultural difference while preparing the individual for citizenship;
- How teaching in a college or university can recognise the diversity of students in the lecture hall;
- The consequences of a clash between the culture of the educational institution and that of the pupils' or students' home or ethnic community.

This process of self-definition will be approached in terms of specific (and not exhaustive) contested issues, defining differences within:

- the nation;
- the nature of society;
- evolving national identity;
- citizenship;
- multicultural society and education;
- adaptation or not to the host culture.

Having done this, the chapter will pause for a reality check to consider the possible consequences of this rationally presented uncertainty, in particular, a rejection of the process of perpetual self-definition and finding relief and comfort in fundamentalism.

The problematic nature of the nation and identity

Clearly, the child at home and at school is exposed to many influences, both intended and unintended. In terms of formal educational interventions at school, as will be discussed later, citizenship education in the UK carries a considerable agenda, both as the transmission of knowledge deemed as pertinent and relevant, and as a means by which, echoing Hay (1998) to inculcate or reinforce a sense of relational consciousness, albeit in a secular manner. But encouraging children to find such relationships through a shared national identity is no simple matter.

For, when seeking national identity, it is worth noting that the term 'nation' is itself complex. Anderson (1983) has discussed the 'non-inevitable nature' of conceptualizing a nation. Ringrose and Lerner (1993) have taken this further to note that nation (and community) building is a continuing and constant process of reworking. While modernist views of society seek clarity—Bauman (1991) has spoken of modernity's 'quest for order'—these attempts are perhaps undermined by contemporary societies' own expressive individuation, which Taylor (1989), for one, has seen as the 'cornerstone of modern culture'. Nations (and with them discernible identities) can also exist while stateless, as can be argued for, say, Scotland and for other 'nations' within an alternative hegemony as can be seen for the Asian immigrants groups in Britain who retain their own culture and, most importantly, in some cases, their own language. Some of the lines in the atlas that determine nations are preposterously straight; however, they are illustrations of the imperialist mind-set that drew boundaries to the convenience of the invading colonist rather than to the 'tidy', unilateral borders. The continent of Africa is a case in point; and the partition of India is another. As is the Palestine/Israeli conflict.

Thus, no matter how the prevailing hegemony presents itself to the contrary, the nation state is never homogeneous and cohesive. (Nevertheless, it can operate as though there were certainties about a cohesive society that members are prepared to defend.) Thus, the construction of a national identity is not automatic and is certainly contested. In this construction, choices of historical events and their interpretation will have to be made. Nation building and national identity are not objective tasks: how people see themselves on a subjective basis—the stories they tell themselves and their children about themselves and each other—rather than objective historical fact (if there is such a thing) will be emphasized. So national identity is no static and reliable social fact, to be picked up and examined in a Durkheimian fashion. To be a particular citizen or nationality may mean that an individual belongs to a certain religious group or adhere to certain cultural practices, or it may not. We are all wary of stereotypes. But what are the implications if a *new* national identity, reflecting new political and societal realities, are the order of the day, either through a conscious political and government decision or through migration and other demographic realities?

The nature of society

Examining such a phenomenon is predicated on the need to contexualise the discussion in a context, within a particular society, so that institutions, processes and experiences can be identified. That task itself, on the face of it, seems simple enough, and in this case, the context is British. However, it is when the debate about the nature of that society is addressed that a minefield of definitions and suppositions is immediately entered. The label of convenience to be placed on society to 'sum up' its current stage of development is no easy matter. In the definition of Giddens (1991, 196, 2000), British society is no longer traditional and has moved through to a late modern phase. Agriculture is in serious decline, the population lives mostly in cities and conurbations and church attendance in mainstream Christianity has fallen to an all-time low. Manufacture, the trigger and driver of industrialization, that once needed and sought cheap migrant labour, is also in decline. As globalization takes a hold, the necessity for cheap labour costs has resulted in manufacture being taken abroad to the developing countries of the South. The education system gears itself to these new economic realities, and governmental policy documents dehumanize our children into 'human capital'. From a choice that also includes post-modern, post-industrial and post-colonial, Giddens calls British society post-traditional. This might be so; but in a society that is rightly proud of its democracy, the apparatus of government in the UK is headed by an unelected monarch (be it simply symbolic or 'technical'), and 'major inequalities' in terms of life chances and outcomes 'exist among different classes' (Giddens, 1996, pp. 54–5). To such a choice of descriptors must be added multicultural and in passing it is noted here that a 'society [that] contains different forms of ethical life is far from being particularly modern' (Gray, 2000, pp. 3–4). He goes on to say that: 'On the contrary, in their diversity of ways of life late modern societies have something in common with the ancient world' (Gray, 2000, p. 4). But to adopt a 'wide sweep' (to which it is freely acknowledged that there are distinct and significant exceptions), it is also clear that the seeming cultural 'simplicity' of traditional societies in which received values are handed down automatically has not beaten a complete retreat or been completely replaced by a succeeding paradigm. After the presence of over 1 million people on the streets of London for the Queen's Jubilee weekend (in June 2002) perhaps a lingering of something 'unmodern' or 'traditional' in the English psyche is indicated.

Evolving national identity

It is contradictions and complexities of this type that the school has to deal with constructively, coherently and inclusively. For clearly as societal compositions change, so do linked concepts such as national identity. In response to these changes, it has increasingly become the task of government to promote social cohesion and shared values. Lessons can be learnt from two examples at the macro and micro levels and from two very different societies. At the macro-level, in post-apartheid South Africa, the 'Rainbow Nation' has been invented; and, as has been mentioned, in the

UK citizenship education has been introduced into state schools. However, in both instances, the nature of national identity is not unproblematic and this has implications for those who are responsible for the implementation and management of government policies.

At the macro-level (1)

Early in 2004, ten years after the end of apartheid, Archbishop Desmond Tutu was asked about South Africa's greatest successes in this period. He replied that a 'very diverse society with a painful history of racial conflict ... [is] managing to walk the path of forgiveness and reconciliation'. Importantly, it is doing this 'as a viable and stable nascent democracy' (Hawthorne, 2004). So both in Africa and in Europe the nature of societies is changing, and though in some instances linked through colonial history, the complexities of the situations are very different. However, what is shared would seem obvious: societal mono-cultures are being replaced with something more diverse and far less repressive. Baines, of Rhodes University (1998, p. 2), has written of identity and nation building in South Africa in these post-apartheid times:

> The past has shown that the assertion of a single national identity has precluded the assertion of others. National identity is invariably defined by the dominant group which excludes others from the locus of power.

At the micro level (2)

As the nature of British society has changed in terms of its increasingly multicultural and multi-ethnic basis, enhanced through substantial movements of postwar immigration both from countries belonging to the former British Empire and from other parts of the world, citizenship education has become a *mandatory* subject in schools. The hegemonic assumptions that generations once seemingly absorbed without question are now under serious strain. Significantly, it is particularly in the area of national identity that the intentions and interventions of government are clear (Crick *et al.*, 1998). However, as has been seen, such an identity in contemporary Britain is not unproblematic. Thus, citizenship teachers in the classroom and school leaders, responsible for specific and whole-school approaches are not presented with 'taken-for-granted', unquestioned perspectives and assumptions in the social order that Norval (1996) has described, in the South African context, as being 'constituted by difference, as opposed to otherness'. Baines notes (1998, p. 3) that 'a new South African identity is being constructed discursively through the media and other forms of public discourse'. There may be fewer explicit parallels in British society (there is, after all, no written constitution that sets out the values of the British nation). However, in this uncertainty, it is likely that the conceptualization of national identity, promoted and embodied by policy implementers may be based, at least in part, on how they have constructed the narratives around their own.

As has been seen, the boundaries—geographical, legal, constitutional, behavioural and emotional—of the nation state have been a means by which a ruling class has defined and controlled a hegemonic culture. It has prevailed over the 'indige-nous' and acted as a recognizable host culture to new arrivals. In England specifi-cally, through the presence of an established church, namely the Church of England, it is possible to identify, within this culture, a state-promoted religion, membership of which placed adherents within the social mainstream. Other reli-gious groups were latterly tolerated though suffering social, economic and educa-tional disadvantages. With the passage of time through the nineteenth and twentieth centuries, minority religious groups such as Irish Catholics, drawn from mass Irish immigration, have been accepted by the host culture and established their own schools. In most aspects save that of religion, the price of such acceptance has seemingly been their assimilation into the hegemonic host culture through the adoption of a 'British' identity.

Supporting identity or inhibiting relational consciousness?

However, it would appear that *contemporary* movements of people to the UK have retained loyalties to their own religion, and in some instances to their own language, and what they perceive as their own identity. Education is a particular example, as demands for schools, within the state-funded system, for minority religious groups have intensified. After conforming to official state standards, certain of these religious groups, some Christian others not, have recently obtained their own schools and have become part of the long-established dual system in which voluntary, faith schools and maintained schools function side by side. (In the acrimonious debate that surrounds faith schools, there are significant differences among liberals. In the *Guardian*, jour-nalist Polly Toynbee has mounted an unrelenting campaign against such schools, seeing them as essentially middle class and socially divisive. In contrast, the journalist Darcus Howe, writing in the progressive *New Statesman*, has argued that state funding for Muslim schools is a victory against Islamophobia.)

The importance and problematic nature of citizenship

Much has been written about the problematic nature of the concept of citizenship (e.g. Johnson & Holness, 2003), and world, European and British political events, including the Bradford riots of 2001 (Hussain & Bagguley, 2005) that have problem-atized the concept, already contested by different ideological and professional perspectives. Under New Labour, in reforms of the welfare state and the public services in general a concept is employed of citizenship as empowered, active, partic-ipatory and declared, as opposed to a state of marginalization or social exclusion, based on a passive acceptance of the supposedly 'taken-for-granted' or 'we know it when we see it' Britishness. In this, the complicated and essentially political nature of British citizenship is clear even in a legal context (Johnson & Holness, 2003). It becomes even more so when we turn to note some of the social and cultural realties of a post-modern and post-colonial world, in which the UK has become both a focus of immigration and a historic origin of emigration.

The acceptance of multiculturalism

To live in a contemporary Western society is to live in a society that is both pluralistic and multicultural. But as noted earlier, the latter term is also problematic. Charles Taylor makes the point that:

> our identity is partly shaped by recognition or its absence, often by the misrecognition of others, and so a person or group of people can suffer real damage, real distortion, if the people or society around them mirror back to them a confining or demeaning or contempt-ible picture of themselves. (Taylor, 1994, p. 25)

So, a discussion about multiculturalism is not 'just academic' and its definition has impact on the lives of real people, their children, and how they are addressed and taught to see themselves in learning situations.

Such learning now carries with it another change in contemporary society: the understanding and expectation that each of us should have an *authentic* identity in which you and I are 'true to [ourselves] and [our] own particular way of being' (Taylor, 1994, p. 28) engage in the process of self-recognition and definition. The educational, emotional, spiritual developmental and political implications of this are clear. But in this, the role of the state is problematic as its hegemonic impulses are increasingly inef-fectual. It does have a role in the politics of equal respect which it can support through its being 'inhospitable to difference' and in which 'the survival of members of distinct societies' (or groups) cannot be accommodated (Hermans, 2000, p. 4); the state can also take a different tack and be 'hospitable to difference' which, according to Taylor, opts to 'be in favour of the cultural survival of a particular nation, culture, religion' (Hermans, 2000, p. 4). It is in the choice of these responses that the state is making decisions about the form in which societal culture will survive and be perpetuated.

The modern state and the maintenance of 'its' culture

As has been seen, societal culture, again, is no simple term, for:

> A society's culture is closely tied up with its economic, political and other institutions. No society first develops culture and then these institutions, or vice versa. They are all equally vital to its survival, emerge and develop together, and are influenced by each other. (Parekh, 2000, p. 151)

Perhaps to the surprise of some English readers to whom 'English' and 'British' are synonymous, cultural difference has always existed for other groups who also inhabit these islands. For some, including a former Welsh nationalist MP:

> The unspoken discourse of the 'multi-cultural' debate is one that goes to the heart of the nature of British society and the British state itself. Diversity and plurality has to be seen as 'recent'. (Dafydd Elis Thomas, quoted in Hickman, 1995, p. 4)

The political consequences of such an admission could be uncomfortable; he goes on:

> To admit otherwise is to admit that the whole history of Britain *internally* as well as exter-nally has been about imperialism, racism, colonialism, linguistic and political domination. (quoted in Hickman, 1995, p. 4; emphasis added)

It seems that the discourse of silence about the *historic* lack of homogeneity is coming to an end, in the awareness of the incorporation involved in the more recent, 1950s and onwards, immigration to the UK 'from Britain's ex-colonies in Africa, the Caribbean and the Indian sub-continent'. Hickman is adamant (1995, p. 6) that the 'whiteness' and 'Europeanness' of Irish immigrants to England (and by implication that of the Scots and Welsh) has hidden their experience of English cultural imperialism. This 'new' awareness, she argues, has been brought about by explicit and visible ethnic differences.

Incorporation and adaptation strategies in the face of the host culture

The reception of these comparatively recent arrivals takes us directly to the issues surrounding the absorption of 'indigenous', minority and migrant people. *Incorporation* refers to interventions by the state to ensure some form of uniformity and standardization. Two examples, one historic and the other contemporary, are:

1. Through language policies to discourage the speaking of Scottish Gaelic and Welsh, such policies (now reversed) illustrate the British state in its full hegemonic pomp, when inhospitable to difference and attempting to crush minority cultures, as recently as the twentieth century;
2. Through the introduction of some form of formal citizenship education, either as mandatory in schools or as a condition of the granting of citizenship.

Other terms such as 'assimilation' and 'integration' address the strategies adopted by minority and/or migrant peoples *themselves*. In a Canadian context but with applicability elsewhere, Berry (1993) has found four main adaptation strategies in respect of the host culture for migrant groups:

- In *integration* and *assimilation,* there is contact with the dominant group but the choice of assimilation means loss of the original culture;
- *Separation* means no contact with the dominant group or host culture;
- In *marginalization,* there no contact with either the host or original culture.

Multicultural education

While citizenship education has specific aims, schools and other educational institutions have responded in their own ways to such changes in the conceptualization of national identity, the challenges of multiculturalism and the nature of incorporation and responses to it. What happens in the classroom is also supported (or undermined) by the organizational culture and climate of the whole school, for: 'central to the concept [of culture] is the idea of value, that which is regarded as worthwhile by members of the group' (Hoyle, 1986, p. 3). The personal values of individuals, be they pupils or staff, within the school and its supporting community may be expressed overtly in a number of ways or allegiances, some of which are political, some social and some religious. Less consciously but perhaps even more importantly, these values will be transmitted in the 'ordinariness' (Goffman, 1969) of everyday behaviour, relationships and interaction.

So it would seem that change and a differentiated society now seem an inevitable part of contemporary life. As Ziebertz (2000) notes of Habermas and Lyotard, neither sees 'a way back to the unitary society or unitary culture'. However, parents will have to make definite choices about how they want their children prepared for and to relate to a society that perhaps no longer has consistency and predictability, and that contains many spiritual and moral positions. Minority groups, in particular immigrants, will have to make decisions about their long-term future (perhaps in terms of Berry's typology, above) in the host culture.

In the choices made there is likely to be present a liberal duality and contradiction that is derived from what Gray (2000) calls 'the two incompatible philosophies' embodied in the paramount ideal of liberalism, namely toleration. One view, to quote Gray again, is that 'human beings can flourish in many ways of life', and that communities (and schools) can have a role in creating positive identities that express living religious and cultural traditions. Other liberals, contradictorily, seek a 'rational consensus on the best way of life' and perhaps a shared, increasingly globalized, identity. Whatever the tensions or confusions engendered by this duality, as Gray (2000, p. 1) states, it can be said the toleration that is the essence of liberalism 'has contributed immeasurably to human well-being'. He also issues a timely warning that such toleration cannot be taken for granted and 'that it is an achievement that cannot be valued too highly'. Liberalism and its concomitant toleration have a long philosophical history. For John Rawls (1973), liberal toleration and its concomitant intellectual neutrality cannot mean a retreat into comforting certainties; but for Rawls, the real test is between 'reasonable' and 'unreasonable' behaviour. Interestingly, he notes that most of the major doctrines are not neutral: 'Except for certain kinds of fundamentalism, all the main historical religions … may be seen as reasonable comprehensive doctrines' (Rawls, 1973, p. 170). The crucial issue within liberalism would seem to be whether or not the expression of your rights infringes my freedom, and vice versa. Essentially, what is or should the liberal state be privileging? The answer to that question is further complicated by the expression and promotion of the multicultural agenda.

As we have previously touched upon, first, linked to the liberal emphasis on the rights of the individual, there is a multicultural perspective that argues for the toleration and active support of a shared culture within the group to which individuals elect or perceive themselves as belonging to. Ironically enough, these groups may or may not promote socially liberal values. The real difficulty occurs when they fail Rawls's test about being a 'reasonable' doctrine and so could be seen as subverting the liberal environment and society that allows them to exist. Second, there is a multicultural perspective that allows cultural diversity within the context of, what was called earlier a 'shared political identity'. (This could be in terms of the nation state or, increasingly, a supra national identity such as being a citizen of the European Union or a globalized 'citizen of the world'.)

Both models have the same practical outcome—one as its final stage and the other as a stage of transition—of producing citizens, who are 'hyphenated', belonging to both the subgroup and society as a whole. This echoes John Dewey's promotion of a 'hyphenated American' (Dewey, 1988, p. 27), in which US citizens possessed 'an ancestral and an American identity'. In this way, in the view of Lyotard and Habermas, with no retreat possible into a unitary culture, Britain may be becoming more 'American'.

Event

In the real world—perhaps far from the abstraction and spectator-status of the liberal intelligentsia—in July 2005, the London underground railway system was bombed by British-born Muslim terrorists.

A reality check

Underpinning the above discussion has been an acceptance of modernist and post-modernist ideas; but what if an individual is disinclined to engage in an endless process of self-definition and acceptance of the game of self-construction? And what if this societal tolerance of uncertainty, ambiguity and relativism leads, first, to hopelessness, a passivity, and then frustration, in individuals and groups? This could be despair at the seeming futility of life derived from a lack of philosophical, religious, spiritual or political certainty; or perhaps dissatisfaction with an insatiable materialism (or an economic inability to join in); or an anger at a globalized economy that peddles a mass popular culture of unspeakable vulgarity and salaciousness; or a hostility at the self-enslavement and debasement of self-commodification needed to 'sell yourself' on the market; or indeed a failure to agree and identify with certain Western countries' foreign policy and its implementation in one's own country of origin or in one that shares one's religious tradition. In response to such conceptual, political and moral greyness comes anti-modernism and fundamentalism. The latter are found in many religious groups and can be considered as a return to the fundamentals—the basic, defining principles—of a religion. Such fundamentalists, though belonging to their main religious groups, distinguish themselves (establish difference) from the mainstream by 'building a wall of virtue' to protect themselves not only from alien religions, but from the modernized, essentially 'compromised' form of their own religion. So an essential component in such fundamentalism is alienation from both their own traditional group and society in general. In Berry's (1993) terms, far from wanting to relate to the society in which they live, some young people who are British-born and who have been educated within its liberal and open-minded educational system are actively *seeking* marginalization.

The leap from fundamentalism to terrorism is immense (and rarely made). But within this alienation and adoption of 'pure' values the necessary emotional work and the closing of the mind has been done (Fromm, 1960). 'Having all the answers', and so being 'special' or 'chosen' be it in the form of Christian, Muslim, Marxist, secularist or something else, fundamentalism can dispel the sense of insecurity, uncertainty and perhaps worldly failure. Terrorism is the ultimate, totally unreasonable self-assertion over the feelings, beliefs and lives of others. It is the categorical refusal to relate to others and society in general. It offers the perpetrator a conclusive and confident response to any feeling of futility and despair brought about by a poor education, a model of unreconstructured masculinity, low economic and social status and few, if any, positive expectations about the future. (They may be anti-modernist but not all terrorists are anti-modern; for example, the Internet is an essential part of the operations of Al Qaeda (Gray, 2003).

It is clear that certain groups within British society in their marginalisation look beyond the host culture to an idealized culture and religion of origin; but despite 'visits back', they remain 'imprisoned' in the host culture (Ali, 2003).

Tentative, and admittedly simple, conclusions

But what does this discussion of difference mean? What is the use of all this complexity? And what does this debate *do*? The decisions at the macro level cannot be reached. But at the micro level, where there is interaction between individuals, well, perhaps it helps us to release ourselves (partially, at least) from the temptation to find security in the self-repression of the closed mind by seeking challenges, advice and guidance from a variety of others (some we know and some we only know through their writings for scrutiny and discussion). Exemplifying this, Karen Armstrong (writing in the *Guardian*, 27.7.2005, p. 25) reminds us pertinently that:

> Liberal-minded atheists can be just as strident as fundamentalists if their idea of faith is challenged in any way, even if they know next to nothing about religious history or theology. Their opinions seem to have a psychological importance that renders accurate information irrelevant and obscurely threatening.

We try to keep up with the current thinking but we can also seek guidance from an older source. Karen Armstrong also reminds us that, while

> [o]pinions change with each generation ... [the] best way of countering the clashing dogmatisms of our time is to be suspicious of any *idée fixe*—including our own. Socrates made it his life's work to compel people to question their most fundamental assumptions. True knowledge was acquired only after an agonising struggle that involved your whole self.

So there we have it. Much about modern life in a sophisticated city can offer comfortable shortcuts through what can seem to be the crushing weight of complexities and uncertainties, with 'readymade' this and 'carry out' that. But clearly, from this discussion of the terms we use every day, there are no easy solutions—either as adults or as school children—to finding knowledge and truth; but we must proceed perhaps through the rigour of dialectical process and with a sense of humility in the face of what we do not know. In that we are supported by the liberal education (and within it, general approaches and particular initiatives that are concerned with the relational consciousness that some would call spirituality). After all, as C. Wright Mills (1963, p. 367) reminds us that:

Its first and continuing task is to help develop the bold and sensible individual who cannot be overwhelmed by the burdens of modern life. The aim is nothing more and can be nothing less.

Endnote

Some final thoughts are:

At the end of July 2005 ... it is likely that for many of us, we are lucky to live in a context that we enjoy and feel at home: in short, we have a sense of belonging. In that, we also are aware of difference, perhaps on the basis of ethnicity and religion but more likely we use the criterion that has the most significance for us: hence my awareness about the differences between generations, the passing of time and getting caught out with fixed and out-of-date ideas. (In short, my age!) But while my fellow travellers and I do not know what each is thinking about (perhaps, the nature of liberalism ... the time of the next appointment ... what's in the fridge for dinner), we know from our acculturalization (derived in a lesser or greater degree from religious traditions, our schooling and from a manifold variety of other sources) that what really matters is how we relate and behave towards each other in ordinary, everyday situations. Sometimes there is the briefest of relationships in the offer of a seat to a middle-aged woman from a kind young man on his way to college with a backpack, full of files and books. But at the most minimal level, we know that the tube journey—and living in the city—only becomes possible and comfortable if we respect each other, are hospitable to difference and do not harm each other.

Notes on contributor

Helen Johnson is Reader in Education at Kingston University, UK. Her research interests include faith schools, citizenship education, emerging trends in educational leadership in education institutions and learning and teaching in higher education.

References

Ali, T. (2003) *The clash of fundamentalisms: crusades, jihads and modernity* (London, Verso).

Anderson, B. (1983) *Imagined communities: reflections on the origin and spread of nationalism* (London, Verso).

Armstrong, K. (2005) Certainty isn't a sure thing, *Guardian*, 21 July, p. 21.

Baines, G. (1998) *Mots Pluriels No. 7.* Available online at: http://www.arts.uwa.edu.au/MotsPluriels/MP798,gb.html (accessed 8 August 2005).

Bauman, Z. (1991) *Modernity and ambivalence* (Oxford, Polity Press).

Bauman, Z. (2003) *Liquid love: on the frailty of human bonds* (Cambridge, Polity).

Berry, J. (1993) *Indigenous psychologies: research and experience in cultural context* (Newbury Park, CA, Sage).

Crick, B. *et al.* (1998) *Education for citizenship and the teaching of democracy in schools: final report* (London, DfEE/QCA).

Dewey, J. (1988) *Democracy and education* (London, Macmillan).

Fromm, E. (1960) *The fear of freedom* (London, Routledge & Kegan Paul).

Giddens, A. (1991) *The consequences of modernity* (Cambridge, Polity).

Giddens, A. (1996) *In defence of sociology* (Cambridge, Polity).

Giddens, A. (2000) *The third way and its critics* (Cambridge, Polity Press).

Goffman, E. (1969) *The presentation of self in everyday life* (Harmondsworth, Penguin).

Gray, J. (2000) *Two faces of liberalism* (Cambridge, Polity).

Gray, J. (2003) *Al Qaeda and what it means to be modern* (London, Faber).

Hawthorne, P. (2004) *Voices from the rainbow nation*. Available online at: http://www.time.com/europe (accessed 3 February 2005).

Hay, D. with Nye, R. (1998) *The spirit of the child* (London, Fount).

Hermans, C. (2000) The challenges of multiculturalism, *International Journal of Education and Religion*, 1(1), 1–18.

Hickman, M. (1995) *Religion, class and identity* (Aldershot, Avebury).

Hoyle, E. (1986) *The politics of school management* (London, Hodder & Stoughton).

Hussain, Y. & Bagguley, P. (2005) Citizenship, ethnicity and identity: British Pakistanis after the 2001 'riots', *Sociology*, 39(3), July, 407–426.

Johnson, H. & Holness, M. (2003) The complications and possibilities of citizenship education: confirming identity and meaning to enhance emotional and spiritual resilience in a post-September 11 world, *International Journal of Children's Spirituality*, 8(3), December, 215–226.

Mills, Wright C. (1963) Mass society and liberal education, in: I. L. Horowitz (Ed.) *Power, politics and people: the collected essays of C. Wright Mills* (New York, Ballatine Books), 353–373.

Norval, A. (1996) *Deconstructing apartheid discourse* (London, Verso).

Parekh, B. (2000) *Rethinking multiculturalism: cultural diversity and political theory* (Basingstoke, Macmillan).

Rawls, J. (1973) *A liberal theory of justice* (Oxford, Clarendon Press).

Ringrose, M. & Lerner, A. (1993) *Re-imagining the nation* (Buckingham, Open University Press).

Taylor, C. (1989) *Sources of the self: the making of the modern identity* (Cambridge, Cambridge University Press).

Taylor, C. (1994) The politics of recognition, in: A. Gutman (Ed.) *Multi-culturalism: examining the politics of recognition* (Princeton, NJ, Princeton University Press), 25–74.

Ziebertz, H.-G. (2000) Religious education in a multi-cultural society, *International Journal of Education and Religion*, 1(1), 178–197.

Praxis

Introduction

Mark Chater

Among those whose work is directly with children's or young people's spirituality—religious educators, teachers with an interest in the spiritual, those in youth ministries and those who train them—there is a perennial concern with the practical that is problematic in several ways.

First, successful practical activities are wanted. The search for 'something to do' with a group or class seems never ending and often anxious. Often, the search is for something that will 'work', be 'relevant', avoid 'preaching' and include 'fun'. This is all very well. It creates a commercial market in resources. Many professionals feel impelled to seek and use off-the-peg materials, because time does not allow them to reflect and, in some cases, because of a lack of confidence originating in the fact that the professional is locked into a role in which s/he delivers someone else's curriculum—even someone else's religious or spiritual agenda—with unease. Because technology and youth culture are rapidly changing, resources and practical approaches appear to date just as rapidly, the market continues to turn over and the professional's sense of anxiety does not go away. The new, the relevant and the successful seem, at times, like a mirage. In this way, much of the desperate consumerism around children, analysed in the first section by Zygmunt Bauman, Mary Grey, Joyce Mercer and Raven LeFay, becomes also the behaviour of the spiritual carers of children.

Praxis is the place where the fevered questing stops, and the more sober questioning begins. What is successful, and how would we know? What skills, values and attitudes are rather more enduring in spiritual education? How can we identify the attributes needed by the teacher or leader that will enable her/him to teach or lead well? Praxis demands that professionals create the space for critical reflection on these and other questions. Praxis is the place of intersection between the theories and assumptions we all carry, the questions we dare to ask ourselves privately, the critical pathway from those questions and the changing practice we inhabit.

Coming from many national contexts, and from differing religious, ideological or pedagogical starting-points, these articles share a concern with critically examining practice in order to promote its authenticity. The first three papers are concerned with context in its broadest sense. Ping Ho Wong, drawing on Chinese, Hong Kong, Vietnamese and Western sources, critically examines the nature of spiritual education in relation to other forms of education and the systems that encase them. He believes that spiritual education can authentically happen only when it addresses its social context honestly. Daniel Scott's contribution employs a metaphor of wrestling as an analytical picture of the tasks of the spiritual educator in relation to him/herself: here the context is not so much national as universally individual, and the task not so much a critique of systems as a rigorous examination of one's own motives. Joyce Bellous uses her own Christian theology to develop a sense of the spiritual educator's relational way of being with her/his pupils as a stance for equality and inclusion, and against discrimination, alienation, isolation, addiction and violence. Joyce's five steps of the spiritual educator are a fluid flow of theology and developmental psychology.

Jacqueline Watson, writing in the English education system, issues a call for discourses of religious and spiritual education to be more democratic in their treatment of content. Cathy Ota, working in the same system, argues that dynamic forms of groupwork in teaching have the potential to unlock ability, challenge unhelpful pedagogical practices and to transform the life chances of the economically and spiritually most disadvantaged. Clive Erricker's critique of models of pedagogy in religious education, and of the assumptions about religion and spiritual experience that lie behind them, sets down challenges for those who work in systems claiming objectivity and liberalism as their core values. In particular, the need to be honest, and to empower children to be honest, about religious and political difference involves a struggle to overcome the liberal and modernist desire to disguise difference.

Writing from post-apartheid South Africa, Cornelia Roux tackles the invisibility of spirituality in her country's curriculum, and narrates a situation in which a heritage of religious privatization, coupled with current economic and medical emergencies, relegates whole-person considerations to the margins. Marian de Souza, with her experience of the Australian interest in spirituality, explores three qualities that overcome political expedience, crude dualism and models of difference. From the USA, Karen-Marie Yust investigates youth camp ministries and questions the value orientation of these highly successful events.

The diverse contexts of these contributions raise a small number of recurring questions which must be for all practitioners to address: when we speak of the spirituality that we wish to find in children and young people, how do we position it? What is its relation to religious traditions, to experience and to our various identities (familial, communal, ideological, ethnic, national)? Are we seeking, in the young, a spirituality that merely affirms culture, for instance, a 'nice' spirituality that promotes moral conformity, invites a polite appreciation of nature or stimulates a 'responsible' or 'realistic' political programme? Have we allowed critical perspectives, such as globalization critiques, ecofeminist activism, liberation theologies, to inform our own spiritual models? And have we, after this, done the necessary digesting to enable us to share those perspectives appropriately with the young? Have we set out on the journey that distances us from the hegemonic curriculum values (social success, academic performance, technical skill, national identity, economic necessity)?

We may never complete such a journey. Yet even if we begin, have we noticed that spirituality changes from useful accessory to pilgrim partner? Sometimes it changes again and again: recurrently, spirituality practitioners claim the right to shift epistemological models as they seek to give expression to the invisible without being bound by the rules of the academic game, or the pedagogical game.

A conceptual investigation into the possibility of spiritual education

Ping Ho Wong*

Into the maze of the concept of spirituality

To look into the possibility of spiritual education begs the question of what 'spiritual education' and, ultimately, 'spirituality' are understood to be. Despite the caution that 'attempted definition [of the spiritual] is not only futile but totally counter-productive' because 'it is a characteristic of spirit and the spiritual that it is dynamic' (Priestley, 1985, p. 114), it is necessary to provide some brief indications of certain aspects of the idea of 'spirituality' with which I can personally connect, and which are also commonly included in various formulations of spirituality.

Transcendence

One commonly mentioned aspect of spirituality is transcendence. For example, Emmons puts 'the capacity to transcend the physical and the material' (1999, p. 164)

*Department of Educational Psychology, Counselling and Learning Needs, The Hong Kong Institute of Education, 10 Lo Ping Road, Tai Po, N.T., Hong Kong. Email: phwong@ied.edu.hk

at the head of his list of five characteristics displayed by spiritually intelligent individuals. While Emmons construes transcendence as being related 'to a person's capacity to engage in heightened or extraordinary forms of consciousness', such as 'rising above our natural world to relate with a divine being', or 'going beyond our physical state to effect a heightened awareness of ourselves' (1999, p. 164), I would venture to suggest that a more mundane form of transcendence is also possible, and indeed more common, which simply involves one's awareness of and commitment to values beyond the physical and material realms, or the pursuit of goals that go beyond the self.[1] The commitment to non-materialistic values and the pursuit of self-transcending goals, in turn, give a sense of meaning and purpose to an individual's life, and are the sources (or at least, the close allies) of other features that are commonly associated with the concept of spirituality such as perseverance in the face of hardship and the capacity to be virtuous.

Raised awareness

Experiences that are profound or mystical, and heightened states of consciousness, are one area that has attracted the attention of a lot of researchers, William James being one of the most prominent among them. Hay with Nye (1998) put forward three 'categories of spiritual sensitivity': awareness sensing, which is 'characterized by a sharply focused attention to the here-and-now of one's experience' (Hay, 1995, p. 19); mystery sensing, which involves the 'awareness of aspects of our life experience that are in principle incomprehensible' (Hay with Nye 1998, p. 66); and value sensing, which is the direct perception of value and meaning. Furthermore, Nye's research with children highlighted the salience of 'relational consciousness'—the sense of oneness with the self, with people, with the world and with God—in children's spirituality (and probably not only in children's spirituality). Just as it is conceivable that there might be a 'spectrum of transcendence' ranging from the mundane to the extraordinary, so I would speculate that there are different degrees of 'mystical' experience too. Our ordinary experience is already mystical in a very dilute sense, and it is this weak but pervasive mystical quality of everyday experience that provides the basis that makes it possible for us to make sense of descriptions of the heightened forms of these experiences that warrant the term 'mystical'. For example, an everyday conversation that opens up a space of intersubjectivity where two or more individuals engage each other in an encounter with open hearts and minds is a spiritual experience, in the sense that each participant has in some, albeit small, degree transcended himself or herself and achieved oneness with the other. Every act of understanding is a minor miracle. Admittedly, such a conversation (and the understanding it makes possible) may fall far short of a genuine dialogue involving a full I–Thou relationship, a form of dialogue that is 'an unusual phenomenon, since the I meets the Thou merely by grace' (Yaron, 1993, p. 2). However, this merely reinforces the point I wish to make: spirituality comes in different degrees and shades, like the colours in a colour circle, and for some purposes at least, no radical break should be assumed to exist between spiritual and unspiritual states such as the I–Thou and the I–It relationship. It is possible to imagine, Buber notwithstanding, a conversation that does not feature a full-fledged I–Thou relationship between the participants, and yet is not a totally I–It non-encounter.

Associations between spirituality as transcendence and spirituality as heightened states of consciousness are apparent. 'Raised awareness' (Hay with Nye, 1998) is transcendence of ordinary experience. The direct perception of value in a heightened state of consciousness transcends any intellectual appraisal of the pros and cons, committing one to the value thus perceived with the force of emotion and despite oneself (in a restricted sense of the self: see n.1, above). Similarly, an intuitive grasp of some profound meaning and point in existence provides the inexhaustible impetus for the dedicated pursuit of one's vocation. And the self is infinitely expanded or transcended in relational consciousness.

Spiritualism

Another domain that is also often denoted by the term 'spirituality' covers spiritual phenomena such as activities of the soul or spirit as distinct from the body in a separate spiritual realm, and contacts and interactions with spiritual entities or forces, It posits the literal reality of a spiritual plane of existence, as distinct from a metaphorical spiritual dimension of human existence. Again, I would like to suggest a continuum of 'spiritual phenomena' in this sense, from weak to strong. An example of a 'weak' spiritual stand would be the position labelled 'transpersonal, a term that Jung had coined to describe experiences in which we transcend our individual identities and tap into a "collective unconscious" shared by all humans'[2] (Horgan, 2003, p. 160). 'Stronger' spiritual positions might more properly be labelled spiritualist, paranormal or even occult, such as Rudolf Steiner's anthroposophy. This sense of 'spirituality' is related to the other two senses, in that both 'raised awareness' and the value and meaning deriving from and driving transcendence cry out to be further accounted for and made sense of,[3] and one plausible way in which this can be done is to posit a separate spiritual realm as the venue of mystical experiences, and where all ultimate values reside and emanate.

Perhaps all sincere spiritual pursuits would ultimately have to face up to and answer the question of the ontological underpinnings of mystical experiences and of meaning and value. However, in practice, the three 'strands' of spirituality can be addressed relatively separately. Very often, in investigations of mystical experiences and of meaning and value, the question of their ontological underpinnings is 'bracketed'. And the distinction between spirituality as mystical experience and spirituality as interactions with spiritual forces is blurred. For example, in *The secret spiritual world of children*, Hart (2003) has gathered together a wealth of accounts of children's spiritual experiences, one of which is about the interactions his daughter, Haley, had with her angel, who provided Haley with guidance. Hart himself raised the question of the ontological nature of such encounters: 'Does she really see an angel?' (2003, p. 22); 'Would it be more accurate to think of Haley's angel as part of herself, "a fountainhead from within"?' (p. 23). However, in the end, Hart evades (or, should we say, transcends?) the question he raises:

> The source of guidance and knowledge, like Haley's, may indeed be thought of as on the inside—an inner fountainhead—or on the outside—the muses of the ancient Greeks or maybe a guardian angel. What is most significant is not the concept we use to describe this knowing, but the fact that, by whatever name, it is available. Its value is measured by the quality of what is heard and how it impacts a life. Haley is able to tap a source of insight, loving comfort, and guidance. (Hart, 2003, p. 23)

In the adoption of an agnostic stance and the bracketing of the question of the reality of spiritual beings or spiritual forces, my own stand is similar to Hart's. And I will not even touch upon any paranormal experiences such as the one reported by Haley about her angel. This is controversial territory, and anyway I am temperamentally not attracted to such matters—but neither am I for the view that spiritual beings or forces definitely do not exist. There is simply insufficient ground for me to take any side. The most that I am comfortable to positively believe is that there is a voice in our heart telling us the right things to do—if only we can still ourselves, listen for its faint utterances and hear it.

The value of the mundane

To conclude, to me spirituality is the capability of and the disposition to transcendence and raised awareness, including relational consciousness (and human qualities and their manifestations associated with transcendence and raised awareness), with these terms being understood both in their mundane and profound senses. In practice, my emphasis would be on their mundane senses, since what I am concerned with is education, for most people, not just for a few spiritual geniuses. In focusing on the weak and mundane forms of spirituality, I may be accused of underestimating everyday folk's spiritual potentiality, and also of adopting a compromising and compromised position with regard to the properly stringent requirements of spirituality, a position that condones and encourages mediocrity, and is thus not spiritual at all. In my defence, I can only say that I do sincerely believe if we focus mostly on the profound expressions of spirituality, particularly as the aim of spiritual education, we run the risk of sacrificing the majority without necessarily benefiting the spiritual development of the few who do have the potential for great spiritual achievements.

Furthermore, even if I do indeed underestimate the everyday person's spiritual potentiality, my misguided estimation is made not out of arrogance and snobbery, but based on self-reflection. I do not think I can aspire to a profound spirituality featuring, for example, an exalted ultimate concern or intense mystical experiences. With regard to spiritual potentiality, I consider myself representative of, if not actually less 'spiritually intelligent' and more mediocre than, most people. And I do believe the mundane and 'weak' forms of spirituality are no less valuable than the profound forms, though probably they are valuable in slightly different ways.

What is 'spiritual education'?

As a corollary to my understanding of spirituality, spiritual education, in its broadest sense, would be any intended or unintended circumstance or effort that promotes the development and flourishing of spirituality, in particular, the capability of and the disposition to transcendence and raised awareness, including relational consciousness. Examples of qualities associated with these two forms of spirituality that should be promoted include commitment to non-materialistic values; pursuit of self-transcending goals; a sense of meaning and purpose in life; perseverance and resilience in the face of hardship; being virtuous; the capacity to feel curiosity, wonder and awe, even in everyday life; and openness to relations.

The importance of social ethos

What forms can and should spiritual education take? The African proverb 'It takes a village to raise a child', popularized by Hillary Clinton's book, *It takes a village* (Clinton, 1996), provides a convenient entry point into our consideration of the issue. The proverb can, of course, be variously interpreted. It reminds us that 'raising the next generation is a shared responsibility' (Bateson, 2000, p. 153), requiring the active involvement of numerous people in the community. It also hints at the crucial role played by the social ethos in a child's education, a point well recognized in the Chinese tradition. The popular Chinese practice of consulting geomancy (*fengshui*) masters for the selection and arrangement of residence with a view to the promotion of prosperity and good fortune is now well known, but ever since antiquity the Chinese sages have been advising people about the careful choice of the community of residence based on a consideration not of its material, but its moral and spiritual impact on the residents. Confucius once remarked that 'It is Goodness[4] that gives to a neighbourhood its beauty. One who is free to choose, yet does not prefer to dwell among the Good—how can he be accorded the name of wise?' (Confucius, 2000, p.94) It is said that Mother Meng (Mencius's mother, who was widowed) moved the family three times in Mencius's childhood until they:

> lived next to a school. [The young] Mencius then played by setting up sacrificial utensils, and performing the rituals of a guest bowing, giving way, entering, and departing. Meng's mother said, 'Truly I can reside with my son here.' And so they lived there. (Wang, 2003, p. 150)

Mencius's subsequent great achievements are said to have owed a great deal to his mother's wise choice of neighbourhood.

The proverb 'It takes a village to raise a child' can also be 'over-interpreted' as asserting the superiority and wholesomeness of the intimate ethos characteristic of a village community as an environment for children to grow up in. Tönnies, a nineteenth-century German sociologist, called such a village ethos *Gemeinschaft* ('community'), 'a state characterized by a sense of fellow feeling, strong personal ties, and sturdy primary memberships, along with a sense of personal loyalty to one another', in contradistinction to *Gesellschaft* ('society'), a condition that occurs when rural life is displaced by urban living, and is characterized by 'a high division of labour, less prominence of personal ties, the lack of a sense of community among the members of society, and the absence of a feeling of belonging' (Anderson & Taylor, 2000, p. 597). That this by-now globalized movement from rural to urban life, from *Gemeinschaft* to *Gesellschaft*, has greatly compromised the ability of the community to serve as a kind of pervasive 'hidden curriculum' for people's spiritual education, and, to put it even in stronger terms, has turned the community into an agent of spiritual mis-education that actively corrodes people's spirit, has frequently been observed, commented upon and lamented by people of different persuasions from a variety of perspectives, though not always using the term 'spirituality'. For example,

> Buber believed that there had been a movement from relation to separation, that there was a growing crisis of being or existence in 'modern' society. He believed that the relationship between individuals and their selves ... between people, and people and creation was increasingly that of I–It. As a result it was becoming more and more difficult to encounter God. (Smith, 2000, n.p.)

Of course the movement from rural to urban life is only one of many intertwined factors, such as the rapid development of technology and worldwide ideological developments that have culminated at the present point in time in the hegemony of neo-liberalism; and that have acted together to continually reshape the ethos and texture of contemporary social life in a modernized community, like Hong Kong, in such a way as to prompt some commentators to deploy the metaphors of poison and pollution to describe the current social and cultural environment. For example, the Vietnamese Buddhist monk Thich Nhat Hanh pointed out that:

> There is pollution in our consciousness. Television, films, and newspapers are forms of pollution for us and our children. They sow seeds of violence and anxiety in us and pollute our consciousness, just as we destroy our environment by farming with chemicals, clear-cutting the trees, and polluting the water. We need to protect the ecology of the Earth and the ecology of the mind, or this kind of violence and recklessness will spill over into even more areas of life. (Thich, 1997, p. 165)

Garbarino (1995) offers a more systematic critique of the unwholesome social ethos, using the term 'socially toxic environment ... to suggest that the social context of children, the social world in which they live, has become poisonous to their development' (Garbarino, 1995, p. 3). The targets of his critique include television, the erosion of childhood as a protected social space, the decline of civility and the 'monetarization' of daily life, among others.

Limitations of a compartmentalized spiritual education

It is my belief that effective spiritual education is, first and foremost, rendered by the social ethos. By saying this, I do not mean there is no room for more or less 'compartmentalized' spiritual education initiatives, to be carried out in specific and more confined contexts, such as that of the school, including the school curriculum, in the form of a more narrowly defined spiritual education. After all, the social ethos is constituted by the sum of all individual actions, social relations and collective undertakings—without forgetting the significant implications of the crucial fact that this whole thus constituted is larger than the sum of its parts. There is indeed an important role to be played by spiritual education initiatives and activities, for example, sessions set aside for the discussion of spiritual issues or the teaching of meditation exercises, or even regular meditation periods in the timetable. While Buber believed that the education of character 'is not achieved through the direct teaching of ethics', he nevertheless admitted that it will involve some reflection upon ethics (Smith, 2000, n.p.). What must be resisted is the temptation of the complacent assumption that, as Farrell puts it in relation to the problem of moral education, 'our attempts to "educate" (in this case within the moral domain) within the constraints and rituals of formal schooling will somehow produce (or at least can produce, if properly planned and organized) "moral learning" among the subjects of our schooling enterprise' (2003, p. 113). As Erricker observes:

> in the social sphere there always exists a political and economic climate within which relations work and of which those relations are themselves an expression ... Once this is understood we cannot pretend that our ability to relate to one another can be approached educationally without attention being paid to the political climate framing and suffusing relations. To do so would be to create a code of values that breaks down every time it is challenged by that climate, i.e. once there is a politico-social price to pay. Thus, there is a lip service paid to 'warmth', as far as values and relations are concerned, which, since it has no political context, disappears when that political climate changes. Educationally, therefore, the climate is not mentioned. The values are preached or explored in the sterile and irrelevant isolation of the classroom without reference to the social reality in which they are to be employed. (2002, pp. 40–1)

Discrete elements of the spiritual education curriculum work and are made sense of in the context of the overall school and even social ethos, rather than achieve their effect in isolation of this context. A well-intentioned initiative, when carried out against the background of a surrounding hidden curriculum of contrary purposes, will either serve to subvert that hidden curriculum, particularly if the hidden curriculum is explicitly exposed, recognized and critiqued, or be itself subverted by the hidden curriculum, particularly if the latter is unchallenged or seen to be unchallengeable, even contributing to more cynicism. Thus we should always proceed cautiously and not take things at their face value. Another feature of compartmentalized spiritual education initiatives that likely compromises their effectiveness is the compartmentalization itself, which supports a model of the human person as an aggregate of discrete knowledge, skills and attributes that can be assembled together like a factory product, a model that subtly conveys an expectation to pupils of what they are like and how they deserve to be treated that is contradictory to the spiritual understanding of human beings. And this reminds us that the adjective spiritual in the term 'spiritual education' should properly describe the nature rather than only the 'content' and 'intended outcome' of that education. An education in spirituality should itself be spiritual. This is different from the case of, say, geography education, where it makes little sense to describe the education as geographical.

The non-linear dynamics of the spirit

In its essence, the idea that education in spirituality should itself be spiritual is similar to the view that effective spiritual education is, first and foremost, rendered by the social ethos. And they both contain within themselves a paradox that should lead us to rethink their soundness, or at least harbour some reservation about them. This is similar to the Socratic paradox of how on earth it is possible for anyone to learn anything, or, for that matter, for anyone to teach anything to another. To be able to learn anything new, one has to be already in possession of the requisite knowledge about the thing to be learned that is necessary for comprehending and assimilating the new knowledge. Hence it is impossible to learn anything radically new; all learning is nothing other than recollection. Analogously, since education in spirituality must itself be spiritual, there is no way in which spirituality can arise or be cultivated if the social ethos is spiritually toxic. There is simply no point through which the spirit can enter this closed circle. And this seems to be borne out by the fact that, despite the unending flow of critiques of the corrosive effects on human character and spirituality ever since the advent of industrialization and urbanization, to such an extent that they now sound mere platitudes, such critiques have not succeeded in stemming the tide. Despite pockets of resistance in such forms as alternative communities and the counter-culture, the overall trend towards industrialization (and its putative successor post-industrialization) and urbanization continues to accelerate, and the evolving social forms into which we find ourselves moving do not seem less malignant than their predecessors. There is no shortage of memes flowing around that protest the suffocating of the spirit, but they do not constitute the dominant discourse, and industrialization and urbanization, and now technologization and globalization, seem just to follow their own inexorable developmental dynamics like that of a cancer growth. Yes, there is room for the more or less free flow of these dissenting memes— and this is something we must be thankful for—but they do not seem to matter much.

Yet the idea that spiritual education is impossible under current social conditions is, of course, contrary to our understanding of the nature of spirit and spirituality: recall that 'it is a characteristic of spirit and the spiritual that it is dynamic' (Priestley, 1985, p. 114). It breaks out in unexpected moments and places. If we do take the ideas of spirituality and spiritual education seriously, we should not give up on the possibility of achieving something meaningful through less than perfect means, such as meditation classes and discussions of spiritual issues, under less than ideal conditions, and should try to do as much as we can, even as we uphold in principle the ideas that education in spirituality should itself be spiritual and that effective spiritual education is firstly rendered by the social ethos. For one thing, the fact that the proliferation of dissenting memes and subversive initiatives has so far produced no significant effect in stemming the onslaught of forces that make our social environment toxic does not mean that the growth of these memes and practices does not actually matter. We cannot tell in advance when their growth approaches the critical mass requiring only a last straw to tip the scale and reverse or put right the trend, the point at which the spirit breaks open and enters the circle. There may indeed be a dynamic governing all this, but that of non-linear dynamics. In mathematical jargon, 'after the catastrophe [the sudden, huge change that is initiated when the critical mass is reached] then you may end up on an attractor [a stable state, such as a new social ethos] that you never knew existed [you never knew was possible]'[5] (Cohen & Stewart, 1994, p. 211). Gladwell, the writer who popularized the concept of the 'tipping point' with his bestseller of the same title, puts the same point in less intimidating language: in social epidemics 'change happens not gradually but at one dramatic moment' (Gladwell, 2000, p. 9). He advises that: 'What must underlie successful epidemics [roughly meaning "social movement" in this context], in the end, is a bedrock belief that change is possible, that people can radically transform their behaviour or beliefs in the face of the right kind of impetus' (p. 258). Those who are concerned with spiritual education would do well to heed this piece of sagely advice (or platitude, which is probably the same thing).

Bootstrapping spiritual education

Furthermore, there is the argument that features of human character, such as virtue and spirituality, can be cultivated through the pursuit of practices that are initially not completely or properly virtuous or spiritual. At first glance, this view seems to contradict the idea that education in spirituality must itself be spiritual, but in fact the two need not be contradictory, at least not entirely so, as I hope to show in due course. Take the example of language learning. Whereas the possibility cannot be ruled out that, occasionally, an infant might happen to have formed a certain concept in its mind before being taught or discovering its verbal label, thereby learning the word and grasping its meaning, in the majority of cases, an infant just gets immersed in a language environment before there are even vaguely formed concepts in its mind. In the course of language learning, infants are bombarded with pieces of language in the context of real-world interactions. Through initially 'senseless' sound play in imitation of the language pieces they hear or in response to encouragement by adults, or in myriad other ways, they somehow suddenly grasp the meaning of the initially senseless sound-complex and hence the idea or concept it signified.

A moving example of this process is provided by Helen Keller, who told the story of how the persevering effort of her dedicated teacher finally enabled her to grasp the meaning of the word 'water', the first word she was ever able to make sense of, and the enlightening effect this first discovery had on her. This is a mysterious process: meaning arising or emerging out of the engagement in pre-semantic behaviour. However, note that certain conditions must be satisfied for this mysterious process to work. The child must be engaged to and by the language community in active interaction. An infant watching television alone, though heavily bombarded with pieces of verbal language, will never learn the language and be thus enabled to grasp the concepts these pieces of language signify.

What all this discussion of the discovery of meaning and hence the cultivation of the intellect initially through the play or practice of not-yet understood language is intended to suggest is that the cultivation of virtue and spirituality can, if not must, follow an analogous path. Comte-Sponville explains the process of becoming virtuous by quoting the great philosophers:

> There are no natural virtues; hence we must become virtuous. How? 'For the things we have to learn before we can do them', Aristotle explains, 'we learn by doing them.' Yet how can we do them if we haven't learned them? … 'We become just', Aristotle continues, 'by doing just acts, temperate by doing temperate acts, brave by doing brave acts'. But can we act justly without being just? Temperately without being temperate? Bravely without being brave? And if we cannot, then how do we become just, temperate, brave? (2001, pp. 10–11)

That paradox is analogous to the Socratic paradox about the (im)possibility of learning. Comte-Sponville invokes Kant for a solution to this paradox:

> For him [Kant], these first semblances of virtue can be explained in terms of discipline, in other words, as a product of external constraint: what the child cannot do on his own because he has no instinct of it 'others have to do … for him', and in this way 'one generation educates the next'. It is by mimicking the ways of virtue … that we stand a chance of becoming virtuous … If we can become moral (and for morality even to be possible—and immorality, too, for that matter—it must be the case that we can), it is not through virtue but through education, not for goodness' sake but for form's sake, not for moral reasons but for reasons of politeness. Morality is first artifice, then artifact. By imitating virtue we become virtuous. 'For when men play these roles', writes Kant, 'virtues are gradually established, whose appearance had up until now only been affected. These virtues ultimately will become part of the actor's disposition'. (2001, pp. 11–12)

What Comte-Sponville seems to be saying is that an initially hollow, external behavioural form, when deployed often enough, will give rise to the inner substance of character it is supposed to express. This view might be termed an 'emergence' model of virtue development. Here the term 'emergence' alludes to the philosophical idea that reality is a multi-levelled structure, with a higher level of reality being the emergent property of the entities one level below, when these entities are organized in the proper manner. A more sophisticated version of this model of reality posits bi-directional inter-level influences, in the sense that the entities on a certain level not only give rise to a higher, emergent level of reality, but are themselves influenced or conditioned by the higher-level qualities they have given rise to, and, in turn, influence or condition the lower-level entities that have given rise to them. For example, one attempt to solve the age-old mind–body puzzle suggests that the behaviour and interactions of brain cells properly configured give rise to the emergent property of consciousness, the operation of which, in turn, in some way influences or conditions the operations of the brain. The emergence model of virtue development then proposes that actions and practices that are imitations of virtuous actions and practices, when engaged in often enough, will somehow give rise to the imitated virtue as an emergent, higher-level feature of the individual who engages in such actions and practices.

I would suggest that the range of application of the 'emergence model' can be extended beyond virtue development to also cover language development and spiritual development, and possibly other phenomena too. In the case of language, the frequent pre-semantic deployment of language forms (behaviour) will give rise to a grasp of the meaning signified by these forms (cognition). True to the bi-directional nature of inter-level interaction, once the child grasps the meanings signified by the language forms, his use of these language forms will change, in the sense that it will now be informed by the meaning the child wishes to express. In the case of spiritual development, the regular engagement in spiritual practices will enhance one's spirituality as an attribute of one's inner being.

The educative role of the community

In what sense does this not contradict the view that education in spirituality must itself be spiritual? I will argue that in fact not all engagement in spiritual practices will contribute to enhancing one's spirituality. Recall that in the case of language learning, the child must be engaged to and by the language community in active interaction, otherwise no amount of passive immersion in the language will lead to any breakthrough to understanding.[6] Similarly, the mere mechanical performance of a spiritual practice, in a community that does not take the practice seriously, is likely to contribute to alienation rather than spiritual development. At best the child can only learn to engage in the spiritual practice in the same spiritless, if not hypocritical, way as those adults around him do. Confucius was well aware of this danger:

> The Master said, A man who is not Good,[7] what can he have to do with ritual? A man who is not Good, what can he have to do with music? (Confucius, 2000, p. 86)

> The Master said, Ritual, ritual! Does it mean no more than presents of jade and silk? Music, music! Does it mean no more than bells and drums? (p. 201)

Of course, at the outset, a novice can only simulate a virtuous action or spiritual practice. However, the unit of analysis should be larger than the individual novice, just as in language learning, the unit of analysis is the infant and its social circle. In the absence of the support of a social circle, an infant imitating TV sounds will never learn any language. Now argument by analogy is shaky, and I do not rule out the possibility that the mere 'going through the motions' of a spiritual practice such as, say, meditation may produce a spiritual experience in the form of a heightened state of consciousness. This would be particularly likely in the case either of a spiritual genius, or of someone who treats the practice very seriously. However, I believe that the case of language learning can throw important light on how spiritual education is possible and how it is impeded in many cases. A novice can indeed only simulate the form of spiritual practices. However, if the models from whom he copies the form are themselves serious about the spiritual practices, that is their spiritual practices are indeed expressions of the inner spirituality of their character, the inner spirituality of the novice will be ignited through the catalyst of the practice of the form. On the other hand, to take an extreme, hypothetical case, if the teachers of spiritual education are themselves hypocrites, who discuss spiritual issues with pupils because that is prescribed in the school curriculum, but are otherwise uninterested in these spiritual issues, their hypocrisy cannot but be detected by the pupils, resulting in more spiritual harm than good. In this sense, the success of the spiritual education of the common people still depends to a large extent on a spiritual social ethos.

In conclusion, we should heed the advice of the ancient sages to avoid extreme positions.[8] A strong spiritual ethos is not an absolute necessity for spiritual education to be possible, but nor is spiritual education easily realized *ex nihilo* irrespective of the social context. On balance, I believe that, in the absence of a strong spiritual social ethos, spiritual education, though not impossible, will face serious impediments. Trying to transcend these impediments to our pursuit of spiritual education is a way for us to realize our nature as spiritual beings.

Notes

1.   This last phrase is a very rough formulation. There is a sense in which one's committed goal is constitutive of one's (expanded) self. The self grows by transcending itself. Perhaps a better formulation would be 'goals that go beyond the egoistic self', but 'egoistic' might sound redundant as an adjective of 'self', and anyway begs further explication.

2.   Jung sometimes describes the collective unconscious as the product of the evolutionary heritage of the human species, evident in such phenomena as archetypes and universal dream symbolism. In this sense, the collective unconscious is not necessarily a spiritual realm. However, in many other instances, such as in discussions of the phenomenon of 'synchronicity', the collective unconscious as construed by Jung is something that is a properly 'transpersonal' realm that hovers over, or underlies, all individual human beings, constituting a medium through which the separation of individuals can be transcended.

3.   I admit that I may be mistaken on this point. For example, value is directly grasped in a 'value sensing' type of raised awareness, which means that there is a self-contained, holistic perception of the value, its significance and its justifications, if such distinctions are meaningful at all in relation to the experience. The experience itself is the justification for the perceived value. Therefore there may not be any subsequent need to account for the perceived value separately. Still, analytically the ontological status of the source of the value is an issue, only that probably the answer to this is already included in the value sensing perception itself.

4.   'Goodness' is the sinologist Arthur Waley's rendition of the fundamental Confucian concept of *ren*, which has been given different translations by different authors. For example, Fung (1997) translated it as 'human-heartedness'.

5.   The following fuller quote reinforces the point about the unpredictable character of the future, a future that cannot be assumed simply by extrapolating current trends: 'after the catastrophe you may end up on an attractor that you never knew existed. It was busy developing, out in the mathematical space of the possible, but you didn't notice it because the new attractor wasn't being physically expressed. Suddenly it is expressed, and the mathematical fiction gobbles up your own reality and lands you in totally unexpected circumstances' (Cohen & Stewart, 1994, p. 211).

6.   In other words, the child learns the language as it is used by those around it to communicate among themselves and, more importantly, to interact with it in a meaningful way. In this sense, the community and the child born into it are totally committed to the language. This commitment on the part of the community of which the child is a member is crucial.

7.   'Good' is Arthur Waley's translation for *ren*, which has often been alternatively rendered as 'human-hearted'; see n.4, above.

8.   This is, of course, a simplified and distorted formulation for the sake of ease of expression. This advice should not be taken as itself advocating an extreme position of avoiding extreme positions in all cases and at all costs. Instead it recommends giving everything its proper due, no more and no less.

Notes on contributor

Wong Ping Ho is a Senior Lecturer and the Deputy Head of the Department of Educational Psychology, Counselling and Learning Needs, the Hong Kong Institute of Education, Hong Kong, China. He had been a secondary school teacher for ten years before moving into teacher education. He studied for his MEd in religious and moral education at the University of Hong Kong. He is now also a PhD student at the University of Hull, working on the issue of spirituality in education.

References

Anderson, M. L. & Taylor, H. F. (2000) *Sociology: understanding a diverse society* (Belmont, CA, Wadsworth/Thomson Learning).

Bateson, M. C. (2000) *Full circles, overlapping lives: culture and generation in transition* (New York, Random House).

Clinton, H. R. (1996) *It takes a village: and other lessons children teach us* (New York, Simon & Schuster).

Cohen, J. & Stewart, I. (1994) *The collapse of chaos: discovering simplicity in a complex world* (New York, Penguin).

Comte-Sponville, A. (2001) *A small treatise on the great virtues: the uses of philosophy in everyday life* (Catherine Temerson, Trans.) (New York, Metropolitan Books).

Confucius (2000) *The analects* (Arthur Waley, Trans.) (London, Everyman).

Emmons, R. A. (1999) *The psychology of ultimate concerns: motivation and spirituality in personality* (New York, The Guilford Press).

Erricker, C. (2002) *When learning becomes your enemy: the relationship between education, spiritual dissent and economics* (Nottingham, Educational Heretics Press).

Farrell, J. P. (2003) 'Hey Joe ...' Moral education, moral learning, and how could we ever know if and when the first produces the second? *Curriculum Inquiry*, 33(2), 105–115.

Fung, Y. L. (1997) *A short history of Chinese philosophy: a systematic account of Chinese thought from its origins to the present day* (Derk Bodde, Ed.) (New York, The Free Press).

Garbarino, J. (1995) Growing up in a socially toxic environment: life for children and families in the 1990s, in: G. B. Melton (Ed.) *The individual, the family, and social good: personal fulfillment in times of change* (Lincoln, NB, University of Nebraska Press), 1–20.

Gladwell, M. (2000) *Tipping point: how little things can make a big difference* (Boston, MA, Little, Brown).

Hart, T. (2003) *The secret spiritual world of children* (Makawao, HI, Inner Ocean).

Hay, D. (1995) The validity of the experiential approach to religious education, *Hong Kong Journal of Religious Education*, 7(1), 14–26.

Hay, D. with Nye, R. (1998) *The spirit of the child* (London, HarperCollins Religious).

Horgan, J. (2003) *Rational mysticism: dispatches from the border between science and spirituality* (New York, NY, Houghton Mifflin).

Priestley, J. G. (1985) Towards finding the hidden curriculum: a consideration of the spiritual dimension of experience in curriculum planning, *British Journal of Religious Education*, 7(3), 112–119.

Smith, M. K. (2000) Martin Buber on education, in: *The encyclopedia of informal education*. Available online at: http://www.infed.org/thinders/et-buber.htm (accessed 13 July 2004).

Thich, N. H. (1997) The sun my heart, in: A. Kotler (Ed.) *Engaged Buddhist reader: ten years of engaged Buddhist publishing* (Berkeley, CA, Parallax Press), 162–170.

Wang, R. R. (2003) *Images of women in Chinese thought and culture* (Indianapolis, IN, Hackett).

Yaron, K. (1993) Martin Buber, *Prospects: the quarterly review of comparative education*, 23(1–2), 135–46. Available online at: http://www.unesco.org/International/Publications/Thinkers/ThinkersPdf/bubere.pdf (accessed 13 July 2004).

Wrestling with the spirit(ual): grappling with theory, practice and pedagogy

Daniel G. Scott*

Introduction

In engaging the theoretical and personal complexity of spirituality in academic research in this paper, I am also addressing concerns for practice in professional care settings with children and youth. How we study spirituality matters in how we teach it and how our understanding is applied to the lives of children and youth in the midst of their living. In a world marked by so many divides, I hope, by staying in and with the difficulty of spirituality and resisting simplifications and exclusivity, to find ways of understanding the spirit(ual) in children's lives.

Following David Blades's (1997) presentation that used the Biblical account (Gen. 32) of Jacob wrestling with an angel/spirit on the banks of a stream as a metaphor for education, I conceived my (theoretical) difficulties regarding research in spirituality as a similar act of wrestling with the spirit(ual). Although contemporary wrestling is corrupted by images of staged showcase wrestling, I confess that a ring

*School of Child and Youth Care, University of Victoria, PO Box 1700 Stn CSC, Victoria, BC V8W 2Y2, Canada. Email: dgscott@uvic.ca

complete with ropes, white mat and roaring crowd has flashed in my mind's eye as a possible scene. The following scenario of seven 'moves' plays out between Jacob's riverbank and an imaginary arena.

My difficulty arises from my attempts to grapple with the spirit(ual) in research, while simultaneously, believing the spirit(ual) is not something to be firmly grasped at all. Perhaps my attempts to study spirituality academically use techniques that violate the topic itself. Or endanger the nature of children's spirituality. I struggle with that struggle. It has implications for my pedagogy and practice.

Jacob wrestled in the dark until daybreak, refusing to release his unknown opponent until he had extracted a blessing. The shadowy presence I struggle with may be my own demon. If it occupies other academic writing about spirituality, then perhaps my grappling with it and the difficulties of articulating the spirit(ual) will offer some benefit for our work with children.

The seven moves/problematics

Move 1: avoiding the grip of definitions

It begins, as it does in academic work, with defining the terms. My urge is to lunge in and seize the spirit(ual) and pin it down to make clear what exactly I mean by 'spirituality'. The voice of academic tradition in the crowd wants the opponent named: 'Defining is necessary.' But a counter voice whispers: 'In defining there is always an ending'. Wen Song Hui (Curriculum Colloquium, Victoria, BC, Canada) said in July 1997: 'To define is to destroy':

> *definio-ire –li -itus* tr. to mark out the limits of (a place); to limit, restrict; to define; to fix, determine; to bring to a finish, put an end to; and to assign. (*New College Latin–English Dictionary*, 1996)

I hesitate. Do I wish to put an end to the spirit(ual) by pinning it to the mat? Perhaps the spirit(ual) is a site where the need to define and fix should be questioned (or at least doubted). The first foe in the ring is an unexpected one. If I am resisting tradition, maybe I have to avoid being seized by the necessity of definitions. Do I want to make the spirit(ual) certain? Any borders I declare might delimit the spirit(ual). Here is the heart of the problem for me: uncertainty seems necessary in spirit. Is that a sufficient demarcation? In some traditions there is an abiding quality of mystery in that which is just out of reach, beyond grasp. Caputo (1987), borrowing from Heidegger, calls mystery the unencompassable:

> The thing (no-thing?) we cannot get around, both in the sense of something we cannot avoid running into somewhere along the way and in the sense of something we cannot surround, circumscribe or encompass with our concepts. It is what is left over, the radical hermeneutical residuum which conceptual thinking and planning can never exhaust, include, assimilate. (p. 270)

But we try. I have several pages of definitions of spirituality collected from papers in the field. They are all partial; that is, incomplete and favouring some pre-position.

They are all constructs. Each is an attempt to hold the spiritual still for observation and study: spirituality is relational consciousness (Hay, 1998); seeing the invisible, wisdom and between you and me (Hart, 2003); connections beyond the self (Scott, 2004); meeting the Divine in religious traditions; any meeting with the other/Other; or a description of energy and forces (Kovel, 1991). The spirit(ual) is an aspect of inner life, values, morality, or being connected to the self. It may include some or all of these, or things yet unknown. They are glimpses of something and are initially accurate ways of framing spirituality.

Religions opt for metaphors and poetics to offer images that are momentary, referential and incomplete; perceiving spirit as fleeting; and allowing meanings that are multiple. Spirit is wind, breath or fire. A certain wisdom acknowledges that fixing spirituality is a loss of engagement and possibility. Closure is not required.

At dawn, Jacob's unidentified opponent slipped away. So the spirit(ual) must slip out of my grasp as I must elude the grip of the call to definitions. To address the spirit(ual) must itself be a spirit(ual) task: a congruent action that respects its nature, draws from it its way of being expressed and its offer of form. That undefined form holds me in a grip of impossibility. I cannot escape making claims: the spirit(ual) is somehow elusive and powerful. A (contradictory) space must be held open to avoid being caught in the grip of knowledge and certainty, yet simultaneously, being caught by the spirit of the spiritual and not the rules of tradition(s).

As a child, I visited the old Natural Sciences Museum in Ottawa where there were rows of display cases of dead butterflies, all pinned down and well lit. It was a horror for me: beautiful creatures pinned, specimens defined by tags. In medieval iconography the butterfly was a symbol of the soul, a creature of metamorphosis in flight. This has always seemed a spiritual insight to me, worthy of passing on.

Move 2: grappling with what always gets away

The irony of holding on to that which cannot be held sets in. This is a problematic with several layers of difficulty:

1. If a primary quality of spirituality is its elusiveness and its vitality depends on it being in motion, can I study it without altering it to do so? (Think of the pinned butterflies)
2. What methods, what ways of studying spirituality might be feasible, allowing it to stay in flux?
3. Is it possible to study the one/thing whose nature includes qualities of unexpectedness and irruption?

That which is in motion can only be known by the way it is enacted: we see what the wind does even if we cannot see the wind. There is a fleeting quality to knowledge-in-passing.

Jacob's opponent comes without a name, refuses to be identified, yet gives a name in exchange for release. Jacob is altered in the process, left with a wounded hip and new identity. It is a transformational story. Jacob faces an encounter with his estranged warrior brother, Esau, and fears for his own safety. He has to cross a stream: the Yabbok—a word meaning pouring out or emptying (www.sacrednamebi-ble.com/kjvstrongs/STRHEB12.htm#S1238). He is being poured out on the banks of the Yabbok in an all-night wrestle. Who does he wrestle: some part of himself, his own fears, or an other/Other who has come to challenge him to emptying and crossing over? Who leaves him renamed, remade? The answers matter for research and for pedagogy.

There are three challenging connections that arise to express the difficulty of grappling with what always gets away. The first is from Serres's (1982) 'Knowledge in the classical age', in which he concludes that the search for 'knowledge is a hunt. To know is to put to death—to kill' (p. 28). From the La Fontaine fable he is discussing he outlines the process of strategy and devouring: 'Thus it is that the relation between theory and practice, the relation of metaphysics to knowledge, and the relation of the latter to domination come together in the same place, *at the outcome provided by death*' (p. 28; emphasis in original). This is the very place I am trying to work and think: 'between theory and practice.' How am I to understand it? Who dies in the hunt? Jacob? Perhaps the spirit(ual) is always a dangerous encounter, a confrontation that comes (un)invited and slips away. Jacob is strong enough to hold his opponent demanding to know the name of the other/Other and secures a blessing before he lets go. He is renamed: Jacob becomes Israel.

Our quest for knowledge may be the hunt but the spirit will not permit being named (defined). Is the elusive quality an act of withholding? (I shall return to this momentarily via Caputo.) In my wrestling with the spirit(ual), I am worried about killing it to gain knowledge. Something is awry.

A hunt has happened but there is another way of understanding it. In *Christianity rediscovered*, Donovan (1978) describes his unorthodox missionary work with the Masai of Kenya where he attempted to present a theology appropriate to their way of seeing the world, based on their experience. In seeking a word in Kishwahili to describe faith, a Masai elder dismisses the word chosen by Donovan as too distant and disengaged. He chooses instead a word that describes the lion's embrace of its prey in the act of killing that captures the energy and focus of the kill. The elder notes that it is not he who hunts for the Divine, but rather the Divine who hunts for him, and in the end the lion is God. The elder knows he is the prey. Perhaps in wrestling with spirit I need to reconsider. I believe I am hunting, but perhaps it is I who am being hunted? A zebra becomes food for the lion without warning, without design on its part. Who, then, needs to slip away?

I cannot answer that question. I am compelled to stay with the struggle even as the unexpected arises. I thought of continuing with the passage from Caputo (1987) in his tenth chapter: 'Openness to the mystery' on the unencompassable:

> It is the moment of withdrawal (*Ent-zug*) which inhabits everything which is 'given', the absence (*Ab-wesen, ab-esse*) in everything which we try to summon into presence (*An-wesen, prae-esse*). But not just the absence but the play of presence and absence, the unsettled, unsettling fluctuation between the two, so that we can never lay hands on a fixed structure or a stable stuff. (p. 270)

We are in the midst of hanging on to the thing that is not fixed in structure or temporality. It seemed sufficient to acknowledge its slippery nature, the quality of that which exists in/through withdrawal, and that the spirit(ual) includes a tradition of emptiness and abyss, as well as a tradition of presence. There and not there, present and absent, even as I try to grapple with it for the purposes of writing, research and teaching. But what if grasping (knowing) the spirit(ual), insisting on its presence or denying its absence is already to kill, to rupture its fluidity and form?

A second passage from Caputo multiples the complexity and returns me to the Masai elder's question about who is being hunted. Caputo (1987) names the unexpected intrusion in a different way:

> I would say that in the thin membranes of structures which we stretch across the flux, in the thin fabric we weave over it, there are certain spots where the surface wears through and acquires a transparency which exposes the flux beneath. There are certain breaking points, let us say, in the habits and practices, the works and days, of our mundane existence where the flux is exposed, where the whole trembles and the play irrupts. Then we know we are in trouble. The abyss, the play, the uncanny—in short, all hell—breaks loose and the card castles of everydayness come tumbling down. Something breaks through because the constraints we impose upon things break down. (pp. 269–70)

This is Jacob's case: something has irrupted in the shape of a physical opponent. There is trembling. Jacob is afraid to face Esau whom he cheated of his inheritance and has sent gifts ahead, seeking appeasement. The two encounters: one here and one to come, change him. He acquires a new name and identity. He also has loss: a dying of self.

Am I willing to face disruption if I get (too) close to the topic at hand? If I resist the urge to define, if I remain engaged, demand and let go, will I survive? Will the spirit(ual) remain alive and elusive if I succeed in studying it? And what of children? What ways of engaging will they be shown and use to meet the spirit(ual) in their lives? Will spirit retain vitality for them? What dangers does it include for them?

These questions are important for our field. The congruency between our methods of study and what we are exploring matters. Will our methods affect the lives of children and their spirit(ual) realities and experience? What is in their best interest in our curiosity about their spirituality? How much must remain hidden and elusive for their well-being in meeting the spirit(ual)?

Move 3: stripping the other/Other

This move is a series of layers, waiting to be peeled away. It is about laying bare. Research is an act of prying and opening. Its vocabulary of uncovering, seeking, looking into and examining speaks to its goals of exposing patterns, clarifying structure(s) or displaying themes. We seek to bring to light what is hidden. It is not the researcher who is to be exposed, but rather the others/Others—the researched— who are to be laid bare. If my hunch is right and the spirit(ual) requires a degree of hiddenness, a necessary covering—in some inexplicable way, a modesty for existence—and if research has an inherent violation in its laying bare, what is the work of exposure to accomplish?

Again, I turn to metaphors. Serres (1997) tells an odd tale of the Harlequin king, also known as the Emperor of the Moon, who returns from a lunar expedition to tell the assembled crowd that the new land is just like home: 'everywhere everything is just as it is here' (p. xiii) and that there is 'nothing new under the sun or on the moon' (p. xiii). The crowd begins to deride him, demanding he reveal new truth, and mocking his appearance. In response he gradually removes his harlequin clothes that are:

> a motley composite made of pieces, of rags or scraps of every size, in a thousands forms and different colours, of varying ages, from different sources, badly basted, inharmoniously juxtaposed, with no attention paid to proximity, mended according to circumstance, according to need, accident, and contingency. (p. xiv)

The ridicule continues until Harlequin, after peeling away layers of similarly mottled garments is naked. His skin, covered in tattoos, is also variegated: 'striated, iridescent, embroidered, damasked, shimmering' (p. xv). Their demand for novelty and singularity produces nothing and the crowd leaves disappointed. But in the last moment, as the curtain falls, Harlequin is transformed into Pierrot, the fool who is all and entirely white, skin and clothes, and then disappears. Serres's piece of theatre is about ideas, education and the search for knowledge.

I adapt it here to speak to my wrestling match, including its caution about the eager multitude. My crowd has come to hear of a new place—the spirit(ual)—and are promised it is nothing new. It is hard for enthusiastic researchers to hear that the spirit(ual) may not be a site of novelty or simple solutions in practice with children and youth. It is complex and fragmentary, constructed from fragments of life, experience, tradition and culture. Like Harlequin's garb, the spiritual is an assemblage of scraps, historical ideas and gathered cultural pieces. The simple solution the crowd seeks is not there. The demand comes: 'Lay bare. Expose.' Layer after layer is peeled away but the display is a failure. The (re)search for novelty must be abandoned.

What of the spiritual lives of children and youth? Hiddenness may be necessary for them. If a component of their engagement of the spirit(ual) requires secrecy, then their spiritual experiences may need to go on out of sight. If we focus too much attention on them, trying to lay bare their secret lives, perhaps they will lose access to the spirit(ual). It may disappear in the (over)-awareness created by overt attention. Children may lose engagement because, in being self-conscious, they will be unable to be open and attentive. What if they are being laid bare in the (re)search?

In Serres' tale there is a moment of transformation in the disappearance of the Harlequin behind the falling curtain. I can read the Emperor as the spirit(ual) which lays itself bare in response to the demand to be seen. It is never seen as it is expected to be. The exposure does not uncover some new unknown. The crowd turns away, tired of encountering the same old complexities and lack of novelty and misses the transformation. The spirit(ual) is altered, providing a glimpse of the other/Other in its state and at its moment of hiddenness. As it disappears, or withdraws (as Caputo claims), there is a glimpse of a different nature, but one that cannot be seen except fleetingly and falling away.

There is one more risk in uncovering. I may be the one who is at risk of being bared in wrestling with the spirit(ual) in an academic forum. Perhaps I am to be uncovered and exposed. Work in spirituality requires living with necessary respect for the complexity and vulnerability of the topic, as well as an awareness of one's own vulnerability and risk in taking it up. In spirituality (re)search and pedagogy acting from a place of reverence and caution, willing to be shaped by the work may be necessary. And so the fourth problematic of entanglement arises and a growing sense of (r)elation in the middle of the ring.

Move 4: getting entangled

Being entangled in the topic of the spirit(ual) combines the struggle for clarity with necessary elusiveness and the partiality of location and claims. I am caught in a tenacious grip. Threads of ideas flow out in many directions, entwined and knotted: hermeneutic knots. The spirit(ual) is a site of intersection and complication. This too bears on children's experience.

The spirit(ual) is about relations and relationships: all my relations. 'All my relations' is a phrase borrowed from First Nation traditions. It is said as a closing acknowledgement to speeches and stories that all the relations are present across time and species. It is a spiritual recognition of connection and responsibility. The future is present as a witness, as a relation, awaiting how it will be shaped. We have a responsibility to choose and act for those yet to come. The past is also present witnessing our actions. The ancestors are alert to our capacity as are all the other creatures of the world and the world itself. We are related to all things and are accountable to them for word and deed. We are entangled in life. Our choices matter beyond ourselves as the spirit(ual) is connection beyond the self.

Research cannot be a thing unto itself and for itself, especially if its focus is the spirituality of children and youth: those who come after us. Children are at stake in the acknowledgement 'all my relations'. In taking up spirituality, I am in the midst of all that is mystery and beyond self. A great crowd of witnesses entangles me across time, across species and across spaces, leaving me in the middle: in-between.

Being in the in-between has implications. I will mention only two. First, there is the between state of transformation that is evident in rites of passage (Eliade, 1958; Turner, 1967; Mahdi *et al.*, 1987). One leaves a stage of life and enters a new stage. In between lies the liminal state: a threshold or doorway. It is open, dangerous territory where choices get made, where old ways and identities are shed and new ones taken up. There, the spirit(ual) comes into play, as values, meaning and identity are given shape (Eliade, 1958; Mahdi *et al.*, 1987; Turner, 1967).

Jacob's story bears the marks of a rite of passage. He wrestles on the banks of the stream of emptying and crosses over after being given a new identity. It is a passage and transformation that requires struggle. I wrestle in my metaphoric ring, caught between a way demanding clarity and certainty and a way that is not a way, full of ambiguity and uncertainty. I become a site of intersection where contradictory forces meet, pulling in several directions, while I refuse to let go. I am caught in-between, resisting both idealization and simplification.

Second, there is a hyphen that connects: in-hyphen-between. It is a visual connector, a literary cue to the way things are joined. I am in the ring hyphenated, in-between, tied with a myriad of threads, fragments that are active vectors carrying messages out from me and simultaneously transmitting to me messages from all the others/Others around me. It is a two-way flow. Here, at the bottom of my soul, 'at the bottom of the dark' (Smith, 1971), where there is neither below nor further, a window opens to elsewhere. In that opening are passages and links beyond me.

Move 5: the endless round (wrestling in the stream)

The spirit(ual) is not a category of solidity. Any engagement with the spirit(ual) is an entry into flux. It is meeting what is already in motion and always moving in flows of energy and experience. It is not a steady, even flow, but a flux of turbulence, shifting winds, vortices and eddies. As Caputo (1987) notes, flux irrupts, breaking in unexpectedly: 'There is a fine point in the mind where one is brought up short, a moment of midnight reckoning where the ground gives way and one also has the distinct sense of falling into an abyss' (p. 269). It is necessary 'to stay with the flow ... without bailing out when the going gets rough' (Caputo, 1987, p. 273). There is no way out of the ring. I am caught in the flux. Only from the midst of turbulence can I (partially) observe the nature of the spirit(ual). My insight is temporary and incomplete, dependent on from where in the swirl I pay attention. The process and the experience are non-linear and fluid. I rely on metaphors and implication in passing on messages and the impulse of the flux.

Like Jacob, alone in the night on the banks of the Yabbok, there is an edge of terror: facing the abyss, caught in the turbulence, being a site of receptivity; a receiver and transmitter of unintended messages. I seek a way forward and hope for a beneficence of some kind to assist in the journey.

Move 6: winning/losing on the continuum of impossibility

There is a moment in any sporting event when an awareness arises that it will be over soon. It is an insight of quite different quality for the side that is winning and the side that is losing: a growing sense of elation for one and a rather flat, empty feeling for the other. I see no end-point for me, nor an outcome that makes me think there will be a way out. Perhaps Jacob clung so desperately to his opponent, refusing to let go because he could not face either winning or losing. Either way his encounter with his warlike brother would come when the struggle was over. I have no idea what is beyond this struggle. I do not long for victory and I hesitate to lose.

My response to the spirit(ual) is along a continuum of impossibility with a range of responses that all seem inadequate. To win (to know) is to kill. To have a firm grasp of the spirit(ual) would be to conclude something in me and in my knowing, cutting me off from a flow of energy. I would be beyond shifts or perturbations, safe, but cut off in my knowledge.

The spirit(ual) requires ongoing openness: the human as constant receptor, available to messages from elsewhere. Receptivity is not a place of strength, but a way of vulnerability and open access. The risk in be(com)ing so available may be complete loss: the suicide of the self. This is to lose. I struggle to avoid either outcome and cling to the middle. I wish to remain open, to know. I can only do so by staying in the difficulty. How can it end?

I could leave the struggle and sever the relations I have. This would be escaping without knowledge. Jacob did not choose this option, but clung to his opponent until a blessing was given. Perhaps I am clinging on in the hope of being blessed and readied for the next stage of my journey. Can I play for the fourth option of not losing, not winning and not getting away?

I resist the desire to pin down, seize or lay bare, as if in exposing the fragility of the spirit(ual), I might make myself strong. I must, as Daignault (in Pinar *et al.*, 1995) suggests, remain somewhere in the space between murder and suicide: in the tiny liveable space of the narrow way between these terrors of destruction.

Move 7: in the dark

I have imagined an audience watching the wrestling, with at least one commentator narrating the action. Serres's Harlequin had a crowd in the theatre. What if the lights went out and the whole multitude was cast into a confusion of darkness? What could be seen? Jacob wrestled in the dark. Perhaps we all are and have missed seeing how little we can see.

Some difficult questions linger in this struggle obscured by the assumed solidities of research and practice. What of evil in the lives of children and youth? In a world so skilful at deception and seductive images, what grounds might children have for sorting the false from the true, the life giving from the destructive? How can the young sift experience? How do children and youth encounter that which is fleeting, overwhelming, complex, powerful or invisible?

I worry about what passes as the spirit(ual): the false being presented as true. Where there should be doubt, there is certainty. I doubt certainty. I cannot accept the exclusive claims of some spiritualities. But how will I know what is wrong or untrue or evil if I cannot define what is good, right or true? The question of clarity remains. Yet, if I am too sure of what I know and how to know it, will I join that flow of energy that leads away from the difficult simplicity of weakness, fragility, incompleteness and complexity?

I feel required to live in fragility and weakness, wrestling with what I cannot escape nor let go on the shore of the Yabbok, the place of emptying. It is in the dark that I come close to the spirit(ual). I believe experience founded in uncertainty and weakness forms the fabric of the spirit(ual) experiences of the young. That matters for practice and teaching. It requires a pedagogy of care and respect.

Conclusion: a reflective review

In order to learn it is sometimes necessary to take a step out or back, to arrive at what Nadine Gordimer (2000, in Atwood, 2002) identifies as 'extraordinary disinvolvement':

> Powers of observation heightened beyond the normal imply extraordinary disinvolvement: or rather the double process, excessive preoccupation and identification with the lives of others, and at the same time a monstrous detachment ... The tension between standing apart and being fully involved: this is what makes a writer. (p. 29)

She marks the territory a writer's space. Researchers and teachers stand in it as well. In reflection, I have learned two things, perhaps three. First, I have discovered from my own experience and from Jacob that it is necessary to hang on as long as possible in order to learn. My second lesson is also from Jacob who was wounded in learning: injured at his hip changing his gait forever. My struggle with the spirit(ual) has altered me. As my fears take shape, I am forced to cling to them to extract insight. Spirit does not leave me walking in the same way. Being wounded contributes to uncertainty, keeps me doubting what I know and leaves me vulnerable in the process. My learning has not made me stronger. It has allowed me to cross over, to have glimpses of life's possibilities and to face what I can manage in my condition.

A third lesson appears. In looking for a way to know the spirit(ual), I have stumbled into an integrative node where I have been woven/have woven myself into a new fabric of be(com)ing. I was trying to learn. I am being changed. This is the way of the spirit(ual): changing who it touches. The spirit(ual) in its complexity and elusiveness is a reminder of the partiality and temporariness of knowledge and life. Our research and our pedagogy must be formed to this way of being and becoming.

Notes on contributor

Dr Daniel G. Scott is an assistant professor and graduate adviser (for the MA and PhD programmes) in the School of Child and Youth Care at the University of Victoria, BC, Canada. He is currently involved in an international study of childhood peak experiences, and in a project exploring the spiritual lives of adolescent girls, based on their original diary and journal writings.

References

Atwood, M. (2002) *Negotiating with the dead: a writer on writing* (Cambridge, Cambridge University Press).

Blades, D. (1997) *Procedures of power and curriculum change* (New York, Peter Lang).

Caputo, J. D. (1987) *Radical hermeneutics: repetition, deconstruction and the hermeneutic project* (Indianapolis, IN, Indiana University Press).

Donovan, V. J. (1978) *Christianity rediscovered* (Maryknoll, NY, Orbis Books).

Eliade, M. (1958) *Rites and symbols of initiation* (W. R. Trask, Trans.) (New York, Harper & Row).

Hart, T. (2003) *The secret spiritual lives of children* (Maui, Inner Ocean Press).

Hay, D., with Nye, R. (1998) *The spirit of the child* (London, Fount/HarperCollins).

Kovel, J. (1991) *History and spirit: an inquiry into the philosophy of liberation* (Boston, MA, Beacon Press).

Mahdi, L. C., Foster, S. & Little, M. (Eds) (1987) *Betwixt and between: patterns of masculine and feminine initiation* (La Salle, IL, Open Court).

Pinar, W. F., Reynolds, W. M., Slattery, P. & Taubman, P. M. (Eds) (1995) *Understanding curriculum: an introduction to the study of historical and contemporary curriculum discourses* (New York, Peter Lang).

Scott, D. G. (2004) Retrospective spiritual narratives: exploring recalled adolescent spiritual experiences, *International Journal of Children's Spirituality*, 9(1), 67–79.

Serres, M. (1982) Knowledge in the classical age, in: J. V. Harari & D. F. Bell (Eds) *Hermes: literature, science, philosophy* (Baltimore, MD, Johns Hopkins University Press).

Serres, M. (1997) *The troubadour of knowledge* (S. F. Glaser & W. Paulson, Trans.) (Ann Arbor, MI, University of Michigan Press).

Smith, K. (1971) *At the bottom of the dark* (Fredericton, NB, Fiddlehead Poetry Books).

Turner, V. (1967) *The forest of symbols* (Ithaca, NY, Cornell University Press). Available online at: www.sacrednamebible.com/kjvstrongs/STRHEB12.htm#S1238 (accessed 10 May 2004).

Five classroom activities for sustaining a spiritual environment

Joyce Bellous*

Introduction

> Knowledge has two extremes which meet. One is the pure natural ignorance of the infant at birth. The other is reached by great minds which have passed through the entire range of human knowledge, only to find that they know nothing of the truth, and have come back to the same ignorance from which they started. This latter state is a wise ignorance which knows itself. (Pascal)

At its best, spiritual education permits diversity to flourish and allows children to integrate and differentiate themselves within a classroom, so that they are recognized within it rather than estranged from it. To make the case, I describe five activities that promote diversity but ground children in common human experience and also

*McMaster Divinity College, McMaster University, Hamilton, Ontario L85 4K1, Canada. Email: bellousj@mcmaster.ca

provide a comprehensive pattern for children's developing personalities. If teachers welcome diversity through these activities, they draw learners into the heart of what it means to be whole. By building spiritual education through activities that I think are essential, I assume that:

- Every human being has spiritual, personal and material needs.
- The spiritual aspect of human beings is conveyed through object relating.
- Every human being is moved by desire for meaning, love and work.
- The self is a meaning-making activity.
- Personal worldview is a product of spiritual processes: object relating, meaning making.

These assumptions establish groundwork for spiritual education and position mean-ing-making as the central activity of human life. Meaning making is spiritual activity that influences life's other aspects—e.g. approaches to relational labour (effort expended to initiate and maintain connections to other people) and productive labour (effort expended using abilities to get resources to live on).

While spiritual education implies method and content, it also refers to the way teachers know what to do in the classroom. This third aspect is my focus. Spiritual education creates an environment through five activities: including, attending, embracing, releasing and remaining. I define environment as complex, cumulative effects of social interaction that leave an impression in a dominant way of being. The activity of including refers to hospitality offered to difference, so that each child shows up in the environmental landscape; attending refers to a just distribution of attention, so children learn to make meaning; embracing refers to appropriate ministrations of presence, so children become relational; releasing refers to timely regard for enabling children to learn on their own, so that they enjoy being productive; remaining refers to the faithful constancy of 'being there', of dependable availability, as well as to integ-rity—i.e. being faithful to one's own identity and the process of its growth. Without remaining, there is no wisdom. Through these five activities, teachers create a spiri-tually rich environment in which all children feel they belong.

Including: a foundation for showing up

A community is a place to stand, a room in which to abide, a home culture to which participants return for refreshment and strength needed for everyday life. A classroom is a community in this sense if its purpose is to help children feel they fit in its envi-ronment. Children cannot flourish unless they fit to a satisfying degree, so they are visible to others. A feeling of fit is important for spiritual growth, but is it an achieve-ment (completed action due to one's place in a society—i.e. automatically granted) or a task (an ongoing process of learning in which one tries to fit and succeeds or fails—i.e. personal responsibility)? To ask whether fitting in is an achievement or task is to raise the question of spiritual work itself. I suggest spiritual work is communal and personal in the sense that people must learn to individuate from and integrate within a community, in this case, a classroom. The nature of spiritual work is to accomplish both at the same time. Feeling we fit is not the same as being coterminous with an environment: we differentiate ourselves, yet feel at home. Spiritual work makes personal meaning collaboratively.

Robert Kegan suggests the complexity of modern life requires spiritual work, though he does not use that expression (Kegan, 1997, pp. 266–70). In his view, complexity creates opportunity for what I call spiritual education because we have not caught up with requirements of modern (or post-modern) life (Kegan, 1982, p. 7). To him, object relating is an intrinsic interest of persons: ego activity *is* object relating and begins at birth (Kegan, 1982, p. 7). He organizes psychological development and educational transformation around object relations, a view that is useful for understanding how spirituality works because he thinks the essence of humanity is the making of meaning.

Object relations theories assume all learning organizes experience meaningfully. What every organism does is organize; 'what a human organism organizes is meaning' (Kegan, 1982, p. 11). In offering his claim about identity, Kegan interprets Piaget to reveal an omission that matters if we believe young children are capable of empathy and insight Piaget did not seem to think possible. While being faithful to Piaget's stages, Kegan focuses not on developmental plateaus, but on the process of moving from one plateau (stage) to another. He emphasizes the activity of making meaning and thinks plateaus are not the main point, though he is uncritical of them. In exploring human development, Kegan thinks Piaget described the achievement of meaning-made, not the dynamic self engaged in the struggle 'to make meaning, to have meaning, to protect meaning, to enhance meaning, to lose meaning and to lose the self along the way' (Kegan, 1982, p. 12). He focuses on the dynamism: a self as motion—the ebb and flow of loss and recovery regarding the meaning attached to various assumptions we hold to be important. The heart's hard spiritual work is to move through loss to recovery, so that meaning is organized and reorganized sufficiently for life to be hopeful.

Meaning making implies change. If a child's spiritual personality is seen as a static, unchangeable condition, the idea of a self engaged in meaning making is undermined. This is true on two counts: first, spiritual education provides an environment that encompasses fully orbed spirituality (i.e. the four spiritual personalities outlined below); second, meaning derived through object relating (core to spiritual experience) is not static unless individuals shut down or get stuck. Meaning making is an ongoing process in which new experiences inform a worldview that is already in place. Becoming stymied is a sign that something is wrong. Education creates an environment conducive to spirituality by awakening learners to the work of making meaning. Not to mature spiritually is not to grow up at all.

In spiritual education, including implies that teachers account for a propensity in children to focus on interests typical of four personality types described by Corinne Ware (2000). Like adults, children may be animated by:

- Words, content and their correctness; the aim is to expand personal understanding; e.g., Jesus' Sermon on the Mount (Matt. 5: 1–12).

- Music and talk; the aim is personal renewal; action tends towards speaking, witnessing, telling one's story—e.g. Jesus sending out his disciples (Matt. 10: 1–14).
- Images, impressions, silence, hearing, connecting with and spending time alone with God to enjoy union with God: Jesus in prayer by himself, in quiet, solitary places (Mark 1: 12).
- Actions of visionary, single-minded crusaders who aim to regenerate society: Jesus clears the Temple Courts (Mark 11: 12–17).

The young are moved by words, feelings, images or action and relate to one aspect more than others. If classrooms emphasize words over images, for example, a mystical child feels strange, isolated and incomprehensible. She may come to believe she must keep her spiritual sensibilities private, making integration in a classroom unlikely.

Integration (fitting in) plus individuation (distinguishing one's self) constitute spiritual work. But individuation is not separation. To fit in and be different is to be authentic and realize innate capacities (Ware, 2000, p. 19), a process that is interactive:

> We cannot integrate the potentially enriching experiences of others into our own self-understanding unless we first have a self; to gain a self, we must first relate to and then differentiate from community. It is a continuously enriching circular movement of inter-action and definition. Once one is able to accommodate to new configurations of self, the personality remains open to alterations and enrichment. (Ware, 2000, p. 13)

Spiritual education has to do with sensing what classrooms include and invites us to revisit our dominant practices to see if we are comprehensive of difference. Inclusive teachers provide for the study of words, so that children become precise and make cognitive gains; offer opportunities to learn through feeling and open up occasions for telling personal stories and explaining what they mean, using the arts; allow time for silence, wonderment and imagination to set the agenda for interpreting experience; and bring children into settings where they can take specific, focused action aimed at improving the world.

Including, by itself, will not ensure children do spiritual work in class. Integration and differentiation are not simple choices a child makes. If we think choices are free, we have not reflected on the power of community. Without the other activities, allowing children to engage with words, feeling, images and actions that are spiritually satisfying does not provide sufficient resources for the young. We must also give them our full attention.

Attending: a foundation for being and meaning

The activity of attending takes its starting-point in object-relating gaze behaviour between mother and child. Object relating is the heart of spirituality, in my view. Ana-Maria Rizzuto examined object relations theory that Freud uncovered when he asked how people come to possess belief in the existence of God (Rizzuto, 1979, p. 41). Object relations theories explain our need for others, since they are 'theories about our relations to the 'objects'—people and things—to which we are attached and which give meaning to our lives' (Klein, 1987, p. xv). These theories assume that 'personality development occurs in the context of interactions between [a person] and the environment, rather than through the internal processes of maturation alone' (Kegan, 1982, p. 7). Object relating is ego activity; it begins at birth and is ground-work for making meaning. In a classroom, children require teacher attention to orga-nize personal experience meaningfully.

All learning is organizes meaning making is about loss and recovery. Spiritual work moves through loss to recovery so that personal and communal meaning is organized and reorganized over time. Spirituality calls for emotional work based on a human capacity I describe as *a sense of felt connection*. Spiritual work is the effort of sensing and sustaining meaningful connection with objects in the world. Making meaning is a felt experience of motion, of creating, losing and recovering objects layered with meaning and organized into a personal worldview. Spirituality mediates between the self and these objects until we come into being as identities and move through meaning-making to be a fully formed self, capable of meeting the demands of living.

Object relating can convey coldness about these connections but its etymology defies that view. Object signifies motion at its root, as does the word 'eject': the root refers to the activity of throwing and the word object 'speaks to that which some motion has made separate or distinct from, or to the motion itself' (Kegan, 1982, p. 76). Object relating has to do with making things separate or distinct: object rela-tions are 'our relations to that which has been thrown from us, or the experience of this throwing itself' (Kegan, 1982, p. 76). It refers to the motion of a self through life: the experience of being embedded in the world's objects is replaced (hence lost) through differentiating the self from these objects. In making meaning, we are in motion. Meaning making is an evolutionary process that moves forward with respect to significant objects.

As an example, Piaget saw that infants are embedded in impulses and emerge from these impulses by differentiating from them—e.g. in separation anxiety. Gradually a self becomes its own object, distinct from a mother that was previ-ously indistinguishable from an infant's point of view. A child loses her mother and gains her self. Object relations are a continual process of loss and recovery: of losing one's centre and coming back to a home that is not the same as it was before but that remains recognizable. By about 11 or 12 years old, worldviews are constructed though experience into a system that lasts into adulthood (Kegan, 1982, pp. 28–45, 222).

Meaning making is necessarily relational—adults attend to infants and attune to one who depends on that gaze in order to come into being as a meaning-maker. To attend to others is to provide them with the resources of attention, a commodity just like money that may be more important than money to a child's future. Attention is 'one of the great generic currencies of social life', a distinct phenomenon that can be analysed, like money, to establish the value of a person's life (Derber, 2000, p. xxiv). The more attention people are skilled at getting, the more value they have. Those unable to secure other people's attention are impoverished by their lack of skill; their poverty goes very deep—creating the expectation they will neither be heard nor seen and no one cares for them. Attention that counts in creating and sustaining human value is focused on people not behaviour. When adults set limits on behaviour, if children feel recognized and sense adults understand how they experience the event (whether or not adults concur), they find limit setting tolerable, even a relief. If children do not feel recognized, they resent limit setting as a violation of identity (Kegan, 1982, p. 211).

We attend easily to those with requisite skill to draw our attention to them. These children get attention from peers as well. Attention getting grants value; attention keeping conveys that value is secure and permanent. In analysing attention getting, keeping and giving, Derber argues that Western culture is addicted to attention (Derber, 2000, p. xxv) and so engrossed in seeking attention no one is left to give it. The modern self carries a unique distress:

> Each person ... has received the burdensome gift of an overgrown self. We enjoy the positive, attractive features of this self-orientation, but ... fail to appreciate how much it costs us as well. (Baumeister, 1991, p. 10)

Adults are not exempt from an insatiable drive for attention. We only give attention generously on the strength of our commitment to bless the young.

In addition to recognizing people rather than emphasizing behaviour, parents and teachers must be drawn to and stay with a child if attention is to have full effect in paying out value to one who is its focus. Attention getting builds personal currency; as Kegan points out, 'survival and development depend on a capacity to recruit invested attention of others to us' (Kegan, 1982, p. 17). An infant's capacity 'to hold the mother with a recognizing eye is as fundamental [to a child's] development as is the prehensile capacity to hold a physical object' (Kegan, 1982, p. 17). Infants learn to grasp physical objects and human objects in order to achieve their own maintenance—to remain alive in the world. Infants have a biological capacity to get and keep attention so as to recognize and be recognized—activity we are all compelled to continue throughout life. Whether the object grasped is a thing or person, infants make meaning with these objects, that is transitional objects (e.g. a teddy-bear). We grow up with respect to our perception of these objects and the related sense of self that develops over time through experiencing them, which evolves into the meaning they hold for us.

Meaning making is a social, survival activity and depends on someone to recognize and collaborate with the child. Some children are raised by parents that are incapable of providing sufficient attention for them, even if physically present. The essence of inequality in the classroom is children's unequal ability to recruit attention *in them* (Kegan, 1982, pp. 17–18). Yet recruitability is learned; its success can be acquired in spiritually sensitive classrooms if teachers attend to the uneven ability students have to recruit the interest of others in them. Children carry this inequality in their very being by seeming invisible or being demanding. In either case, a child is unsatisfied by human attention and cannot relax. Recruiting requires others, so they need help. They may have learned to be irritating out of desperation or learned to disappear as a way to relieve their disappointment. Human beings are able to recover by making meaning with new experiences. Attending is a spiritually sensitive activity that helps children to recover from the loss of adequate attention for their developing sense of self.

Embracing: a foundation for relational labour

Attending responds to human longing for inclusion and distinctness and is built on a humanizing gaze. Embracing—the appropriate ministration of presence—is conveyed through a metaphor of healthy holding on (Kegan, 1982, p. 126) in which a caregiver unanxiously holds an anxious child. It is not simply a gesture of holding on, embracing is marked by ability and willingness to hold on in the right way, at the right time, for the right reasons; through appropriateness, it lays the groundwork for separation; 'to hold on without constraining may be the first requirement of care' (Kegan, 1982, pp. 126, 162).

Embracing is a way of being present to another, so that the attention we pay *is to them*. We respond to a person not a problem, which conveys that we trust a child: 'An ability to remain present for others when they are anxious, to recognize the anxiety, without becoming too anxious or immediately trying to relieve the anxiety has long been understood to be a feature of competent, professional psychological help' (Kegan, 1982, p. 126). Through embracing the person behind a problem, it is possible for a child to grow up and no longer need the same investment from adults, which is perhaps why some adults refuse to embrace the young appropriately: they do not hold on, they hold children back.

Consider the following thought experiment. A young mother has coffee at a neighbour's house. They each have a child roughly the same age. One child sits on her mother's lap while the two women converse. The child looks at the other child playing. She gets down but keeps a hand on her mother's lap and leans towards an enticing game. She watches, and moves close to the play, toys and a partner her size. Then she climbs back on the lap. Her mother welcomes her but now as she sits on her perch her whole attention is on the game played by the other child. She gets down and joins the play. A pattern of closeness and distance continues until dependence on her mother is distracted by the fun of playing with another child. Being near/moving away is a game children learn under favourable conditions as the beginning of interdependence.

The activity of embracing is built on self-donation—a mother's lap to a child's need for it. A mother gives herself to a child's need, yet has time for friendship. Mother and child relax in their availability to each other. Availability depends on economics. If mother is destitute, she is unavailable; if preoccupied, she is not present. Is her availability a sacrifice of her being for the child's greater good? Is the child more important than the mother? If yes, how could an inferior person hold the child's respect? I say rather that mother and child are equally valuable, even economically. Availability is an offering to a child, expressive of a mother's value. Embracing is a form of self-donation in which both parties enjoy value, although needs differ, particularly with respect to their urgency. Self-donation is giving, losing and regaining the self and structures the parent–child relation.

Tension in self-donation arises as one tries to give oneself without losing one's self entirely. If young mothers appear to get lost for a time, due to a child's urgent, foundational needs, self-donation requires them to regain themselves. We cannot donate what we have lost. Regaining ourselves implies that we do not actually get lost, but temporarily and willingly give priority to another's need. Self-donation is conscious, intelligent action, not enslavement. Slavery has two forms: it carries out action in the interests of others that actors have no interest in, where interests include material resources and values held as ultimate concerns. The second form of slavery is the failure of self-mastery. People are slaves to whatever has mastered them—e.g. their own insatiable desire. Self-donation is not an offence against mothers' interests and is not the lack of self-mastery. The problem for maternal self-donation is its absence of social value.

If all learning is organizing experience from birth, then education begins by observing the child, as Plato suggested. In his analogy of the metals in the *Republic* he took a social risk to say that we should educate the young on the basis of what we perceive they are made of and for (i.e. made for doing) and not on social class. While embracing begins by focusing on children's needs, it raises the question of what sort of selves we need to be, so we are able and willing to donate ourselves without a fundamental loss of self. From a Christian perspective, Jesus gave himself without losing himself (John 10: 17–18). Yet in human self-donating, there is a loss of self of some kind that cannot be evaded. To put one's self at the disposal of another's need is to turn our attention from our own, which might be quite pressing in its own right. While looking after one's own children may be a way of giving attention to our selves (e.g. to demonstrate wealth), how does self-donating apply to embracing other people's children, in whom we have no self-interest?

Caring for other people's children points towards a basic aspect of self-donation; it is:

> the will to give ourselves to others and 'welcome' them, to readjust our identities to make space for them, [and this act of turning our attention to them] is prior to any judgment ... except that of identifying them in their humanity. (Volf, 1996, p. 29)

But Volf asserts that embracing cannot take place until truth has been said and justice done. It is an act of self-giving and not slavery. Self-donation does not permit injustice to go unchecked: 'even if the will to embrace is indiscriminate, the embrace itself is conditional' and always also a struggle against 'deception, injustice, and violence' (Volf, 1996, pp. 29–30).

Embracing is an activity in which someone makes room for others. Making space for others is a priority and rearranges other aspects of self-identity. Those who care for others are willing and able to make room in their identity for intrusions that carry spiritual and material costs and benefits. But if embracing is making room for others expressed by healthy holding on, the activity of releasing is its essential counterpart.

Releasing: a foundation for productive labour

If including grounds being and attending fosters meaning making, embracing is relational labour that prepares the young for separation and releasing is its educational partner. Releasing refers to the timely regard for letting students learn and work independently. Education—*educare* ('nurture') and *educere* ('leading out')—signifies healthy embrace and separation: effective teachers work themselves out of a job eventually. Learning to work is related to recognition that comes with attention. Freedom to work is a function of recognizing and being recognized. Work shapes how we perceive our selves and our place in the world; it is a process and product of spirituality.

Work is an object, like any other; we relate to it, making it meaningful. Releasing learners to engage projects independently enables them to make a distinction as they learn to work. Those who learn to work effectively do so, despite bosses or teachers that grade them, because they separate some people's social power in an organization or school from the psychological power and ownership they retain over their own work (Kegan, 1997, p. 157). Effective workers are not alienated from their labour; they perceive the complexity of modern labour but understand that refusing to feel alienated is part of their work. When we understand how to work, the self as a system developed at 11 or 12 years shows up as an object of attention that we 'have' rather than being a system that has us—since if we are embedded in it, we are unable to reflect upon it.

The classroom is a place where children learn to work as teachers release them to do so. Spiritual education is an opportunity to learn to work personally and collaboratively due to its insistence on differentiation and integration as essential tasks. In spiritual education, learning to work has two phases: the first allows children to identify and acquire basic skills all workers must have; a second phase teaches them to offer personal contributions to collective projects. If spiritual education is to encompass all five activities, releasing must include these two phases. It is only if both phases of releasing are involved that all children learn to work.

Teaching children to work was a focus for reform in earlier eras. Antonio Gramsci (1891–1937) critiqued schooling and thought it 'necessary to enter a "classical", rational phase' and find in the ends to be attained by schooling 'the natural source for developing the appropriate methods and forms', to direct the process of learning to be acquired by the young (Gramsci, 1987, p. 24). I will adapt creative schooling to say we need a classical, spiritual phase that situates rationality within its framework and retains the two phases he proposed for creative schooling.

The first phase of releasing is dedicated to erasing unjust social disadvantage. Creative schooling incorporated active schooling (e.g. Montessori methods). Gramsci did not reject action-based learning *per se*, but he abhorred its inequality. He saw active schools as dependent for their success on middle-class experience. For working-class children it is inaccessible. Inequality is hard to eradicate if dominant practices leave students out and if differences of skill in recruitability, for example, are inadequately addressed.

Inequality frustrates recent approaches to learning as well. For example, the Project Approach[1] excels at teaching children to work, but does not offer the first phase as groundwork for developing the skills implied by cultural and social capital assumed in the programme. Cultural and social capital is knowledge that 'knows how' to arrange for its own increase and is linked to recruitability. Spirituality and spiritual personality are aspects of cultural and social capital that shape one's capacity to enjoy and circulate social trust in an environment and to recruit attention in one's personal and/or family interests. In this way, a first phase is a process of inclusion but it adds to inclusion the structured and intentional aim of helping children acquire requisite skills of learning to work on their own eventually.

The second phase of releasing teaches children to work together. To demonstrate the second phase, Gramsci used a model based on organic solidarity, a sentiment that holds people together so they achieve a common goal, or live together amiably (Hillery, 1972, pp. 226–7). In these environments, people are aware of the expertise of others even if they do not carry out the same tasks, but they appreciate the whole enterprise and identify their role and responsibility in it. He used the example of an editing house to describe collaboration that produces effective workers. In an editing house, each person is an expert in his or her own field; each helps enhance the expertise of the whole. In collective experience, each is required to do his or her proper work well, respectfully of others, focused on truth implicitly and explicitly expressed in the expertise each person brings to the table. In the second phase, creativity is understood in a particular sense: 'to discover a truth oneself, without external suggestions or assistance, is to create, even if the truth is an old one' (Gramsci, p. 1987, 33). Creativity demonstrates mastery over method and indicates learners have gained intellectual maturity.

While Gramsci designed creative education on a framework useful to spiritual education, he omitted religion from a child's school experience. His dismissal was due to misunderstanding how a worldview forms through spiritual processes. In outlining the fifth activity of spiritual education, I propose that we do not mature by abandoning childhood worldviews based on home values. Rather, we mature by remaining connected to them in a way that engenders wisdom.

Remaining: a foundation for wise ignorance

Remaining is an adult activity and refers to the faithful constancy of 'being there', dependably available, as well as to integrity—i.e. being faithful to one's own identity's growth and maturity. It is hard to persuade adults that remaining is a good and wise approach to life. One tension in the activity of remaining lies between individuation and integration that is central to spiritual work. Humanity longs for distinctness and also to belong. How can we have both? In theory, remaining addresses the tension by saying it is possible to remain with and be distinct from others: it is possible to be near and different—socially intimate and psychologically distinct.

A second tension in the activity of remaining has to do with the idea of development itself. There is a strong assumption in developmental theory that an old way of being must fail before a new way can take its place. Development proceeds through loss and recovery—bearable in terms of individual development but with high costs relationally and socially. It explains why people might abandon relationships during mid-life. Abandonment appears justified if an old form must die before a new form comes into being. Relationships tied to the old form become expendable to someone in crisis. In remaining, the conceptual point is the difference between abandonment and renewal.

A third tension erupts between adult and childhood needs. Kegan is clear that remaining in place for children permits them to enjoy healthy development. Children are embedded in a culture that needs to remain in place during their transformation and re-equilibrium, so that what was part of them and gradually becomes not-them can be successfully reintegrated as an object of new balance (Kegan, 1982, p. 129), a home that is different but recognizable. Remaining requires that we comprehend human growth. Growth,

> is not alone a matter of separation and repudiation, of killing off the past. It is a matter of transition. Growth involves as well the reconciliation, the recovery, the recognition of that which before was confused with the self. This is precisely the process of meaning-making that is central to the formation of personality. (Kegan, 1982, p. 129)

If a child's environment is lost during development, the loss can be so great that it is impossible to recover balance. Depression may result. It is common insight that 'the underlying substrate of depression is loss' (Kegan, 1982, p. 131). To lose one's environment is to lose part of oneself:

> For [home] to disappear at exactly the time when the child is experiencing a loss of herself is to leave the child with a kind of unrecoverable loss, a confirmation of her worst suspicions about the life project ... The normal experiences of evolution involve recoverable loss; what we separate from we can find anew. What is unnatural is for a culture of embeddedness to disappear through psychological withdrawal or psychical disappearance ... [particularly during a] critical period roughly nine to twenty-one months of age. (Kegan, 1982, p. 13)

What meaning are we to make of tensions implicit in the activity of remaining?

Between the two books he wrote on meaning making, Kegan reflected on these tensions. On the one hand, he thinks all growth is costly and involves leaving behind an old way of being in the world (Kegan, 1982, p. 215) and 'all transitions involve leaving a consolidated self behind before any new self can take its place' (Kegan, 1982, p. 232). In his second book, largely through paying attention to feminist critique, he emphasizes that 'there is no necessary *identity* between taking command of ourselves and taking leave of our connections' (Kegan, 1997, p. 220). Increasing differentiation can itself be a story of staying connected by continuing to hold on to precious connections while refashioning one's relationship to them, so that one *makes them up* rather than *gets made up* by them. Autonomy does not have to be a story of increasing aloneness. Deciding for my self does not have to equal deciding by myself. Autonomy is self-regulating but that regulation might well be on behalf of preserving and protecting one's connections according to an internal compass or system, since abiding and journeying are contexts for transformational development. Kegan notes the capacity to take a more differentiated position can permit us to move closer to another (Kegan, 1997, pp. 221–2) person or group. The second, collaborative phase of releasing is preparation for this skill of working with others.

Conclusion

Remaining is the glue that holds all five activities together. Through remaining, we mature and provide in our very being the resources children need to live on. I agree with Kegan: we should understand the past, not throw it away. Teaching children effectively is spiritual work for an educator. What matters for teachers who engage in spiritual education is that they perceive their own way of seeing the world as a whole. Kegan's metaphor for the system we were when we were 12 is that of family religion. Until we reflect on it, we take that system to be true. He invites adults to reconsider their family religion, which is not the same as Jewish, Christian or Hindu religion; it is an idiosyncratic form that produced a home environment. In remaining, adults are free to critique their family gods but not free to omit spirituality from a child's environment.

Remaining is adult activity, without which children are not safe to grow up. Previous generations understood that remaining for the children's sake was required, though perhaps they had no idea how to remain authentically. The challenge is to see how to be with children and to move past our critiques of the way things were when we were young, so that we do not lose our selves. Spiritual work awaits teachers, in the activities of including, attending, embracing, releasing and remaining. There is joy in practising these spiritual arts.

Notes on contributor

Joyce Bellous is Associate Professor at McMaster Divinity College, Canada, where she has taught since 1993 in the areas of education, ethics and culture. She has published more than thirty essays in these areas of research and is author of *Gardening the Heart* (Clements Publishing). She also serves as an educational consultant internationally. Her special interest is children and spirituality.

Note

1. For a good example of the Project Approach see K. L. Bellous (2005), Looking at the trees around us, *Early Childhood Research and Practice*, 6(1). Available online at: http://ecrip.uiue.edu /v6n1/index.html

References

Baumeister, R. F. (1991) *Escaping the self* (New York, Basic Books).
Bellous, J. E. (2004) A child's concept of God, in: D. Ratcliff (Ed.) *Children's spirituality* (Eugene, OR, Cascade Books).

Derber, C. (2000) *The pursuit of attention* (New York, Oxford University Press).
Gramsci, A. (1987) *Prison notebooks* (New York, International Publishers).
Hillery, G. A. (1972) *Communal organizations* (Chicago, University of Chicago Press).
Kegan, R. (1982) *Evolving self* (Cambridge, MA, Harvard University Press).
Kegan, R. (1997) *In over our heads* (Cambridge, MA, Harvard University Press).
Klein, J. (1987) *Our need for others and its roots in infancy* (London, Tavistock).
Rizzuto, A. M. (1979) *The birth of the living God* (Chicago, Chicago University Press).
Volf, M. (1996) *Exclusion and embrace* (Nashville, TN, Abingdon Press).
Ware, C. (2000) *Discover your spiritual type* (Bethesda, MD, The Alban Institute).

Spiritual development and inclusivity: the need for a critical democratic approach

Jacqueline Watson*

17:30

Introduction

Since the concept of 'spiritual development' was introduced to schooling in England (and Wales) with the 1988 and 1992 Education Acts, there has been much discussion about what is meant by 'spirituality' and 'spiritual development' in the educational context, and this has been accompanied by a sense of confusion because of 'a lack of clear terminology—we still don't know exactly what we are talking about' (Erricker & Erricker, 1997, p. 3). However, this 'confusion' is somewhat

*Corresponding Address: Centre for Applied Research in Education and Keswick Hall Religious Education Centre, School of Education and Professional Development, University of East Anglia, Norwich, UK. Email: Jacqueline.Watson@uea.ac.uk

disingenuous and the 'contemporary debate regarding the "spirituality" of the 'whole child' does not take place in a vacuum' (Wright, 1996, p. 139). In fact, the Office for Standards in Education (OFSTED) and schools are largely agreed on what is meant by 'spiritual development' for schools, so that at the practical level, we do broadly know what we're talking about. And at the theoretical level, while debate continues on the broader question of what might be meant by a spiritual education, even here educationalists know what they're talking about, they just don't agree with one another.

I attempt here to justify these claims. I will also argue that the form of spiritual education currently practised in state schools is not inclusive, even though it claims to be, and neither are suggested theoretical alternatives. I will then put forward an argument that takes up the ground between the critical realist approach of Andrew Wright and the democratic relativist approach of Clive Erricker, and argue for what I label a critical democratic approach to education for spiritual development, an approach which I consider can offer inclusivity.

Spiritual education as 'spiritual development'

The first principle governing spirituality for state education is that 'spirituality' must be conceptualized inclusively:

> The potential for spiritual development is open to everyone and is not confined to the development of religious beliefs or conversion to a particular faith. To limit spiritual development in this way would be to exclude from its scope the majority of pupils in our schools who do not come from overtly religious backgrounds. (NCC, 1993, p. 2)

Accordingly, 'spirituality' is understood humanistically because, as David Smith has said, even though he is a Christian:

> It would not make much sense to aim for the spiritual growth of all pupils if we did not believe that everyone is in some sense a spiritual being ... This is one reason for focusing on abilities which are uniquely human. (Smith, 2001, p. 5)

This means that, while Religious Education (RE) is important for children's spiritual development, it is more important to recognize opportunities across the *whole-school* curriculum and it also means that the discourse around 'spiritual development' is broadly about promoting the well-being of the whole child through a process approach to education (Watson, 2004). The 'spiritual development' discourse promotes 'a pedagogy of resistance, seeking to challenge, undermine and emancipate pupils from the cultural status quo' (Wright, 1999, p. 13), from objectives models of education in general, and the National Curriculum in particular.

Dissent and disagreement

Although the spiritual development discourse reflects considerable consensus, there has been dissent. It has been criticized from a religious perspective for its humanistic or secularist bias. For instance, Mabud (1992) argued that the very 'neutrality' of this humanistic or secular spirituality in itself constitutes a form of spirituality that is at odds with religious, and specifically Islamic, spirituality:

> As with all faiths or world-views, secularism is based on, and promotes, a certain philosophy of life ... The absolute and immutable norms and values, which for all the major religions are God-given, are denied ... From the Islamic point of view belief in God provides human beings with an unchanging and absolute moral code and the eternal norms and values of truth, honesty, justice, mercy, love, kindness, etc., which are enshrined in God's attributes. (Mabud, 1992, p. 89)

I found similar views expressed by Christians I interviewed in earlier research (Watson, 2000).

It has been criticized by a number of educationalists for detrimentally favouring an introspective and individualistic spirituality over an embodied and communitarian spirituality, which, it is argued, has the power to critique social and political injustice (see e.g. Thatcher, 1991; Hull, 1996). It has been criticized by a small number of educationalists who have championed a spiritual education equated with knowledge and reason (e.g. Carr, 1995; Wright, 1996).

A particular problem I have with the cross-curricular 'spiritual development' approach to a spiritual education is that, oddly, it ends by marginalizing spirituality. Spiritual concerns around meaning and purpose in life and death are only a small element in what is meant by 'spiritual development' (Watson, 2004). But cross-curricular 'spiritual development' is not the only way to conceive of a spiritual education. There has been some debate at the theoretical level about what we might want from a spiritual education and a number of alternatives have been proposed. Here, however, inclusivity is routinely achieved by assuming a *universalist* account of spirituality. In the next section, I will argue that the universalist method of conceptualizing spirituality is equally unable to offer an inclusive approach to spiritual education. I will then discuss a further alternative approach to spiritual education, the pluralist approach.

The universalist approach to spirituality and spiritual education

Some time ago, Nicola Slee observed:

> the meaning of 'spirituality' in any given context will be dependent upon the philosophical and theological framework of the writer, and...this ideological commitment may not always be acknowledged, but may masquerade under a false assumption of philosophical neutrality. Thus ... [there is a] need for critical vigilance on the part of the reader in approaching and assessing the debate about spirituality in education. (Slee, 1993, pp. 10–11)

Wright (1997) has argued for the importance of recognizing the cultural rootedness of spirituality, that there are 'a variety of spiritual traditions' (p. 16). My experience of researching people's understandings of spirituality led me to conclude that a person's account of 'spirituality' will be contextualized in their worldview (Watson, 2000). Slee, Wright and I appear to agree, then, that the word 'spirituality', in these post or late modern times, will *inevitably* be defined, or described, in a contextualized form. In other words, any individual's account of spirituality brings into play a belief system through which that individual's understanding and use of the word 'spirituality' is given its meaning. This means there will be many accounts of spirituality. This observation does not seem to have been taken on board by many educationalists involved in the discussion of spirituality for education. Instead, there is an assumption, across much of the literature, that spirituality is a *universal* phenomenon. I have found educationalists routinely writing about spirituality *as if* it were a *real* phenomenon with ontological status, and claiming to *know* something of its nature. Disagreements between educationalists are characterized as error rather than difference of opinion.

Wright has already raised concerns about this universalist approach to defining spirituality. However, I want to argue that Wright's analysis simplifies what is a more complex picture in stating, 'the recent history of spirituality in education has been almost unanimous in insisting on a universal anthropological notion of spirituality which transcends any specific religious belief system' (Wright, 1999, p. 17). I think Wright's analysis is an accurate description of spirituality for 'spiritual development' as currently practised in education and discussed above. But at the theoretical level, academics are not putting forward *one* universal account of spirituality. Instead, they are working within a universalist meta-theory. In other words, each of the theoretical accounts of spirituality is a universalist account in its own right, but each is different. Wright has concluded there is a 'contemporary consensus' (Wright, 1999, p. 11, and 1997) on what is meant by spirituality for education. I would argue, however, while we can talk of a consensus in relation to spiritual education through 'spiritual development', and to a large extent even within the academic discourse (Watson, 2003), none the less, at the theoretical level, discussion of what might be meant by a spiritual education continues to reflect considerable difference.

This conclusion is based on reading across the whole spiritual education literature but, in particular, on a close examination of recent papers and books by six academics prominent in this field. A comparative analysis of these authors' arguments led me to make the following broad observations on four out of these six accounts of spirituality, from David Hay and Rebecca Nye (1998), John Hull (2002), Jack Priestley (2000) and David Carr (1995, 1996, 1999):

- each author claimed to know what spirituality is;
- each account was universalist;
- each account was significantly different from the others.

I also concluded:

- each account was contextualized in the personal beliefs of the author;
- no one account should be privileged;
- each of these accounts, and the issues they raise, is valuable for education for spiritual development.

The arguments of two of the six authors, Andrew Wright (1999, 2001) and Clive Erricker (Erricker & Erricker, 2000; Erricker, 2001), did not fit this pattern and I will discuss these arguments later.

Unfortunately, I do not have the space here to give detailed descriptions of the educationalists' accounts of spirituality I examined, or to do them justice, but I hope examples of their major points will illustrate both their diversity and, importantly, the value of points they raise in their arguments.

Varieties of universalist forms of spirituality and spiritual education

David Hay has long argued for 'a notion of spirituality as something biologically built into the human species', and though linked with religion, 'logically prior to religion' (Hay with Nye, 1998, p. 57). Spirituality, he says, 'refers to a more reflexive process—being attentive towards one's attention or "being aware of one's awareness"' (p. 60). Along with Rebecca Nye, Hay also states spirituality is about relationship, and Hay and Nye refer to spirituality as 'relational consciousness', a term coined by Nye (1998, p. 113).

John Hull, on the other hand, dismisses Hay's disembodied spirituality in favour of an embodied spirituality that transcends 'the merely biological' (Hull, 2002, p. 171). He also claims that 'the spiritual person does not live by duty and obligation but by freedom and joy' and children are 'spiritually educated when they are inspired by freedom and love to live in solidarity with others' (p. 174). In Hull's 2002 article, as elsewhere, he denounces what he calls the false spirituality of contemporary capitalism and, although a strong supporter of *religious* pluralism, argues that *spiritual* pluralism represents a spiritual market, 'driven by the money madness which grips us today' (Hull, 1996, p. 43), which is symptomatic of the sick spiritual condition of contemporary, money-orientated Western society.

Jack Priestley has long argued that spirituality underpins curriculum (Priestley, 1985); he has also argued that spirituality 'should remain always fluid, always in the making', because it uses a language which is 'essentially imprecise' (Priestley, 2000, p. 124). He says spirituality underpins and gives constancy and consistency to the contingent material world, and he proposes a mystical metaphysics, perceived through the solitary spiritual experience or 'the original vision' (2000, p. 126) as the 'proper point of reference for education' (p. 132), because it is 'the essence of education' (p. 127). He states corporate religion always starts from 'the inner experience of an individual in solitude' (pp. 125–6).

David Carr points to the need for 'greater analytical clarity' in the discussion of spiritual education (Carr, 1995, p. 83) and does not accept that definitions of spirituality should focus on 'the sublime or ineffable' (Carr, 1996, p. 163). He seeks a knowledge base for spiritual education and puts forward the notion of spiritual propositions suitable for objective enquiry, such as 'no man can serve two masters', 'sufficient unto the day is the evil thereof', 'what does it profit a man to gain the world and lose his soul' and 'man does not live by bread alone' (Carr, 1995, p. 91; Carr, 1996, p. 171, and 1999). He rejects non-religious approaches to spirituality, because 'they are not focused on transcendent or spiritual experiences in any relevant sense' (Carr, 1995, p. 90) and offer no positive cosmic perspective for despair; and he rejects negative conceptualizations of spirituality, since he says, for instance, 'although we can speak of the spirit of Nazi Germany ... we can hardly speak acceptably of the values of Nazi Germany ... as *spiritual*' (p. 89).

Each of these authors' claims is contentious and highly conjectural. Yet each author makes claims to know what spirituality is for everyone. It seems, in becoming detached from its traditional, historical link with religion, the word 'spirituality' has taken on an essentialism or universalism suggesting there is a real phenomenon 'out there' that the word 'spirituality' points to. It seems it is easy to mistake one's subjective vision as universal rather than partial. It then feels comfortable to apply, or really to impose, this partial view on *all* children. Such an approach cannot be considered inclusive.

An inclusive education for spiritual development would need to begin from the fact that spirituality is inevitably defined in the context of the beliefs and values of the person defining it and that, therefore, spirituality is pluralist. Spiritualities, therefore, could include the enlightenment quest, existentialism, and hedonism, and even Nazism, as well as various forms of religious faith and the ideas expressed by the authors referred to here. An inclusive spiritual education would need to make room for assessing and challenging these alternatives, including darker forms of spirituality (Earl, 2001).

However, finally and crucially, although universalists' claims for spirituality are conjectural and partial, they are fascinating and worthy of consideration. There is no basis for privileging one set of conjectures over another but, at the same time, in an inclusive and challenging education for spiritual development, any of these ideas could be put up for consideration.

The pluralist approach

Clive Erricker and Andrew Wright set themselves apart from this universalist meta-theory. Each promotes a pluralistic approach to spiritual education: Erricker through the relativism of the spirituality of the individual child and Wright by contextualizing spirituality in religions or worldviews; however, Erricker and Wright strongly disagree with each other (see Erricker, 2001; Wright, 2001). In the following sections of this paper, I examine their approaches and then explain how this examination led me to develop an argument for a further alternative approach, which I have called a critical democratic approach to education for spiritual development.

Clive Erricker: listening to children's narratives

Spiritual freedom is the starting-point for Erricker. He argues education should involve children in a process rather than merely fill them with knowledge. Spiritual education should not teach religious truths but encourage children to construct narrative meaning for themselves by listening to each other's views and experiences and recognizing 'the script is constructed in the classroom rather than by predesign' (Erricker & Erricker, 2000, p. 6). Currently, schooling is too concerned with delivering bodies of knowledge and skills. Knowledge is a 'leprosy of the mind' (ibid, p. 72) and 'feeding children a diet of epistemology (in the form of curriculum) in order to ensure economic profit (or wealth) from their future activity as an intellectually and practically skilled but politically and socially compliant workforce does not constitute a sufficient (or even justifiable) education':

> There is no 'chart', no fixed map to journey by. There is only activity itself, of which conceptualisation within conversation is a part. This leads us to recognise the unfounded-ness of scientific and religious claims to knowledge as fixed points to which return can be made ... The point I am making is simple: conceptual and linguistic constructions have no relationship to a reality that is not cognisable. It follows that the use of language to describe such a reality—true, real, absolute, objective and so on—is mythical or fictional. (Erricker & Erricker, 2000, p. 71, 74)

Wright criticizes Erricker's approach because it offers no tools to grapple with spiritual conceptual thinking. While he acknowledges children's fledgling spirituality should be nurtured, he says, 'Erricker at times appears to come close to suggesting that this initial stage is all that is required' (Wright, 1999, p. 44).

I agree with much of Wright's criticism of Erricker. Children do need knowledge and language to challenge the coherence of their own spiritual thinking and to engage with alternative spiritual worldviews, and also for their general knowledge and, in the end, for their personal spiritual development. It is surely perfectly possible to hear the voices of children and young people, without ejecting *all* knowledge. There are some fixed points, as Wright says (Wright, 2001, p. 123, 127). We do have a (provisional) map: the Earth is undergoing 'global warming'; the Holocaust did happen; and people do need to eat to survive. I tend to share Wright's conclusion that Erricker 'opens the door to a resurgent confessionalism' into a 'single non-negotiable worldview' (Wright, 2001, p. 121).

Andrew Wright: spiritual literacy and critical realism

However, while I agree with much of Wright's argument for a critical form of spiritual education, and agree with his claim that a 'spiritually educated child' should be 'informed, articulate, [and] literate', I have problems with his approach when he adds, as he does here, that the spiritually educated child should also be 'above all real-istic' (Wright, 1996, p. 148).

Wright is a critical realist. He seeks 'a communal spirituality within a framework of critical realism' (Wright, 1996, p. 140), acknowledging 'the possibility of contingent rationality through which knowledge, however provisional and open to revision, is obtainable precisely because we are inheritors of intellectual traditions whose power structures are open to critical scrutiny' (Wright, 2001, p. 122). His critical realism assumes a 'true nature of reality' and a 'proper relationship with the actual order of things' (Wright, 1996, p. 146) for both material *and* ultimate reality. Wright slides from talking about provisional knowledge of what he calls the 'brute facts' of material reality, such as cancer and the Holocaust, to talking about provisional knowledge of absolute and ultimate reality. For Wright, it seems, theologians' provisional knowledge of ultimate reality is equivalent to the scientific community's provisional knowledge of material reality. Spiritual literacy would 'provide pupils with the skills and sensibilities ... that will enable them to begin to learn to bring their lifeworlds into an appropriate relationship with the order of things (the traditional, though currently unfashionable word for which is, of course, "truth")' (Wright, 2001, p. 132).

Wright scoffs at Erricker's claim that there is no such thing as reality. because 'It is impossible to ignore the brute fact of the way things actually are in the world' (p. 123). However, absolute reality is not brute fact, and the relationship we actually have with provisional 'knowledge' of (what Wright refers to as) 'ultimate' reality and truth, is not the same as our relationship with knowledge of material reality. This can be demonstrated with two examples.

First, for instance, Wright is of the opinion that God exists, while I am of the opinion that God does not exist. We are both, presumably, willing to accept one of us must be wrong, and therefore our knowledge about God's existence could be said to be provisional. Similarly, there must be true answers to the questions whether Jesus is the Son of God or Muhammad the last Prophet of Allah since, as Wright says, Jesus 'cannot be a false Messiah, God incarnate and a prophet of Allah at one and the same time' (Wright, 1999, p. 20), and, again, present knowledge about this matter could be said to be provisional. In the meantime, however, Wright may refer to himself as a Christian, while I may refer to myself as an atheist, and someone else might refer to themself as a Muslim. The provisionality of our respective 'knowledge' claims about God (and ultimate reality generally) is altogether different from the provisionality of our respective knowledge claims about, say, life on Mars, for while we may be willing to suspend our judgement—to be agnostic—about life on Mars, we may not be willing to suspend our judgement about the existence of God.

Secondly, the truth of religious hypotheses is not established by testing against the real world in the *same way* as scientific hypotheses. For instance, Jesus' teachings, such as turning the other cheek in the face of hostility, *can* be tested against the realities of the world we indwell, as Wright suggests. However, if the real world is not supportive of Jesus' vision, which it tends not to be, this may not lead us to conclude we should reject its truth and wisdom. The real world is not necessarily a very good 'test' for the 'truth' of much of religion's 'knowledge' base. The reality is that, in this meanwhile of provisionality of religious knowledge and truth, each of us makes spiritual judgements and spiritual choices, and these affect the way we live and, in certain, ultimate respects, how we make sense of the world we indwell.

Wright criticizes Erricker for refusing 'to differentiate absolute and contingent knowledge' (Wright, 2001, p. 122), but, in my view, neither Erricker nor Wright makes such a differentiation and there remain unresolved issues around knowledge and truth. Nevertheless, Erricker and Wright's pluralist approach must be right for an inclusive spiritual education, and I want now to suggest it may be possible to achieve a form of spiritual education that is both critical and democratic.

A critical democratic approach to spiritual education

As currently conceived, education for spiritual development in state education in England (and Wales) is chiefly about human development, seeking a holistic pedagogy to promote the well-being of the whole child. However, this conceptualization of spiritual education as cross-curricular 'spiritual development' has marginalized spirituality itself; that is, it has given small space to traditional spiritual concerns, such as meaning and purpose in life and death. Further, spiritual education in this sense has remained (largely) in its traditional place in the curriculum area of Religious Education. RE, meanwhile, although more religiously plural than in the past, continues to largely ignore non-religious spiritualities, despite a strong British tradition of atheism and humanism and, therefore, spiritual education through RE cannot be inclusive. The most recent National Framework for RE (QCA, 2004) now suggests, for the first time, that atheistic worldviews be included in RE, but the mention is brief, the framework is non-statutory and, for the time being at least, no GCSE examination course includes atheism. Spiritual education needs curriculum space, but RE needs to be re-conceived and renamed, if it is to offer an inclusive education for spiritual development.

A critical democratic approach to education for spiritual development would be a worldviews education that would both critically inform and encourage choice. In line with Wright's views, it would include a critical examination and knowledge and understanding of worldviews, but not with the aim of making progress towards increasingly less provisional knowledge about ultimate reality, as suggested by Wright's critical realism. Additionally, in line with Erricker's views, it would include opportunities for dialogue—a hermeneutical approach—taking the form of a Rortian conversation united 'by civility rather than by a common goal, much less by a common ground' (Rorty, 1998, p. 318).

An inclusive approach to contemporary young people's education for spiritual development cannot be limited to teaching about a handful of traditional religious worldviews. Although spiritual educationalists tend to be highly pessimistic about the condition of Western society today, and associate choice and change with cultural decay and decline, others would argue young people are happy with this fluidity and wish to choose their own, sometimes eclectic, spiritual paths because of the prevalent individualism of Western culture. I believe we should celebrate this. Young people, along with the rest of us, live in a pluralist culture in which they are exposed to and are keen to investigate so much more (Watson, 2001; Beck & Beck-Gernsheim, 2002; De Souza, 2003; Tacey, 2004).

A critical democratic approach to education for spiritual development for state schools would not use the word 'spirituality' as if to label a real phenomenon with ontological status. It would use the word to denote a general area of discourse, and include a variety of spiritual beliefs both materialist and non-materialist, encompassing cognitive and emotional responses to, and personal expressions of, meaning in life and death and the human condition. In this way, spiritual education and values education might re-engage children and young people in what is fundamental to our human being.

Spiritual education through Religious Education

In RE, the introduction of spiritual development has meant pupils are expected to learn *from* religions, not just *about* religions. My main concern is for spiritual education through 'RE' to be more inclusive, to demonstrate in 'RE' that *all* children can take part in the spiritual discussion whatever their religion and whether they are religious or not, otherwise education for spiritual development is pointless for many children who do not have a religious belief (Rudge, 1998). However, thinking back to the comments of Mabud, quoted above, for those who (like Mabud) wish to set up separate faith schools (Mabud, 1992, p. 95), my approach to spiritual education would presumably be as unacceptable as the humanistic spirituality currently deployed in cross-curricular spiritual development. That is perhaps a separate argument; but I would prefer all our children to share in a multi-cultural state education, and within a multi-cultural (and therefore multi-faith) educational model, any form of spiritual education must be inclusive.

For me, the major current problems with delivering spiritual education through RE are the lack of diversity of worldviews on offer to pupils and the assumption pupils will be exclusively interested in *religions* as a source of spiritual opportunity. Like Erricker I want to argue for a world view approach to this curriculum subject which does not 'undermine religious faith positions', but nevertheless places them 'alongside non-religious alternatives as the appropriate range of enquiry that should be engaged within an educational system that concerns itself with spirituality and values' (Erricker & Erricker, 2000, p. 58). We need to go beyond *religious* education if we are to achieve a *spiritual* education. The new non-statutory national framework for RE (QCA & DfES, 2004) goes some way to addressing these concerns and my hope is that RE teachers will pick up on this new guidance.

I should like to add that while I agree worldviews education is important to cultural and religious understanding, I would not wish to see this become the main purpose of worldviews education, as is sometimes suggested. And although an atheist myself, I do not agree with the atheist, Blake, that spirituality only makes sense in the context of a religious institution (Blake, 1996). Defined broadly, spirituality *can* be inclusive, and I would seek to retain it, as part of worldviews education in state schools, precisely for the reasons Blake would abandon it:

> It puts in question precisely the kinds of assumption that have to be taken for granted in the mundane world of the institutional, and highlights their mere contingency ... Spirituality, if it is anything, is an escape from, or at least distancing from the very world of experience that education addresses or serves ... Spirituality escapes the institutional; just as a truly free person may escape her education, once she has one. (p. 454)

Spiritual education has the potential to be radical.

Notes on contributor

Jacqueline Watson is a Research Associate in the School of Education and an Associate member of the Keswick RE Centre at the University of East Anglia, UK. She was a secondary RE teacher for 12 years and her research interests are exploring discourses around spiritual development for state secondary schools, citizenship education and religious education.

References

Beck, U. & Beck-Gernsheim, E. (2002) *Individualisation: institutionalized individualism and its social and political consequences* (London, Sage).

Blake, N. (1996) Against spiritual education, *Oxford Review of Education*, 22(4), 443–463.

Carr, D. (1995) Towards a distinctive conception of spiritual rducation, *Oxford Review of Education*, 21(1), 83–97.

Carr, D. (1996) Rival conceptions of spiritual education, *Journal of the Philosophy of Education*, 30(2), 159–178.

Carr, D. (1999) Spiritual language and the ethics of redemption: a reply to Jim Mackenzie, *Journal of Philosophy of Education*, 33(3), 451–461.

De Souza, M. (2003) Contemporary influences on the spirituality of young people: implications for education, *International Journal of Children's Spirituality*, 8(3), 269–280.

Earl, M. (2001) Shadow and spirituality, *International Journal of Children's Spirituality*, 6(3), 277–288.

Erricker, C. & Erricker, J. (1997) Prospects for spiritual development in schools, *International Journal of Children's Spirituality*, 2(1), 3–4.

Erricker, C. & Erricker, J. (2000) *Reconstructing religious, spiritual and moral education* (London, Routledge Falmer).

Erricker, C. (2001) Shall we dance? Authority, representation, and voice: the place of spirituality in religious education, *Religious Education*, 96(1), 20–35.

Hay, D. with Nye, R. (1998) *The spirit of the child* (London, HarperCollins).

Hull, J. M. (1996) The ambiguity of spiritual values, in: J. M. Halstead & M. J. Taylor (Eds) *Values in education and education in values* (London, Falmer Press), 33–44.

Hull, J. M. (2002) Spiritual development: interpretations and applications, *British Journal of Religious Education*, 24(3), 171–182.

Mabud, S. A. (1992) A Muslim response to the Education Reform Act 1988, *British Journal of Religious Education*, 14(2), 88–98.

National Curriculum Council (1993) *Spiritual and moral development: a discussion paper* (York, NCC).

Priestley, J. G. (1985) Towards finding the hidden curriculum: a consideration of the spiritual dimension of experience in curriculum planning, *British Journal of Religious Education*, 7(3), 112–119.

Priestley, J. G. (2000) The essence of education: Whitehead and the spiritual dimension, *Interchange*, 31(2), 117–133.

Qualifications and Curriculum Authority (QCA) and Department for Education and Skills (DfES) (2004) *Religious education: the non-statutory national framework* (London, QCA).

Rorty, R. (1998) *Philosophy and the mirror of nature* (Oxford, Blackwell) (work originally published 1980).

Rudge, L. (1998) 'I am nothing'—does it matter? A critique of current religious education policy and practice in England on behalf of the silent majority, *British Journal of Religious Education*, 20(3), 155–165.

Slee, N. (1993) Spirituality in education: an annotated bibliography, *Journal of Beliefs and Values*, 13(2), 10–17.

Smith, D. (2001) *Making sense of spiritual development* (Nottingham, The Stapleford Centre).

Tacey, D. (2004) *The spirituality revolution: the emergence of contemporary spirituality* (Hove and New York, Brunner-Routledge).

Thatcher, A. (1991) A critique of inwardness in religious education, *British Journal of Religious Education*, 14(1), 22–27.

Watson, J. (2000) Whose model of spirituality should be used in the spiritual development of school children? *International Journal of Children's Spirituality*, 5(1), 91–101.

Watson, J. (2001) Experience of spirituality, experience of school: listening to young people, paper presented at the eighth *Education, Spirituality and the Whole Child Conference*, Roehampton University of Surrey, 21–23 June.

Watson, J. (2003) Preparing spirituality for citizenship, *International Journal for Children's Spirituality*, 8(1), 9–24.

Watson, J. (2004) Spiritual development: a crusade for hearts and minds in the dark days of National Curriculum schooling, paper presented at the *BERA Conference*, UMIST, September.

Wright, A. (1996) The child in relationship: towards a communal model of spirituality, in: R. Best (Ed.) *Education, spirituality and the whole child* (London and New York, Cassell), 139–149.

Wright, A. (1997) Embodied spirituality: the place of culture and tradition in contemporary educational discourse on spirituality, *International Journal of Children's Spirituality*, 1(2), 8–20.

Wright, A. (1999) *Discerning the spirit: teaching spirituality in the religious education classroom* (Abingdon, Culham College Institute).

Wright, A. (2001) Dancing in the fire: a deconstruction of Clive Erricker's postmodern spiritual pedagogy, *Religious Education*, 96(1), 120–135.

A risky business: the potential of groupwork skills for spiritual education in a classroom of difference

Cathy Ota*

Introduction

> The police announcement that Thursday's explosions on the underground and on the Number 30 bus were, apparently, the work of British suicide bombers is the most shocking news to come since the attacks themselves. It is also the bleakest possible development ... The realisation that Britons are ready to bomb their fellow citizens is a challenge to the whole of our society. (Jonathan Freedland, *Guardian*, 13.7.2005)

> The tragedy of July 7 demands that all of us, both in public life and in civil and religious society, confront together the problems of Islamophobia, racism, unemployment ... and social exclusion—factors that may be alienating some of our children and driving them to

*Working with Others Research and Education Unit, Education Research Centre, Mayfield House, University of Brighton, Falmer, Brighton BN41 1GD, UK. Email: cathy.ota@workingwith-others.org

the path of anger and desperation. (extract from the Muslim leader's statement at the Islamic Cultural Centre, London, UK, 15.7.2005)

Living and working in Brighton, on the south coast of England, I am a couple of hours away from London. On 7 July 2005, I was working in the office and by late morning people were talking across desks and logging on to websites to find out more about something big happening in London. Within the hour the same people were calling partners, sons and daughters away at university and colleagues who had travelled to London for meetings.

I count myself fortunate that for me the shock and impact of the London bombings earlier is far less than that of many other friends, colleagues and relations. Alongside this, I acknowledge that for other communities, countries and contexts this situation and fear of sudden violence occurs far more regularly and brutally. This challenges me, alongside many others, to confront and question the difference and diversity that is part of our lives today; a difference and diversity that we too easily assign to leave hovering in the shadows, acknowledged, yes, but at the same time rarely central to how we relate to and engage with others.

This article considers what it means to expose this reality of difference in the class-room. But to sit with simply exposing a reality does not bring us very far and may only serve to foster fear of uncertainty and the 'other'. What I am more interested in (and passionate about) is how through accepting and confronting difference we can sustain dynamic and inclusive relationships with others that embrace the ambiguity of our different lives. And what are the implications of this for the classroom? For what might be called spiritual education? What does this mean for teachers and pupils in their present classrooms, as well as equipping and enabling pupils with the skills needed to live and work in this way in the future (DfEE, 1999)?

The article explores our research and practical work in this area at the University of Brighton, first, as part of a four-year research project looking into effective group-work skills,[1] which then, in the last 18 months, has led to the establishing of the Working with Others Research and Education Unit by Lucia Berdondini and myself. Through our continuing collaboration with pupils, teachers, teaching assistants and parents, difference is explicit and negotiated. This is difficult, challenging and risky, but it also offers a practical process that can address difference through inclusion, relationships, identity, citizenship and spiritual education.

The challenge of a divided world and a classroom of difference

By widening access to power, people feel able to tackle problems affecting communities themselves. Neighbourhood renewal provides a platform for building strong and cohesive communities in which local people—regardless of race, faith, gender or age—have a say over how local needs are best met.

Just like society, the Muslim community is not a homogeneous blob. We need to remember that it is part of our wider community and society.

I'm not excusing the bombers, but addressing educational needs, social deprivation, the role of the media, the aspirations of the Muslim youth and the need for positive role models could be steps in the right direction to address the disillusionment with life in the UK they so clearly felt ... This problem has to be faced by all of us. (Sadiq Khan, *Guardian*, 14.7.2005)

Sadiq Khan (Labour Member of Parliament for Tooting, south-west London) wrote the above within days of the London bombings and in highlighting the complexity of multi-layered difference within our communities and society calls for a broad acknowledgement of responsibility for working with such difference and division—it is indeed, 'a problem ... to be faced by all of us'. The problem here is not only about preventing such atrocities as the bombings ever being repeated. For those of us concerned with the education of the whole child, with offering pupils opportunities to explore and develop relationships that enable their learning and growth, that engage them in a spiritual education, then our problem, or challenge, is, among other things, philosophical, spiritual and practical.

I want to focus on the practical aspects of difference and division, so let us move in this direction, starting with the notion of difference and division in society. If it exists writ large around us, then the microcosm of the school and classroom duplicates this. We can accept this as a point for discussion but how does this work in classroom practice? On the one hand, division and difference is accentuated in the classroom: ability-based groups and seating arrangements around tables for four to eight pupils at primary level (ages 5–11) pervades the majority of classroom organisation in the UK and beyond. For those pupils who are 'too' different, for example, through academic ability, disruptive classroom behaviour or through conditions such as Austism or Asperger's syndrome, then the division is even more enhanced as they will frequently be removed from the classroom and class group in order to work separately with an adult either on their own or with a small group of similar pupils. Here we enter the realms of 'what I do and what I say', for although many classrooms and class groups operate in this way on a daily basis, very little is explicitly discussed with pupils. The adult organizes the children and decides who is located where. If difference, in pupil form, interrupts the already crammed and pressured curriculum, then it is removed, so that the rest of the class can continue its progress.

What is the impact of this? A fairly homogeneous group of reasonably compliant and conforming children who let the teacher get on with their task. Within this remaining group difference is rarely brought together: from our work with teachers and class groups we know that even within a class of 30 young children there is likely to be a small group who never interact or have worked together: they are seated on their ability-based tables and these are the social networks they develop and where friendships are formed. As a consequence, the same children will then spend their time together in the playground and out of school. It is quite feasible that within that class of 30, even at the end of one or two years, some children will still not have spoken or worked with one another.

Crucially, there is nothing in this kind of class that deals with difference, that helps the class (adult and pupils) acknowledge and address what this means for them both as a group and individually. Instead we are left with inequality, exclusion, isolates and children who are not given the opportunity to develop the skills they need to be part of their classroom community. While I appreciate and recognize the valuable contribution that the citizenship agenda and PSHCE (personal, social, health and citizenship education) makes to education in the UK, the sheer volume of disaffection and exclusion at all ages clearly points out that there is still some way to go before we can feel confident that we are offering an education that builds self esteem for all pupils and enables them with the skills to deal with and utilize the difference in their lives.

Practical ways of being explicit about difference

All children and young people work as part of a group in their classrooms, whether seated around a table in small groups, working in pairs or participating in a whole-class discussion. Indeed being able to work with others can be seen as a key life skill, something which employers are keenly aware of and make considerable efforts to develop and foster in their teams. Our research and work at Brighton over the past five years began with an exploration into how pupils could work most effectively in groups; just sitting round a table does not mean that anyone (adult or child) has the skills to contribute and participate themselves and enable other members of the group to work with them.

Our research with 40 teachers from across the south coast investigated whether training in specific skills, such as communication could help, and whether space to reflect and talk with the teacher could enable pupils to develop better strategies for working together. Reports from the 40 or so teachers collaborating with us have highlighted greater social skills, self-esteem, social inclusion, confidence and ownership within their classes, even with children as young as 5 (see Ota & Berdondini, forthcoming, for general overview of project; Berdondini & Ota, forthcoming, for more about our work with very young children).

Five years later, and we now have a process that explicitly focuses on the whole-class group, adult and pupils, their relationships and how they experience being part of that group. This process has two main strands:

- *Strand 1*: developing and training in essential skills—trust, communication and problem solving;
- *Strand 2*: pre- and debriefing as a group.

Strand 1 focuses on training and building trust, communication and problem-solving, and is explicit about key skills for working with others and on the relationships among the class group. There are a number of games and activities that many teachers already use in circle time, PSHCE and PE lessons that address these areas. Having drawn together many of these games, we encourage the schools and teachers we work with (currently over 55 schools in the UK) to try to do at least three a week, even if they are only a few minutes in length. Initially, teachers are asked to look at *trust* within the class. Once they feel comfortable that trust is better established within the group they are asked to introduce more *communication* activities that build upon the trust. As this level of skills becomes more secure the teacher is then asked to introduce *problem-solving* activities, a more complex and demanding skill.

We do not to suggest a rigid framework for week 1, trust, then week 2, communication, etc.; neither do we suggest that 'as soon as trust is established then you can move on to communication'. Instead we perceive these skills as interdependent and requiring continuing support and reinforcement. Combined with the professional and reflective judgement of the teacher, each level of skill is initially introduced as and when the teacher feels that they and their class are ready. They then have the rest of the year together to refine and explore what each of these skills means for their group.

The concept of training in groupwork skills as a whole-class activity is one aspect of our approach that makes it different. A second aspect is Strand 2, the use of pre- and debriefing with pupils. Five or ten minutes spent on a trust or communication activity is an enjoyable game, or more rarely, a complete disaster if everyone ends up arguing. However, by including pre- and debriefing as part of this process, the activity becomes something much richer and more valuable for all the group, pupils and teacher.

Pre-briefing prefaces the activity of the class; the teacher sits with the whole group and explains *what* they are going to do, *how* they will do it and *why*. For example, the teacher might tell the children that they are going to do a blindfold walk exercise around the hall, in pairs, and try to see how they can work together and help each other. The teacher can then ask the class if they have any comments or questions, as well as using the opportunity to reinforce ideas about working together, such as 'Remember last time we did this, we talked about how we needed to help our partner'.

Debriefing follows after an activity and is used by the teacher to reflect with the class on the content of what they have done (what has been produced), as well as the process of working together. In the role of a facilitator, and using open questions, the teacher can elicit responses about how the pupils have got on together, what worked well and what difficulties were encountered. When problems are voiced by the class, they have the opportunity to talk together to find possible strategies to help them in the future. For example, if a pupil reports that their partner did not join in, the teacher might ask the class to think what they could say to a partner in the same situation.

Here the class group together enters new territory: divisions and differences among the group become overt and explicit. Through the facilitation of the teacher pupils are given permission and invited to talk about the differences they experienced among their group. This demands time and commitment from the teacher: to be available to have these conversations with pupils on a regular basis and to support the group as pupils develop their awareness and vocabulary to discuss these experiences and relationships. It is also risky for the teacher. Initially, pupils may be reluctant to participate in activities or talk during pre and debriefing, either through lack of vocabulary or because they are unsure of the new boundaries for honesty and giving feedback to the teacher on how they enjoyed their lesson. Once through this, however, there can be a surge in problems or difficulties ('I don't like working with girls', 'I'm not doing it!', 'It's boring!'). This is where both strands interweave in enabling relationships that work with the differences and divisions in a class. The activities enable skills, sensitivity and awareness and then the pre- and debriefing on any class activity offer an opportunity to identify individual learning and experiences, and to reflect and develop strategies for the future.

The role of the teacher as a facilitator here is fundamental; teachers do not have to carry the burden of being able to solve any problem presented by the group; instead they need to develop the confidence and trust in the class, to reflect it back to them and allow them to come up with strategies and solutions—and they always do! What we also have noticed here is that a different notion of power is engendered, as the whole group together become co-creators of learning and understanding. This can be aligned with the same kind of knowledge construction described by Erricker (2000):

> We are suggesting that children can be allowed to know as much as or even more than the teacher, can publicly claim the position of the repository of that knowledge and have it acknowledged by the former holder of that exalted rank—the teacher. (Erricker, 2000, p. 192)

These varied demands and changes to practice are challenging ones for teachers and we are aware that teachers need ongoing supervision and support if they are to confront these challenges, continue to develop their practice and enable their class to deal with the differences they encounter. Because of this our work with schools also includes regular support and supervision sessions where we employ a teacher-centred approach that aims to help them reflect, support each other and find ways forward for them and their class (Ota, 2005).

Some general outcomes and feedback from teachers and pupils

Through our initial research[2] at Brighton, the impact of this approach on literacy and numeracy levels for 5–7-year-olds has been shown to be statistically significant when compared with control classes of children. A similarly positive impact was found for older pupils in science and higher-order and abstract thinking skills.[3] Beyond this, teachers also report impact on pupils in terms of confidence, communication, self-esteem, inclusion and prosocial skills that, within a short time-frame, extend beyond the classroom to the playground. Individually pupils are recognized as participating far more in the class and in their learning. As a group they are more sensitive to one another and more aware of what each brings to the group. Through this recognition of difference inclusion is more genuine and embedded in the class relationships: instead of focusing on one or two ostracized pupils, the whole class recognizes their responsibility for themselves and each other as part of that group. Here Mandy,[4] a Year 2 teacher (6–7-year-olds) reflects on her class:

> I don't think we do much independent work really ... well, I think they're just doing it all the time and I listen to the class next door and they're really quiet, and I look at my class and I see them all chatting away, but actually they're all on task and supporting each other and helping, even if its an independent activity they're doing ... they're still, sort of, helping each other, and 'how do I do this?', and it's nice because it's not just, sort of, copying answers quietly, they are helping each other ... which is good. (Longitudinal interview with teachers, April 2004)

Where some children might previously have been out of the class for considerable periods of time, teachers adopting this approach have reported that not only can the one child cope with being part of the group, *but that the rest of the class are more able to accept and include them as part of their group.* Mandy's discussion about her 6–7-year-olds provides an example of this:

> We had a kind of incident yesterday and it was brilliant because I split the class into two, because I only had 20 in, and I briefed them a little bit about a science investigation, and then I said, 'right go away and sort yourselves out and do it'. And I sat back and thought [*makes excited noise*] 'they're doing it! Fantastic!'

> But then there was Charles who struggled and he sat there and I could see him looking at the clock, waiting for his special needs assistant to come in and that was like in about 40 minutes, and he was looking around to see where I was and the rest of the group were really good because they included him, and Sophie was in charge and sort of took the lead and said, 'right, has everybody done something?' And she made sure that he had done something. (Longitudinal interview with teachers, April 2004)

Here we arrive at what we have been seeking: the difference is explicit, discussed, explored and strategies to live with and use it developed and used.

I have already highlighted how the key to this working effectively resides with the teacher, and with teachers being able to develop their practice and class relationships in this way. Coping with children who find working with others challenging in the classroom has been cited as a difficult area for many teachers (e.g. those with emotional or behavioural difficulties, as well as the very able pupils who find it hard to see the benefit of working with others). Surpassing this, however, it is without doubt the process of developing pre- and debriefing with pupils that has been the most demanding as well as most valuable aspect of our approach. Having the space and permission to discuss, talk openly and support others, we have seen how classes of children become more cohesive, supportive and understanding of one another. Through this each pupil is recognized not just in their own equal right to be part of the class group, but also in their equal right to have a voice and be the different individual that they are:

> I am important, and what I think and say and do is important as well ... I 'make a difference' to more than myself. What I say and what I am and do matters ... whatever there is in the world around me, that world would be poorer, less interesting and less promising were I suddenly to cease to exist or go elsewhere. (Bauman, 2003, p. 80)

As difference is negotiated among the group teachers report that by the end of the year any child can work comfortably with another in the class and that they naturally monitor and support each other, both in class and in the playground. So what is going on here? In terms of how Faulks describes citizenship, are these social groups providing an experience of citizenship in action?

> Citizenship must be rooted in a notion of the social group. Citizenship cannot be purely an individual status because citizenship only has meaning to the individual in the wider cultural context of the group. (Faulks, 2000, p. 90)

Yes, I would claim that this is on offer to these pupils, but also a lot more besides. For the purposes of this piece we are concerned with engaging with difference and how this can be understood as spiritual education. For the remainder of this article, I want to draw out how this process of being explicit about difference in the classroom addresses different aspects of pupils' education and development, especially spiritual education. To take us there we can draw on six ways in which this practical process engages with difference:

1. it focuses on building relationships among the whole-class group through activities and pre- and debriefing;
2. it allows pupils and teachers to acknowledge and assume personal responsibility for oneself as well as group responsibility for one another;
3. it enables pupil sensitivity to confront uncertainty and recognize difference among one another;
4. it develops pupil skills to respect, include, listen and respond to one another's different characters, personalities, feelings and experiences;
5. it develops pupil vocabulary to express their feelings, experiences and relationships in the class;
6. it encourages the teacher to empower pupils and share with them the co-creation and co-construction of knowledge, meaning and identity.

Working with difference in relationships: a spiritual education

> Inherent in what has been said about the nature of the person, the interrelationships among people in community and communication, and social control, there is an implicit attitude, a tone infusing the whole. For Dewey, education is a moral undertaking and … is not a separate, idealized domain. It is present and a part of everyday living. (Cuffaro, 1995, p. 52)

> Ordinary education is transformed into spiritual education at that point when learning ceases to skim over the surface of a subject and instead begins to grapple with issues of ultimate meaning and truth that constitute the very marrow of our humanity. (Wright, 2000, p. 11)

Our list of six points, above, outlines how our approach to groupwork can work with difference in the classroom. Can it also point us in the direction of spiritual education? Does this also offer one way of understanding the spiritual in classrooms as they are really experienced by pupils and teachers? Can it help identify a different avenue into addressing spiritual education, that is through relationships the work with difference among the class group? In the above perspective, Cuffaro (1995) is exploring Dewey's contribution to early childhood classrooms and highlights the moral as underpinning and infusing education. Might we instead substitute the word 'spiritual' here? Perhaps, Wright's (2000) comment is also pertinent (quoted above). Building on these ideas and our work described so far, I suggest that:

1. spiritual education can be understood as a mark of quality in education.
2. spiritual education is intrinsic and underpins 'good' education. By good education, I mean that which engages with personhood and identity, enables meaning-making and is characteristically relational and about community.

I do not propose the above as absolutes or a defining model of spiritual education. What they can provide, however, is a way of finding spiritual education in today's real classrooms and a way of understanding how spiritual education might be recognized in the relationships and communication that are being constantly negotiated and evolving.

The paradox of moving into a discussion of the spiritual is that this somewhat relatively recently examined and defined term, for education and children, is both at the same time both less defined and over-defined, with a wide range of debate offering a range of definitions (see e.g. Peters, 1967; Erricker & Erricker, 2000; Watson, 2003; Pridmore & Pridmore, 2004; Webster, 2004). This piece has already discussed practical processes for spiritual education. Instead of leading me to a neat definition, I want to dwell on a description, again focused on processes, practicalities and experiences. I return to pre- and debriefing as a way of highlighting a spiritual education, where conversations and relationships include the whole-class group in what can be an uncomfortable, difficult and challenging situation as adult and pupil are required to develop the skills and strategies, to listen to each other's difference, respond honestly and find a way forward together in their learning and relationship. In confronting power and uncertainty, in entering the risky domains of establishing, negotiating and building relationships that are open, respectful and inclusive, such spiritual education is enhancing; but it is also political, difficult and makes demands on the individual person as well as that person in relationship with others. This, then, is not a fluffy, candy-coated spiritual education. In becoming a living democracy and embracing citizenship, its empowerment reaches beyond the confines of classroom and school. There is a public knowledge where the inchoate becomes choate, and there is increased intelligence and connection/reconnection to community through face-to-face interaction (McAfee, 2004). Using Dewey in her exploration of public knowledge, McAfee pointedly remarks: 'Because they know where the shoe pinches they can point to what problems need to be addressed' (McAfee, 2004, p. 149). Paraphrasing this, what we have observed is that even very young children are perfectly able to both point to what deeper problems and learning needs should be addressed *as well as* finding the solutions to overcome them. What limits this, and the spiritual education that could be taking place, is the courage of the teacher and school to engage on this level and offer the skills, opportunities and permission to do so. In such circumstances, this is when true learning, that engages and enables growth of the person, can take place. And it is this learning and these relationships that speak of spiritual education.

Self-love: more spiritual education

In *Liquid love*, Bauman talks of 'togetherness dismantled' (2003, p. 151) to describe the nature of different relationships in today's society. This term aptly conveys the impact of a practical process that offers pupils space to reconsider, to take apart and rebuild their relationships with one another. The impact of such experience, learning and knowledge enable life skills, but also demonstrate the power that resides within the group as a whole. For these classes their togetherness as a group does not deny their individuality or difference, but recognizes, encourages and enables different individuals to have relationships that truly engage with the other:

> The fact that others disagree with us ... *is not* an obstacle on the road to human community. But our conviction that our opinions *are* the whole truth, nothing but the truth and above all the sole truth that there is, and our belief that other people's truths, if different from ours, are 'mere opinions'—*are* such an obstacle. (Bauman, 2003, p. 151)

As well as dismantling togetherness, Bauman's (2003) work also addresses two further relevant themes, namely self-love and love:

> In order to have self-love we need to be loved. Refusal of love—denial of the status of the love-worthy object—breeds self-hatred. Self-love is built out of the love offered to us by others ... Others must love us first, so that we can begin to love ourselves. (p. 80)

> Loving our neighbours as we love ourselves would mean then *respecting each other's uniqueness*—the value of our differences that enrich the world we jointly inhabit and so make it more fascinating and enjoyable a place and add further to the cornucopia of its promises. (p. 81)

We are brought back again to the importance of relationships; the fundamental role of others in enabling the individual to value, respect and love themselves. In engaging with the relational and the individual, we have described a process that exposes difference but also offers a spiritual education that provides a way forward for equipping individual pupils in our classes with the skills they need for life.

Concluding remarks

Our continuing work with schools means that we have the valuable opportunity to explore what can be achieved in a very practical and relevant way in today's classrooms. Our work so far demonstrates that by exposing and working with difference, one avenue for spiritual education is opened up, for teacher and pupils together. There are risks involved—for the pupils and most definitely for the teacher—but also clearly evident are the personal benefits and opportunities that exceed SATs scores and league-table placings. Far beyond this there are possibilities: first, to take further the notion of quality in education and secondly, to seek out where that same quality touches on and engages with the spiritual education of pupils and teachers. To refuse to engage with this possibility, to continue to deny the difference surrounding our young people, will have consequences for us and them. July 2005 forcibly showed us in the UK where exclusion, alienation and desperation can lead, and that is a very big risk, which we all need to take responsibility for:

> the survival and well-being of communitas depend on human imagination, inventiveness and courage in breaking the routine and trying the untried ways.

> They depend, in other words, on the human ability to live with risk and accept the responsibility for the consequences. It is these abilities that are the supports for the 'moral economy'—mutual care and help, living *for* the other, weaving the tissue of human commitments,

fastening and servicing interhuman bonds, translating rights into obligations, sharing responsibility for everyone's fortune and welfare. (Bauman, 2003, p. 73)

Notes

1. Funded by the UK Economic, Social Research Council. ESRC-TLRP reference no. L139251046. The project was a collaborative research project exploring groupwork across all key stages of education (ages 5–16) between the Universities of Brighton, Cambridge and London. The team at Brighton was led by Professor Peter Kutnick and researchers included Lucia Berdondini, Linda Rice, Nadya Henwood, Jen Smith and myself.
2. SPRinG Project, 2000–4.
3. Universities of London and Cambridge, also part of the SPRinG Project, with a focus on key stage 2 (8–11-year-olds) and key stage 3 (12–14-year-olds) respectively.
4. Not her real name.

Notes on contributor

Cathy Ota is co-editor of the *International Journal of Children's Spirituality* and Senior Research Fellow at the University of Brighton, UK, where she is currently leading the Working With Others Research and Education Unit with her colleague Lucia Berdondini. The unit works collaboratively, both nationally and internationally, with pupils, teachers, parents and staff teams, exploring and developing practical strategies to enhance group processes through self-awareness, social communication, peer support, problem-solving and conflict resolution. Her current research and work is focused on developing effective groupwork in early years and higher education settings. Recent publications include joint authorship of *The education of the whole child* (Cassell, 1997), and co-editing *Spiritual education—cultural, religious and social differences* (Sussex Academic Press, 2001) and *Spiritual education—literary, empirical and pedagogical approaches* (Sussex Academic Press, 2005).

References

Bauman, Z. (2003) *Liquid love* (Cambridge, Polity Press).

Berdondini, L. & Ota, C. (forthcoming) Comunicare le emozioni: contento o triste? [Communicating emotions: happy or sad?], in: M. L. Genta (Ed.) *Io sono, tu sei: competenze infantili e scoperta dell'altro a 4 anni* [*I am, you are: children's competence and discovery of the others at 4 years old*] (Italy, Carrocci).

Cuffaro, H. (1995) *Experimenting with the world: John Dewey and the early childhood classroom* (New York, Teachers College Press).

Department for Education and Employment (1999) *All our futures: creativity, culture and education* (London, DfEE).

Erricker, J. (2000) A collaborative approach to researching teacher work in developing spiritual and moral education, in: R. Best (Ed.) *Education for spiritual, moral, social and cultural education* (London, Continuum), 187–198.

Erricker, C. & Erricker, J. (200) *Reconstructing religious, spiritual and moral education* (London, Routledge).

Faulks, K. (2000) Citizenship (London, Routledge).

Freedland, J. (2005) After the aftershock, *Guardian,* 13 July.

Khan, S. (2005) This problem must be faced by us all, *Guardian,* 14 July.

McAfee, N. (2004) Public knowledge, *Philosophy of Social Criticism,* 30(2), 139–157.

Ota, C. (2005) Spirituality and the reflective practitioner in education, paper presented at the *6th International Conference on Children's Spirituality,* Rabat, Malta, 12–14 July.

Ota, C. & Berdondini, L. (forthcoming) Building bridges and right relations: a study in fostering spiritual, moral and social growth through groupwork skills with young children, in: M. de Souza (Ed.) *International handbook on the religious, moral and spiritual dimensions of education* (Dordrecht, Kluwer Academic Publishers).

Peters. R. S. (1967) *The concept of education* (London, Routledge & Kegan Paul).

Pridmore, P. & Pridmore, J. (2004) Promoting the spiritual development of sick children, *International Journal of Children's Spirituality,* 9(1), 21–38.

Watson, J. (2003) Preparing spirituality for citizenship, *International Journal of Children's Spirituality,* 8(1), 9–24.

Webster, S. (2004) An existential framework of spirituality, *International Journal of Children's Spirituality,* 9(1), 7–19.

Wright, A. (2000) Spirituality and education (London, Routledge Falmer).

If you don't know the difference you are living with, how can you learn to live with it? Taking difference seriously in spiritual and religious education

Clive Erricker*

Introduction

This discussion questions how we can approach difference seriously in education when considering religious worldviews that present the possibility of division. It argues that an extrinsic purpose of RE, in England and Wales, has been to play down difference in order to accentuate a sense of moral homogeneity within religions that has given a proclaimed educational value to the subject and social benefit to its

*Havant Local Education Office, River Way, Havant, Hampshire, PO9 2EL. UK.
Email: clive.erricker@btopenworld.com

subjects. In turn, this has given RE a modus operandi that has defended it from criticisms of pedagogical insufficiency and a lack of a body of knowledge with which to defend its curriculum credentials. My contention is that RE is pedagogically insufficient and that this is related to deficiencies in the way it represents its subject (religions). As a result, it does not exhibit the necessary academic rigour in relation to its body of knowledge. Also, RE has seriously weakened its credibility in claiming to promote children's spiritual development through wedding that aim to promoting the inculcation of moral values (Keast, 2005).

My contention is that RE has not served a sufficient educational purpose because it has been negligent of its educational responsibilities by seeking to replace them with a social and moral justification of its worth. One result of this is that, despite it being well positioned to address the significant societal impact of religious and cultural differences, it has been wilfully neglectful of this responsibility and has, as a result, confined the concept of spirituality to a benign sense of liberal well-being and charitable giving: awe and wonder and Mother Teresa.

Approaches to addressing diversity or difference in religious and spiritual education

Two particularly important advocates of the study of religion in the late twentieth century offer disparate reasons why religion is a necessary area of study. Ninian Smart, an influential figure in promoting the study of world religions in religious education, wrote:

> A multicultural or pluralistic philosophy of religion is a desideratum, and it has been amazing how culture-bound so many Western philosophers have been: an unconscious (to be kind) imperialism ... We have surely passed beyond a stage in human life when national values stand supreme, after all the horrors national wars have caused during this passing century. Nationalism sometimes makes good politics: but its dangers are well advertised. We need to see religions in the same sort of context: just as democracy is a way to eliminate violence in the choice of policies: so a kind of spiritual democracy should eliminate inter-religious and inter-ideological violence ... we need an overarching worldview for all human beings. (Smart, 1998, pp. xii–xiii)

In citing the strong religious components involved in bitter conflicts John Bowker notes that this destructive characteristic of religious ideologies constitutes an important reason why religions need to be studied:

> it would be the strongest possible argument for devoting far more time ... to the attempt to understand such insanity a great deal more clearly than we do. Insanity can be a lethally dangerous phenomenon. (Bowker, 1987, pp. 4–5)

Plus ça change ...

Smart and Bowker offer useful starting-points in considering what approach we should employ in the study of religion in schools. The contrasts in their justifications alert us to some of the most difficult issues we face. Smart's desideratum reminds us that liberal thinking of the kind he advocates is no longer the prevailing cultural climate, just seven years later. Neo-liberalism, as it is called, and the free market capitalism it espouses, have brought a different caste of mind not only to whether such a liberal desideratum is possible but also to whether it is desirable. Bowker's insistence on the destructive ideological nature of religion has been evidenced through the attack on the twin towers in New York, the trend towards 'terrorism' generally, 'suicide bombings', the Israel-Palestinian problem, wars in Afghanistan and Iraq and, more recently, the London bombings in 2005. Smart's call for 'an overarching world-view for all human beings' has, at least for the present, receded over the horizon. How could we expect such a possibility now?

However, at the same time, the British government is seeking to pass a law against religious discrimination as it also seeks to combat terror through passing laws that create greater national security despite their impact on civil liberties. Following the London bombings in 2005, a young Brazilian man was shot five times in the tube as he sought to flee from the British police. Mistakenly, the police thought he was a terrorist. The mistake was defended as the sort of event that is bound to happen and likely to happen again, justified by the primary need to ensure the strictest security. It is as difficult to imagine such a justification not causing outrage from the press and the public in 1998[1] as it is to imagine Smart's desideratum being greeted today as a timely reminder of our common humanity.

… le même chose

Despite the new caste of mind we experience now in the middle of the first decade of the twenty-first century, religious education in England and Wales has not changed. John Keast's lecture to the National Association of SACREs (Standing Advisory Councils for Religious Education) in 2005, 'Clever devils and how to avoid them', pursued a well-established theme. His main point was that 'education has to be … provided with a moral dimension … and requires promotion of fundamental ethical concepts'. He continued by arguing that these invoke beliefs, for example about human nature, and that this legitimizes the study of philosophy and religion. Religion, in Keast's view, is synonymous with 'worldview' and inclusive of traditionally 'non-religious' systems such as atheism and humanism. It follows, Keast argues, that the study of ethics and religion are inextricably linked. If education is not to be just about cleverness but also about morality, then, religion in society and religious education in schools should be the vehicles to serve this purpose. He concludes by stating that 'Religion's role in society is to prevent unhealthy coalitions of vested interests and promote a greater appreciation of human life and purpose' and that 'RE's role in the curriculum is to provide that coherent and specialized provision of spiritual and moral development that enables children to understand the roles of religion in society and take their place in it in a responsible way', and he warns us that, 'if we do not actually believe what we teach our children to believe, we become the cleverest devils of all' (Keast, 2005, pp. 6–11). Comparing Keast's exhortation with that of Smart's need for an overarching worldview, it would seem that nothing has changed at all.

Focusing on the use of the term spiritual we can note that Smart refers to the need for a spiritual democracy that would be an antidote to inter-religious and ideological violence. Keast refers to 'the duty of moral and spiritual care' in schools and the need to 'take more seriously their [children's] moral and spiritual development, which means taking more seriously the role of religion in society' (p. 11). These are the only times the spiritual is referred to by Keast, both times accompanied by 'moral', which is a term he uses throughout his address. It is clear that the use of 'spiritual' by both Smart and Keast is as a subsidiary to morality, that it has no clear meaning of its own and that it is anti-ideological. For Keast 'religion' has a broad compass based on worldview, and though he does not say this, it is axiomatic in his argument that worldview is in no sense an ideological term since it serves a pan-religious moral purpose. Similarly for Smart, but here stated explicitly, the 'overarching worldview' is anti-ideological.

This reading of the messages of Smart and Keast provides us with some interesting semantic conclusions. Religion can be judged as both morally good or bad. It is good if it strives for a pan-religious cohesive moral purpose. It is bad if it is ideologically divisive or violent. This distinction alerts us to a judgement being made upon religion, but the judgement is made from a pan-religious moral perspective. In and of itself, religion is neither good nor bad, it depends what end it serves. Alternatively, from a specifically religious ideological perspective, the judgement may go the other way. Religious ideologies may oppose the world around them, and in many respects often do, in which case such ideologies will be in tension or even conflict with that world. The moral judgement changes in accordance with the perspective: the pan-religious is opposed to the specific, separatist ideological religious view, and vice versa. The term 'ideology' is used by Smart in a shorthand way to identify religious worldviews that oppose a mainstream pan-religious consensus or 'overarching worldview' based on democracy. Thus, democracy becomes the anti-ideological vehicle toward a pan religious moral (global) society. Nationalist ideologies, when they are also divisive, suffer the same judgement as religious ideologies. For Keast, explicitly (though for Smart the same is implicitly true) religion means worldview, which, in turn extends beyond religions to include their historical opponents: atheists, humanists, etc. The message is clear: ideologies of all kinds are to be rejected if they in turn reject a democratic, moral overarching worldview by considering their own separatist truth to be superior. Religious education should be understood as a vehicle for striving towards and nurturing this pan-religious, non-ideological, moral worldview in children and schools. Thus, the 'non-ideological' perspective does exhibit ideological tendencies in two respects: in relation to the representation of its curriculum subjects, and in relation to the pedagogical aims and procedures to be employed in order to achieve its desired objective.

While it is necessary for all curriculum representation and pedagogical procedures to be value laden (see Bordieu & Passeron, 1990), it is worrying that this approach to RE justifies itself through the rejection of that aspect of its subject that it regards as not in accord with its moral desideratum and aligns any notion of spiritual development with the pursuit of the same consensual moral conclusions. This leaves us with severe representational and pedagogical problems since the representation of the subject is biased and the agency of children, in relation to the opportunity to arrive at their own evaluative judgements within such an approach, is clearly compromised. These deficiencies significantly damage the academic integrity of RE and its claims to effectively address young people's spiritual development.

Nevertheless, government agencies for education in the UK appear supportive of this enterprise in that it fits well with the drive toward social cohesion. Robert Jackson's work in RE, focusing on the positive nature of plurality and the possibilities of a dialogic approach to the subject, has emphasized the importance of addressing social cohesion as an important aim of religious education, and he is the foremost advocate of this among contemporary theorists (Jackson, 2004). I shall not dwell here on a critical scrutiny of this position, but have offered one elsewhere that can be seen as complementary to the argument presented in this paper (see Erricker, 2006). Jackson can be identified as offering a more sophisticated method, but within the multicultural diversity model, that builds on Smart's phenomenological position but in a revised fashion. The further danger of this approach is that RE lacks any potential to critically consider the values of the mainstream democracy of which it has become an expression.

To summarize, approaches to RE based on the premises of religion understood as an aspect of multicultural diversity (or plurality) and promoting moral homogeneity are ineffective in addressing the phenomenon of religion or spiritual development due to their:

- lack of critical scrutiny of religion and the role it plays in modern society.
- lack of critical scrutiny of mainstream democratic society and its values.
- biased representation of religion that does not sufficiently address the impact of ideological difference.
- lack of pedagogical sufficiency in compromising the agency of the learner and therefore the opportunity for spiritual development.
- lack of definitional clarity as to what constitutes the scope of the curriculum, through the elision of the terms 'religion' and 'worldview' that, intentionally or otherwise, seeks to de-ideologize the nature of religions.
- lack of concern for the key conceptual reference points that identify the core doctrinal propositions or truth statements that characterise the distinctiveness of religious traditions.

In brief, for idealistic, pragmatic and political reasons the ideological aspects of religion, so emphatically emphasized by Bowker (1987), have been ignored. As a result, religious education cannot sufficiently address the divisive encounters experienced at the beginning of the twenty-first century, primarily involving militant Islam and Western, neo-liberal capitalist ideologies. Its alternative recourse has been to a naïve, outdated and liberal view that ignores the ideological forces at play in favour of advocating that 'real' or 'true' Islam is not ideological in character, nor are Western democracies. Despite what we witness of the influence of religion in society, we have reversed the order of things. Ideologies, the repositories of truth and doctrine, are rendered non-existent as we scrutinize the veneer of cultural expression in festivals, family life and benign rituals. Beneath this surface, we pay scant attention to the edifice, shaped and reshaped by tradition, upon the basis of which these expressions are maintained but which constitutes a more rigid and carefully defined framework of spiritual values—its ideological constitution. What devout Muslim will willingly substitute democratic values for a theocracy based on sharia? What fundamentalist Christian will willingly accede to the equal rights of homosexuals in marriage given his or her understanding of the teachings of scripture? What the liberal multicultural/ pluralist approach to religious education demands in order to achieve an 'overarching moral worldview' is the modernization of religion.

Ideological difference and the modernization of religion

In an article entitled 'Muslims unite! And bring your faith up to date', Salman Rushdie (2005) critiques the attitude that those who are committing 'terrorist acts' are not real Muslims. Below, I have cited some important passages from his argument to consider:

> When Sir Iqbal Sacranie, head of the Muslim Council of Britain admitted that 'our own children' had perpetrated the July 7 London bombings, it was the first time in my memory that a British Muslim had accepted his community's responsibility for outrages committed by its members ...
>
> Instead of blaming US foreign policy or 'Islamophobia', Sacranie described the bombings as a 'profound challenge' for the Muslim community. However, this is the same Sacranie who, in 1989, said that 'death is perhaps too easy' for the author of the *Satanic Verses* ...
>
> The Sacranie case illustrates the weakness of the Government's strategy for relying on traditional, but essentially orthodox, Muslims to help to eradicate Islamist radicalism ...
>
> ... many traditional Muslims lead lives of near-segregation from the wider population From such defensive, separated worlds some youngsters have indefensibly stepped across a moral line and taken up their lethal rucksacks.
>
> The deeper alienations that lead to terrorism may have their roots in these young men's objections to events in Iraq or elsewhere, but the closed communities of some traditional Western Muslims are places in which young men's alienations can easily deepen. What is needed is a move beyond tradition – nothing less than a reform movement to bring Islam into the modern age. (Rushdie, 2005)

Following Rushdie's article, *Panorama*, a respected UK TV programme, with a history of controversial reporting treated Muslim leaders, including Sacranie, with the methods of investigative journalism (*Panorama*, 21 August 2005), following which a Muslim public meeting on 'A question of leadership' was convened to discuss the role of the Muslim Council of Britain (Sacranie is its secretary-general) and *Panorama*'s treatment of Islam (see Bright, 2005).

Rushdie's (2005) hard-edged demand for the modernization of Islam is no different in aim, though different in style, to the liberal multicultural/pluralist approach to RE that accepts diversity but not divisive ideology. Religious tradition must accommodate itself to the modernist project, but religions such as Islam know that there is an ideological cost involved. Religions are aware that their representation in the West is dependent on their compliance to this model and, as far as representatives of religions on Standing Advisory Councils for RE (SACREs) are concerned, this compliance is readily understood as being represented through their agreement to what they have in common with regard to sharing a similar moral purpose for society; the opposition, in this context, is secularism and materialism. The ideological face of religion has to be subsumed beneath an appearance of common purpose. But within the communities themselves there are generational tensions.

The issues emerging out of the 'terrorist' events concerning the character and purposes of Islam and how it should be represented are not new. Beneath the surface, within Muslim communities themselves, tensions have existed for a considerable period of time developing as the first generations of British-born Muslims have emerged (see e.g. Erricker, 2001, 2005). Caught between the twin concerns of assimilation and marginalization, Muslim communities have sought to reconcile a new national British identity with the maintenance of a core Islamic identity. Different communities have done this in differing ways but the most politically astute and able have been aware of the need for representation in national affairs in order to be influential. The Muslim Council of Britain is a result of this process, beneath the surface of which the difficulties of representation of various Muslim groups still exist.

With the critical onset of the terrorist crisis we might surmise that this so far largely internal struggle over reconciling national identity with the preservation of religious identity has spilled out into the larger domain of national politics, resulting in a more focused scrutiny of allegiances through political, public and media interest.[2] As a result, those who act as the leadership representatives of Islam are under greater scrutiny from outside the Islamic community and, concomitantly, from within it. The key issue emerging in this debate is whether Islam is willing to modernize or not. One of the key indicators in this is whether Muslims in leadership roles in British society will denounce 'extremist' acts. The climate has changed from one of acceptance of diversity to scrutiny of difference.

Acceptance of diversity has been a hallmark of government policy preserved by the term multiculturalism. In education this term has been a means to propagate the idea that diversity is enriching to our society and should be positively promoted. But difference is different. Difference implies difficulty and potential division, whereas diversity, as it is used, implies the celebration of new forms of expression that do not threaten the core values of the nation. In this distinction we can recognize a problem that multiculturalism is not equipped to handle but which, until now, it might be expected to conceal.

The problem for schools

Religions are political institutions involved in economic affairs, as well as being part of culturally diverse phenomena. Here I am suggesting that religion can be understood within two distinct and specific frames of reference. If within education religion is understood as being expressed through cultural diversity, it is no more than a difference of expression of similar values to those of the mainstream society of which it now forms a part. Thus, for example, it is possible for schools to celebrate festivals of different religions, have performances by 'Caribbean' steel bands, welcome faith speakers and visit places of worship as *cultural* experiences (religion being understood as part of 'culture'). However, if we are to investigate religious and faith differences, then we must deal with conceptual formulations of world-views that prohibit certain activities and promote others, and can undermine the celebration of diversity as inclusiveness. For example, as far as Islam is concerned, this affects provision in relation to artistic and musical expression, physical education and religious education. This is registered, in terms of the way teaching and learning is planned in schools, in relation to Muslim pupils and students whom parents ask to be withdrawn from music, PE or lessons on faiths, such as Hinduism, that are not considered appropriate. Of course, it is not just Muslim parents who request such withdrawal and not all Muslim parents do request withdrawal, but schools ask for advice on a regular basis regarding requests of parents from different faiths—most recently, in my experience, with regard to objections brought by both Pagan and Christian parents.

At the school level, the distinction between the promotion of diversity and dealing with difference is acute. If they can teach religions as enriching forms of diversity (emphasizing culturally differing forms of expression), the result is positive because it promotes inclusion; however, if religions become ideologically divisive forces and emphasize their exclusivity, the result is seen as educationally damaging.

Pedagogical implications for guidance to schools

In summary, my argument has been that in religious education, since the inception of a 'world religions' approach to RE, schools have been encouraged to promote a multicultural diversity rather than a religious difference model of teaching and learning. The tendency has been to avoid controversy by relating religious diversity to differing cultural forms of expression, while emphasizing core moral values that all religions can be said to espouse. These values are generic: right against wrong; good against evil; preservation of life against forms of violence, appreciation and sustaining of the natural world; and living in harmony with other creatures. Thus, a phenomenological approach to RE, influenced by Smart in its inception, has become reduced to the inculcation of idealist moral values expressed within selected stories, teachings and other practices, and cultural expressions of faith, that can promote a homogeneous moral disposition which accords, at a naïve and superficial level, with Smart's desideratum and Keast's view of the purpose of RE.

Where this approach has varied, it has largely been influenced by the experiential method of Hammond and Hay. This approach recognized the lack of attention paid by the phenomenological model to the promotion of young people's 'spirituality'. It sought to introduce a universalist approach to the idea of promoting spirituality by focusing on the learner's ability to draw on their own experience in order to appreciate more subjective responses to existential encounters, for example, through guided fantasy strategies. It has relied on a differing 'phenomenological' approach, evidenced in the writings of Eliade (1959) and others, with a more psychological orientation that questioned the spirituality of Western society in relation to its more religious antecedents who were in touch with the sacred nature of the world. Again, however, there is no intention to engage with religious difference since this, at an ideological level, can be presumed to be inferior to the universalist insights of the mystics, contemplatives and academic interpreters on whom they draw.

Addressing difference

The above summary of phenomenologically influenced RE is indicative of how diversity has been positively addressed while ignoring the issues of difference within religions. To ask teachers to address difference does not amount to just a pedagogical issue at the level of delivery. It involves adjusting from one implicitly apolitical but morally infused approach to another that promotes significantly different assumptions about teaching and learning by explicitly contextualizing religious worldviews within situations that raise social, political and moral issues. The latter approach requires radically re-conceiving our pedagogy at the level of both theory and practice. The most significant pedagogical change is to acknowledge that difference, at an ideological and political level, has to be addressed, rather than just diversity, at a cultural level. This means that we must understand ideological and conceptual bases as the premises on which we address differences in worldviews. In practice, this means we must focus on the key concepts that inform and motivate expressions of faith, beliefs and religious practices. For example, rather than making young people conversant with hajj and eid, we should be identifying the motivations for them. This involves concentrating on key concepts such as tawheed, jihad and ummah. It also means we need to incorporate the sorts of interpretation that Muslims bring to an understanding of these concepts and how they should be acted upon in the context of the modern world, especially when living in, or engaging with, differing Muslim and non-Muslim societies. In effect, this means engaging with a hermeneutical complexity within religions and across religions. It also means students need to be supported and challenged to respond in an informed and evaluative way by reflecting on their own experience and enculturation. The idea of spiritual development or the development of students' spirituality should not be divorced from this engagement, but be an outcome of it: an engagement with difference in order to establish their own beliefs, values and convictions and begin to articulate their own conceptual worldview with its accompanying ethical characteristics.

Pedagogically,[3] the rationale for this approach is based on recognizing that religious worldviews differ according to the key concepts religions use to interpret the world. From this follow the RE-related pedagogical principles of:

1. enquiring into the key concepts that constitute religious worldviews;
2. interpreting and evaluating the implications of conceptual differences in religious worldviews through recognizing ways in which they influence the motivations and behaviour of believers;
3. responding to religious worldviews as distinctive conceptual constructs in order to develop students' reflections upon the construction of their own beliefs and values.

These three principles underpin the teaching and learning process, or pedagogical procedure, within the new agreed syllabus for RE in Hampshire, Portsmouth and Southampton's Living Difference (Hampshire, Portsmouth and Southampton SACREs, 2004).[4]

The pedagogical process or procedure constitutes a methodology for teaching and learning based upon conceptual enquiry (see Figures 1 and 2). The categorization of concepts, moving from those that can be readily accessed within pupils' and students' experience (type A), through those used in the study of religion (type B) to those particular to specific religions (see Figure 2), provides a systematic basis for continuity and progression related to pupils' and students' conceptual and affective development.

The aim, expressed in the attainment target, is interpreting religion in relation to human experience, emphasizing the two complementary aspects of the pedagogical

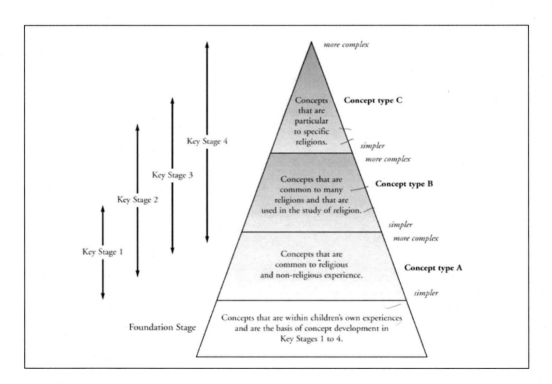

Figure 1

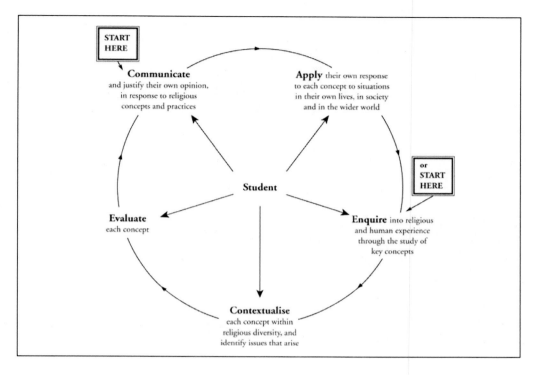

Figure 2

intention, enquiry into religion and reflection of students on their own experience and the experience of others as a result.

Pedagogical strategies then need to be devised that can be effective vehicles for learning within each element of the methodology such that the overall enquiry progressively deepens and gives rise to complexity within each cycle and across cycles of learning.

By taking the example of jihad as a key concept in Islam that has had a significant recent political effect, we can identify in outline how a particular cycle of learning might be conceived. Understanding jihad as both a striving towards Allah (greater jihad) and a striving against the corruption of Allah's creation (lesser jihad), these can be explained at the point at which conceptual enquiry begins (Enquire). If it is thought more appropriate, students can first enquire into the subsidiary concept of 'striving' within the context of their own experience (Communicate and Apply). Contextualization of Jihad needs to progress students' enquiry into the issues and implications differing forms of interpretation of this concept can take. On the one hand, a routine practice of jihad can be to perform salat but, in a more socially sensitive context, it is a motivation for the wearing of different forms of hijab. Expressed in a more radical, political fashion, jihad is claimed as a justification for the events of 9/11 or for violent martyrdom in the Palestinian cause. The issues and implications enquired into within the Contextualize element of the cycle provide the opportunity

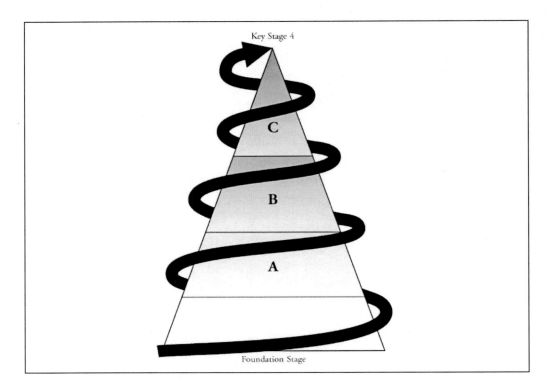

Figure 3

for the evaluation of the concept, both as an appreciation of its importance within Islam and an evaluation of its differing interpretations and potentialities in the wider domain of social and global affairs. If the opportunity to introduce the concept of 'striving' has not been taken at the beginning of the cycle (within Communicate and Apply), or if the learning can be further progressed by returning to the subsidiary concept of striving under Communicate and Apply, for a second time, then this can complete the cycle. What matters is that the cycle is satisfactorily completed such that students' enquiry requires them to engage with the skills required for interpreting, evaluating and negotiating difference in terms of the expression of key concepts within differing religious worldviews.

Conclusion

In conclusion, I am not suggesting that promoting difference, at an ideological level, is the only means available to RE to address the development of young people's spirituality, but that we must not accede to an approach to religious education that ignores or sublimates its importance. The various pedagogies that Grimmitt (2000) presents all have their virtues but with the caveat that, as approaches for the curriculum delivery of RE, they must balance the method they use; for example, socio-anthropological in the case of Jackson, and theological in the case of Wright (see Wright, 2004). And their epistemological stances: interpretative and critical-realist respectively, in these two examples, against the influence of extrinsic socio-political factors such as the celebration of multicultural diversity or the desire for social cohesion that can compromise the academic credentials of the subject and result in a lack of scrutiny in relation to the way its subjects should be critically, as well as empathetically, represented. The pedagogical methodology, presented above, does not, theoretically, divorce itself from the practical presentation of different methods of approach to the subject. However, what it does seek to do is ensure that the subject does engage with the hermeneutical complexity that religion generates, and thus offer the opportunities for a spiritual development of young people that is informed and challenged by that complexity. There is a danger that, as I have argued, there are clear indications that the desideratum of multiculturalism and social cohesion, towards an overarching modernist worldview, has imposed itself on the delivery of RE as a simulacrum for the way that religions operate in the modern world. In turn, this desideratum affects the way in which we conceive of spiritual development as compliance to its wishes rather than as opportunity for young people to reflect upon and voice their own opinions and convictions. We cannot expect that enforcing compliance will bring an end to difference and therefore also to division.

Notes

1. Foreword in Smart, *Approaches to the study of religion* (1998).
2. One of the most notable and widely reported examples of this internal tension becoming public was the violent demonstration by Sikhs against a play staged in Birmingham that had been written by a Sikh woman but offended Sikh leaders and traditionalists by including a rape scene within a gurudwara. The subsequent reporting on this revealed generational tensions existing between Sikhs in the UK in relation to the issues this play provoked, as well as tensions between religious representation and the creative process. For one of many examples of reportage see Harriet Swain's article, 'Talks with Sikhs backfired on theatre', *Guardian*, 29 December 2004.
3. Michael Grimmitt's exposition of pedagogy has been important to me at this point, and I follow his brief outline of what constitutes the various levels of pedagogy here; see Grimmitt (2000), pp. 16–21. Grimmitt provides a critical commentary on a number of influential theoretical approaches to RE assessing their pedagogical sufficiency.
4. A SACRE monitoring body is established within each local education authority (LEA) for ensuring that schools comply with the law regarding legal requirements for and quality of religious education. Agreed syllabuses are produced b SACREs as legal documents that provide statutory guidance as to provision for religious education. The SACRE is the author of an agreed syllabus on behalf of the county or city council. Inspectors/advisers in religious education are provided by the LEA to assist SACREs through providing their professional advice and support, and ensuring support for schools in meeting the requirements of the locally agreed syllabus for RE

Notes on contributor

Clive Erricker is Hampshire County Inspector for RE, joint editor of the *International Journal of Children's Spirituality* and co-director of the Children and Worldviews

Project. Among his publications are *Reconstructing religious, spiritual and moral education* (with Jane Erricker) (RoutledgeFalmer, 2000) and *When learning becomes your enemy* (Educational Heretics Press, 2002). *Living difference: the agreed syllabus for Hampshire, Portsmouth and Southampton* was published in 2004 and is available from: linda.elliott@hants.gov.uk

References

Bordieu, P. & Passeron, J.-C. (1990) *Reproduction in education, society and culture* (2nd edn) (London, Sage).

Bowker, J. (1987) *Licensed insanities: religions and belief in God in the contemporary world* (London, Darton, Longman & Todd).

Bright, M. (2005) Let's shed more light on Islam, *Observer,* 28 August, p. 23.

Eliade, M. (1959) *The sacred and the profane* (New York, Harcourt, Brace & World).

Erricker, C. (2001) The spiritual education of Khoja Shia Ithnasheeri (KSI) youth: the challenges of diaspora, in: J. Erricker, C. Ota & C. Erricker (Ed.) *Spiritual education: cultural, religious and social differences* (Brighton, Sussex Academic Press).

Erricker, C. (2005) Faith education of children in the context of adult migration and conversion: the discontinuities of tradition, in C. Ota & C. Erricker (Eds) *Spiritual education: literary, empirical and pedagogical Approaches* (Brighton, Sussex Academic Press).

Erricker, C. (2006) Religious education and spiritual development: pedagogical insufficiency and possibility, in: M. De Souza (Ed.) *International handbook on the religious, moral and spiritual dimensions of education* (Dordrecht, Kluwer Academic Publishers).

Grimmitt, M. (2000) *Pedagogies of religious education: case studies in the research and development of good pedagogic practice in RE* (Great Wakering, McCrimmonds).

Hampshire, Portsmouth and Southampton SACREs (2004) *Living difference: the agreed syllabus for religious education,* Hampshire County Council/Portsmouth City Council/Southampton City Council.

Jackson, R. (2004) *Rethinking religious education and plurality: issues in diversity and pedagogy* (London, RoutledgeFalmer).

Keast, J. (2005) Clever devils and how to avoid them, *SACRE News,* 13, Summer, 6–11.

Rushdie, S. (2005) Muslims unite! And bring your faith up to date, *Sunday Times,* 14 August, p. 16.

Smart, N. (1998) Foreword, in: P. Connolly (Ed.) *Approaches to the study of religion* (London, Cassell).

Wright, A. (2004) *Religious education and post-modernity* (London, RoutledgeFalmer).

Children's spirituality in social context: a South African example

Cornelia Roux*

Introduction

I would like to start this article with a quotation from one of the most remarkable and well-known painters in South Africa, Fr Frans Claerhout:

> During my years in Africa spirituality was the driving force of soul and beauty and fallibility ... The Africa sun supplied warmth to my spirituality, made it human, gave it life force ... Africa fashioned my spirituality so that I can go to God through others, with others. (Du Toit, 1996, p. viii)

The following issues will be outlined to demonstrate the context of the above quote:

- A critical and thorough review of spirituality in religious and religion education in the South African context, past and present.

*Department of Curriculum Studies, Faculty of Education, Stellenbosch University, Private Bag X1, Matieland 7602, Stellenbosch, South Africa, Email: cdr@sun.ac.za

- The new approach to personal well-being: is that spirituality?
- The social context and spirituality: an educational approach.

A critical and thorough review of spirituality in religion education in the South African context

Before 1994

Children's spirituality has been one of the most interesting and widely debated topics in education and especially in Life Orientation programmes and Religion Education[1] in South Africa since 2003 with the publication of the policy document *Religion and education* (2003). In the previous dispensation, before the democratic elections in 1994, the only options in handling children's spirituality were either through Bible Education[2] or Religious Education classes. In South Africa, Religious Education was defined as a *single-faith confessional moral education* programme. In the period 1960–1970 it was also understood as a form of catechism in Christianity in many schools (Rossouw, 1995, p. 2; Roux, 1998). Religious education in all the different provincial departments of education prior to 1994 was mainly a confessional Christian National Education approach (Roux, 1997, 1998), which alienated many South Africans from different religious and cultural groups. Non-religious learners or non-Christian learners were exempted from the religious education classes. Private religious schools, however, could teach their own religious conduct.

Spirituality was never mentioned as a concept for facilitation or teaching in the curriculum. Spirituality was also never given an opportunity to develop as a new approach in Christian, Bible or moral education, as, for example, in Britain, in the Education Reform Act 1987 (Watson, 1987) and developments thereafter (Best, 2000, p. 27). In South Africa spirituality is still discussed mainly in the context of theology in general. Spirituality was and is still seen as a religious domain within a religious institution. The same notion occurs in comparing spiritual development with religious development and spirituality with religion, as argued in some British literature (Hay, 1999; Thatcher, 1999; Drees, 2000; King, 2002).

Spirituality and the reflection of learners on their spirituality and/or religion was never part of any religious education curriculum in South African schools. The effect was that spirituality, in the broader sense of understanding religion and personal wellness from a holistic point of view, was not part of any school or tertiary curriculum or teachers' training programme. A thorough examination of the curricula for religious education in schools, prior to 1997[3] and 2003[4] showed that content was mainly linked to values and morals in the religious society and embedded in the teacher's own religious views. In public schools mainly Christian values from the religious education curriculum were presented and discussed. The result was that learners never questioned the validity of certain values and morals in a changing or non-religious society, nor worldviews other than their own. Spirituality was also never seen as part of moral education and learners were not exposed to the opportunity to become spiritual in a broader sense, except from a Christian religious point of view.

One may argue that spirituality was regarded only as part of the religious worshipping components within the whole-school curriculum.

After 1994

Since the democratic elections in 1994, a new education model has been adopted. Outcomes-based education, with eight learning areas, forms the basis of the new curriculum. In *Curriculum 2005* (1997) and the *Revised National Curriculum statement* (2002) outcomes and assessment standards were provided for all learning areas for grades R–9. The guidelines for the curriculum and learning areas for the Further Education and Training phase (grades 10–12) have been finalized for most of the learning areas and subjects. This new phase will be implemented in 2006. These outcomes and assessment standards form the core of the curriculum of the different learning areas. The learning area Life Orientation as a *fundamental*[5] in the school curriculum consists of four major elements, namely personal well-being; citizenship education; recreation and physical activity; and careers and career choices.

It is, however, interesting to note that the concept *spirituality* was removed from both the first drafts on education and the curriculum (*Curriculum 2005*, 1997) and did not surface in the later policy documents or revised curricula (*Revised National Curriculum statement*, 2002). I believe that the obvious reason is the lack of knowledge of the meaning and opportunities spiritual development requires from teachers and in teachers' training. Another question that arose is whether the evasion of the term *spirituality* was meant to avoid confrontation within the academic, education and public domains. Although whole-child development is a fundamental approach both in Outcomes-based education and the curriculum (*Revised National Curriculum statement*, 2002), there was still no discourse, rigorous critique or discussions on spirituality in education. It still seems to be still a theological and religious domain.

Outcomes 2 and 3[6] (grades 3–9) in the learning area Life Orientation in the curriculum are the only outcomes where an awareness and a holistic approach to education and spirituality can be facilitated in the understanding of social and personal development. However, in principle, spirituality, just like wellness, is significant in all the outcomes as assessment standards of the Life Orientation learning area. In the Further Education and Training-band outcomes 1–4 deal with personal well-being. The concept of spirituality was only mentioned in grade 11 as part of the competence descriptions and described as follows: 'debate a wide range of contemporary moral and spiritual issues' (National Curriculum Statement [Life Orientation Subject Guidelines], 2005). There are no guidelines for teachers on how to handle these *spiritual issues* or what it entails. In the assessment reports on Curriculum 2005 (*National Curriculum statement*, 2002) it seems that *spirituality* was confused with aspects of mysticism in religions only, and not with the holistic approach that is generally understood in academic circles (Watson, in Carr & Haldane, 2003, p. 157). Another reason may be that the political and social public debate against multi-religion education at that time urged the curriculum designers to change the wording to a less controversial (then) issue.

At present and with the implementation and functioning of the outcomes-based model, the education perspective shifts from *indoctrination* in values and beliefs to *information* about values and beliefs—from a *product-orientation* to a *process-orientation* model. Why, then, was there a change in the educational approach in South Africa after 1994? The main reason was to engage in a holistic approach to learners from all societal structures for the sake of personal and educational development. The previous South African social structure was crumbling and learners from different cultural and religious environments could now attend the school of their choice. The normalization of society supported the idea of a holistic approach to personal development and education. However, disparities in social structures and the differences between economically advanced and economically deprived schools are still a huge problem, and there is no solution in the near future.

One must argue that learners should develop a sense of critical enquiry and engage intelligently to understand their own questions on humanity, society, truth and meaning. They need to engage in dialogue on values, worldviews, belief systems, economics, themselves, the environment and most of all, their own spirituality. They should engage in religious and spiritual questions in an informed, sensitive and intelligent manner. The multicultural South African society, with its social and economic differences, therefore urges teachers to facilitate the concept of spirituality in social context and in everyday life for the benefit of their learners. Although spirituality is not named as a specific concept in the outcomes in the Life Orientation programmes, there is a desire that in-service and pre-service teachers' programmes will be equipped with these notions to empower them to facilitate learners in schools. However, the question is: *Are teachers in Life Orientation programmes aware of the fact that children need to engage in dialogue on issues where they should understand their personal life stances, different beliefs, value systems and spirituality?*

Defining spirituality in a social context

The reason for arguing for a definition of spirituality in social context is that the ambiguity of the concept *spirituality* creates so many different points of departure. The arguments in the definitions of the term seem to be rightfully embedded in a specific theoretical notion. It is, however, also interesting to note that many arguments and definitions on spirituality originate from a religious frame of reference. Drees (2000) argues that spirituality 'is not only how we think about God, but also how we see ourselves and our responsibilities, how we live with our failures and accept life's darker sides'. King agrees that there are many definitions for spirituality, and takes another line by asking if spirituality should not be declared in what it *does* instead of what it *means* (King, 2002). Kourie (in Du Toit, 1995 p. 3) emphasizes the fact that, for many people, spirituality 'is identified with piety or otherworldliness'. He argues that this narrow definition is not in line with the post-modern questions of unqualified activism and the 'glorification of the measurable and replicable'. However, one can contend that the images of humanity as presented by most religious traditions have a crucial role to play. Traditions present models and guidelines for overcoming the present, its conflicts and inhumane practices in societies, but they also give their followers the potential to become human again. Religions can offer to guide humans through the ambiguity of spirituality.

From an educational viewpoint, one can adopt Grey's argument (in Thatcher, 1999, p. 12) that 'it is an illusion to think that theology and spirituality emerge from a timeless, context-free vacuum, or that there is a consensus as to how their insights should be used for education'. When spirituality was considered as part of the school curriculum, Religion Education was the most obvious environment in which to slot it in. Previously, Roux (1999a) also argued that religion education, in the South African context, could be best facilitated in the understanding and expressing of spirituality, diversity, morality and human nature because 'religion is the indispensable foundation of spirituality'.

However, the failure of religious education in schools (Ferguson, 1999; Roux, 2000), and specifically the idea that the single-faith, confessional approach was the sole bearer of children's spirituality, can no longer be defended. The single approach of religious education had a hermeneutical problem. Wrong interpretations led to the moralization of religious content (especially in Christian religious education), which was certainly not an effective means of facilitating values and spirituality in a changing society. Religious Education can no longer be the subject which teaches learners stories from old scriptures and related content, or which urges them to adopt certain behaviours and values. From a hermeneutic point of view, religion, and therefore religion education, has to make more sense to learners in a post-modern world. Although Rouhani (1997) argues that the application of a spiritual or moral principle can cultivate a universal culture of understanding and peace, the two domains are in some instances not compatible. Clive and Jane Erricker (in Thatcher, 1999 p. 129) argue that spiritual development was/is linked to traditional religious nurture, 'and morality was a matter of instruction and appeared to be the prime justification for considering spiritual development'.

Therefore the core of the argument is that, in many instances, religion was moralized in RE, without resulting in a well-behaved *moralized* society. What would the results be if spirituality were only to be defined in religion education? Arguments for a post-modern approach to society and life have made us aware, especially in a democratic South Africa, of social factors, economic situations and disparities, cultural diversities and priorities, and universal values that are not embedded in religions only, but can also be defined from our common history and goals: 'The spiritual can be distinguished from the moral domain insofar as it pays attention to those motivations, or what we might call inherent qualities that constitute our highest aspirations in human beings' (Erricker & Erricker, in Thatcher, 1999, p. 132).

One may ask: *What is the meaning of children's spirituality in the social context in 2005 and beyond?* On analysing this question, I came to the conclusion that curriculum designers—and probably academics—who are not in this field of study (primary and secondary education schooling) must feel the pressure to understand the vibrancies of change and the paradigm shift that the post-modern learner is demanding from teachers and educators.

For years, I have embarked on the most interesting journeys of discovery into children's spirituality, the significance and the influences thereof, in order to discover the meaning of wellness and the expression of experiences of their life stances. Research through literature and experiences in research did not give me a clear description and/or definition of spirituality that explains all the possible aspects of religion, society, education and well-being, personal experiences and social context. Thus, I would like to argue that spirituality, and therefore children's spirituality, consists of more than only personal well-being and personal experiences. It is a whole-person approach, involving the person religiously, affectively, emotionally, cognitively and physically, with all aspects embedded in personal experiences.

In answering the above question, one can also argue for the consideration of a *non-religious spirituality in education*. One can define non-religious spirituality as referring to the spirituality of art, of historical, traditional and indigenous contexts, of the environment, language, literature, music and of science—all the elements that connect with the whole-person wellness. It implies that it is also a means by which, for example, art, music and the sciences contribute to the fulfilment of human nature—the spiritual well-being, the wellness of a person—which can help one to make sense of life and one's life experiences. There are so many dimensions involved in a person's well-being that religion cannot be the sole bearer of spirituality. We must distinguish between that which extends our humanity from that which transcends it. In the post-modern society, religion generally cannot accomplish the transcendence. This is especially true with regard to learners in schools. The implication is that being spiritual is not synonymous with being religious. An increasing number of school children are not believers in one of the main world religions or any indigenous or traditional religious upbringing. This growth of non-believers in school communities has urged educators to rethink religion as a prerequisite for understanding spirituality in a social context.

Does Life Orientation, the new approach to personal well-being, emphasize spirituality?

In the *Revised National Curriculum statement* (2002), the emphasis is on knowledge, skills, values and attitudes as points of departure. This means that the new education model demands a holistic approach to learners' education and their whole-person development. As stated before, personal well-being is part of the fundamental learning area of Life Orientation. What is more important is that in every outcome and assessment standard of this learning area, which includes career, health, emotional well-being, religion, citizenship and recreation, the emphasis is on *the self* and the importance of understanding values and developing skills to handle life issues (life skills). One may argue that the implementation of a spiritual dimension or outcome would help teachers to concentrate on spiritual issues regarding the learners' own experiences and to take note of social structures relevant to the learners. However, irrespective of the arguments for or against the place of spiritual education and religion education as outlined and argued by some academics (Roberts, in Best, 2000,

p. 38; Carr, in Carr & Haldane, 2003, p. 214), it seems that the dangers of understanding the notion of spirituality in a broader social context, is still debatable. Therefore, the fact that elements of spirituality are embedded in the entire Life Orientation programme makes it easier for teachers to concentrate on methodologies to facilitate learners' life experiences, instead of dealing with specific curriculum topics on spirituality. This underlined the fact that in South African school education, there is no *spiritual education* content in the public education sector or in the published curriculum (*Revised National Curriculum statement*, 2002).

According to Wright (2002, p. 76), a critical engagement in spiritual education would allow learners to engage intelligently with the ambiguous claims and counter-claims surrounding questions of ultimate truth and meaning. Is it then possible that schools or learning areas can provide spiritual experiences, when other experiences outside the school are powerful and all-pervasive? Schools and teaching can certainly provide experiences that will affect children's emotions other than by emulating outside stimuli such as those provided by computers and other technological issues. However, according to Taggart (2002, p. 9), the problem is that in the development of critical education, the complex issues are surrounded by spirituality.

One can argue that the general purpose of schooling is to promote human well-being or personal wellness, education for life as well as the development of a critical mind. It seems that one should teach children the skills to acquire knowledge via a sustained contact, but only if the forms are identifiable in terms of distinctive concepts and truth criteria. As schooling takes up a large part of a young person's life and time, the goals of the school should cover a wide range of human wellness. Education and the curriculum should therefore also reflect the priorities of life in general, and the values of society in particular. One can assume that children can then also be critical moral agents in society.

If one critiques the Life Orientation programme, it appears that at least the notion occurs that learners will be able to engage in a humane manner (spiritual experiences?) on social issues in a social context, and in a coherent manner, with concrete expressions of their own social environment. One can thus argue that this is the main aim of the programme in schools.

The social context and spirituality: an educational approach

South African society is exceedingly interesting with its ambivalence on the handling and understanding of values and spirituality. One of the most significant documents on values in education was the publication of the *Manifesto on values, education and democracy* (2001), in which the Department of Education expressed concern about the lack of mutual values in schools and society due to the degeneration and segregation of society that was part of our violent past. The economic and social disparities are vast social constructions that need to be solved. When economic deprivation (poverty), HIV and Aids are main problems in a society, the need for a spiritual awareness seems to be of less consequence. Physical survival is the main issue.

However, with the implementation of the Life Orientation programmes in schools, and in view of the *Manifesto on values, education and democracy* (2001), one should argue that the incorporation of values in the curriculum and thus in school society may also enhance spiritual awareness. It is well known that values cannot be taught, but that they should be embedded and articulated in ideas and behaviour. If children learn to respect different viewpoints, teachers can help them to change the way they behave (Rhodes, 2004). This brings to the fore the fundamental need for respect and caring as a basic value (*Manifesto on values, education and democracy*, 2001), which may reflect on the spiritual experience of sharing, and which manifests in many religions and worldviews as a basic principle and value.

The social and cultural context in South Africa can be clustered in two main groups: a Western orientation and an African orientation. This, however, does not imply that many South Africans from a Western orientation do not respect an African lifestyle, or vice versa. If one wishes to understand the social context of spirituality in South Africa, one is compelled to consider the diverse cultural context within the country. As mentioned before, one can argue that Westerners, and therefore South Africans from a Western orientation, may understand spirituality mainly in a religious and cultural manner. However, the intermingling of Western and African understandings gives the social context a new vibrancy with regard to the meaning of spirituality and humanity.

Definitions and concepts of an African orientation of spirituality are as diverse as Africa itself. One important aspect of African spirituality is that it flows from African mysticism and from the awareness that there is a unity of beings in the universe. This may be one reason why the concept spirituality does not feature in the revised education documents. South Africans from a Western orientation only may feel threatened by mysticism as understood in African religion and culture (Du Toit, 1995). However, the value and concept of *ubuntu* is widely accepted by all South Africans as a fundamental principle in the Constitution and in many policy documents. It also forms part of the desired values in education (*Manifesto on values, education and democracy*, 2001, p. 15). The saying *Ubuntu ngumntu ngabantu*[7] forms one of the core aspects of the values document. Explaining the concept and meaning of *Ubuntu* within the African concept, Bishop Desmond Tutu[8] explains spirituality (Buthelezi, 1987, p. 96) in the following way:

> The African world view rejects popular dichotomies between the sacred and the secular, the material and the spiritual. All life is religious, all life is sacred. (Tutu, 1995, p. xvi)

It is interesting to note the educational and teaching approaches towards spiritual, moral, social and cultural development across different subject matters in the book *Education for spiritual, moral, social and cultural development* (Best, 2000). On reading and analysing the approaches, and trying to read this in a South African context, one wonders whether the following were taken into consideration: the social context; cultural differences; religious differences; economic differences; and differences in the understanding of spirituality (contextualizing spirituality). Taking into account spiritual needs, these are the issues one has to reconsider as one tries to define an approach towards facilitating Life Orientation programmes. An example may illustrate the complexity of the issue, as follows:

> One Xhosa-speaking learner from a deep rural area in the Eastern Cape, attending a school in an informal settlement (squatter camp) in a metropolitan area, may live with an extended family member, have traditional cultural and religious roots (African Religion), and adhere to a great deal of mysticism. The other learners may have been born in the informal settlement (squatter camp), have a Western orientation and function within an Independent African Christian church. Their worldviews on and concepts of spirituality will differ from one another and especially from so-called mainstream traditional religions (churches).

What are the educational approaches and issues that need to be considered when facilitating and understanding the diversity in children's spirituality in the South African context? The reasons for promoting children's physical well-being may outnumber those for advancing spiritual well-being, or do they?

In order to make sense of a complex society and multifaceted education system, some ideas that featured in a small participatory action research programme with a few teachers in 2003 may illustrate the above-mentioned arguments. The following issues were argued by the teachers in an attempt to understand the facilitation of spirituality in a wider context:

1. *The learners' social context has to be taken into consideration*:
   (a) The diversity of cultures and traditions in society, and especially in the school community, from different orientations (Western and African orientations).
2. *The learners' economic stance*:
   (a) Stealing for daily bread may be the only means of survival. How can one judge? What can be done to uplift or manage the spiritual needs that prompt these actions?
3. *The learners' cultural background and manifestation in society*:
   (a) The upbringing of children in African culture by their parents, grandparents or extended family members gives a new meaning to personal well-being in a spiritual manner. The *Ubuntu* value forms the core of this tradition and may be understood in a different manner by teachers who do not adhere to an African tradition. The value of *Ubuntu* is now also part of the values, outlined in the Manifesto (2001) taught in school education; however, the emphasis may differ.
   (b) The traditional upbringing, e.g. what parents expect from a multicultural school and the way to cope with change may differ from one another.
4. *The learners' religious or non-religious worldview*:
   (a) The growing numbers of non-religious believers (learners) in traditional and religious communities.
   (b) How to deal with diversity if the teacher has no knowledge thereof and how teachers can understand their own spirituality.
   (c) The recognition of a *new fundamentalism* evoking in different religions and belief systems.

5. *The learners' understanding of spirituality and mysticism*:
   (a) The diversity of access to educational aids or any other means of the technological world *out there* (the world, society) or *in here* (home).
   (b) The access to different kinds of visual and printed media, the Internet, etc., where children have to make their own choices, while others see that as a first opportunity to be in touch with issues of *the world*.
6. *The learners' dialogical abilities*:
   (a) The traditional upbringing in certain cultures that forbids children to give their own opinions and communication strategies versus educational methodologies and strategies as *good education*.
   (b) The language and expression abilities of the learner in a social context where mother-tongue education (home language) is not an option, or where expressing oneself becomes a problem in dual-medium education.

Spirituality (whole-child development) seems to be an important issue in many societies, cultures, world religions and worldviews. One can argue that ethics is, to some extent, also based on spirituality that has an effect on the interactive contexts of social, economic, political and all other domains of our existential world. This seems to be an indication why there is a dire need for a holistic approach towards children's spirituality, and one that includes every subject or learning area in an education programme.

Conclusion

The social context and school environments in South Africa are changing fast. As a developing country encompassing two worlds, where a wealthy and developed environment has to live side by side with an impoverished and developing social order, the challenges are enormous. The change from mainly mono-religious and monocultural to multi-religious and multicultural school communities has already affected many spheres of teacher education. Teachers formerly trained within the previous education system are trapped within certain religious and cultural paradigms. They are not always willing to redefine their role, especially in support of the new educational programmes (Ferguson & Roux, 2003).

Very little research on the training of pre- or in-service teachers has been undertaken with regard to the processes or approaches towards children's spirituality in Life Orientation programmes. In published Life Orientation textbooks, there is also no indication of any learning material on learners' spirituality, spiritual development or growth. It is imperative that children should engage with a holistic approach to all spheres of life; therefore, one has to create a wellness within, in order to ensure a total physical, emotional and spiritual wellness. Children, irrespective of their social and economic stance, deserve to develop into healthy and happy human beings. The empowerment of children/learners/students to be in control of their destiny, as they travel the road to achieving their full potential, to live a bright, extraordinary life defined by respect and human dignity is imperative.

Notes

1. Religion Education is an education programme that enables learners to engage in a variety of religious traditions in a way that encourages them to grow their inner spiritual and moral dimensions *Policy document*, 2002, p. 9. The subject was previously known as Religious Education (Roux, 1998), but because of confusion with the aim of the new approach, the name Religion Education was adopted in 2003.
2. Bible Education was also known as Religious Education in different departments of education in the apartheid era.
3. The South African government in Parliament adopted the new education model, Outcomes-based Education.
4. In 2003 the South African government in Parliament adopted the new *Policy document on religion in schools.*
5. A *fundamental* is a learning area (grades R–12) that is compulsory for all learners.
6. Outcome 2 = the learner will be able to demonstrate an understanding of and commitment to constitutional rights and responsibilities, and to show an understanding of diverse cultures and religions. Outcome 3 = the learner will be able to use acquired life skills to achieve and extend personal potential to respond effectively to the challenges of his or her world
7. 'A person is a person through other [persons]' is derived from the Nguni (Zulu/Xhosa/Swati), with the noun stem (*-ntu*) meaning 'person'. In adding the Class 14 prefix (*ubu-*), the meaning is changed to 'humanity'.
8. Archbishop Desmond Tutu was Archdeacon of the Anglican Church for many years and a well-known critic of political inequality in the South African society.

Notes on contributor

Professor Cornelia Roux is an Associate Professor in the Department of Curriculum Studies, Faculty of Education, Stellenbosch University, South Africa. Her field of interest is the Social Construct curriculum and inclusivity and diversity in education (religions, belief systems, values and cultures). She has written numerous chapters in books and articles on perceptions and practices in multi-religious and multicultural education. She is also involved in teacher training programmes, including BEd programmes, and postgraduate Master's and PhD students in the respective field of study.

Bibliogaphy

Asmal, K. & James, W. (2002) *Spirit of the nation* (Cape Town, Human Sciences Research Council/ Department of Education).

Best, R. (Ed.) (2000) *Education for spiritual, moral, social and cultural development* (London, Cromwell Press).

Bigger, S. & Brown, E. (2001) *Spiritual, moral, social and cultural education: exploring values in the curriculum* (London, David Fulton).

Brown, A. & Furlong, J. (1996) *Spiritual development in schools—invisible to the eye* (London, Bourne Press/National Society for Promoting Religious Education).

Buthelezi, M. (1987) Salvation as wholeness, in: J. Parratt (Ed.) *A reader in African theology 96* (London, SPCK).

Carr, D. & Haldane, J. (2003) *Spiritual philosophy and education* (London, Routledge Falmer).

Carr, D. & Landon, J. (1998) Teachers and schools as agencies of value education: reflection on teachers' perceptions: part 1, the role of the teacher, *Journal of Beliefs and Values*, 19(2), 165–175.

Drees, W. B. (2000) *Science and Christianity SC14: spirituality or superstition: criteria for quality in science, religion and popular culture* (Oxford, Farmington Institute for Christian Studies).

Du Toit, C. W. (Ed.) (1995) *Spirituality in religions: profiles and perspective* (Pretoria, Research Institute for Theology and Religion, UNISA).

Erricker, C. & Erricker, J. (1999) Spiritual and moral development, in: A. Thatcher (Ed.) *Spirituality and the curriculum* (London, Cassell).

Ferguson, R. (1999) *Strategies for teaching religion in colleges of Education,* MEd dissertation, Department of Curriculum Studies, Faculty of Education, Stellenbosch University.

Ferguson, R. & Roux, C. D. (2003) Teachers' participation in facilitating beliefs and values in Life Orientation programmes, *South African Journal for Education,* 23(4), 273–275.

Hay, D. (1996) *Listening for the spirit of the child: ES14* (Oxford, Farmington Institute for Christian Studies), May.

Hull, J. (2000) The spiritual and the intending teachers, *International Journal of Children's Spirituality,* 5(2), 163–175.

King, U. (2002) *Philosophy of religion: spirituality and post modernism: PR11* (Oxford, Farmington Institute for Christian Studies), November.

Lockhood, A. T. (1997) *Character education* (Los Angeles, CA, Corwin Press).

Rhodes, B. D. (2004) *Values and beliefs in outcomes-based education: exploring possibilities in a diverse school environment.* PhD thesis, University of Stellenbosch.

Rossouw, D. V. (Ed.) (1995) *At the crossroads: perspectives on religious education and biblical studies in a new education system* (Pretoria, Acacia Publishers).

Roughen, S. (1997) Spiritual education: a missing dimension, paper presented at *The Third International Education Conference,* University of Cincinnati, Ohio, USA.

Rouhani S. (1997) Spiritual education: a missing dimension, paper presented at the *Third International Education Conference,* University of Cincinnati, Ohio, 15–17 April.

Roux, C. D. (1996) Paradigm shift: Christian student-teachers in a multi-religious education programme, *Religious Education: South African Journal,* 54(2), 7–10.

Roux, C. D. (1997) *Redefining the role of religious education in a multi-cultural and multi-religious school environment: special research report* (Pretoria, HSRC).

Roux, C. D. (1998) The need for a paradigm shift in teaching religion in multi-cultural schools in South Africa, *South African Journal for Education,* 18(2), 84–89.

Roux, C. D. (1999a) Facilitating religion in Life Orientation programmes: challenges for a developing multicultural society, *Journal for the Study of Religion,* 12(1–2), 113–122.

Roux, C. D. (1999b) Paradigm shift in teaching religion, in: A. Tao & W. Weisse (Eds) *Religion and politics in South Africa: from apartheid to democracy* (Münster, Waxmann).

Roux, C. D. (2000) Multireligious education—an option for South Africa in the new education system, *British Journal of Religious Education,* 22(3) 173–180.

Taggart, G. (2002) Spiritual literacy and tacit knowledge, *Journal of Beliefs and Values,* 23(1), 7–17.

Thatcher, A. (Ed.) (1999) *Spirituality and the curriculum* (London, Cassell).

Tutu, D, (1995) *An African prayer book* (London, Hodder & Stoughton).

Watson, B. (1987) *Education and belief* (Oxford, Basil Blackwell).

Wright, A. (2002) *Spirituality and education* (London, Routledge Falmer).

Wilson, J. (2001) The spiritual, the earthly and the decadent, *Journal of Beliefs and Values,* 22(2), 165–182.

Official government reports

1996. *Norms and standards for teacher education (COTEP)* (Pretoria, Department of Education).

1996. *Lifelong learning through a national qualifications framework* (Pretoria, Report of the Ministerial Committee).

1997. *The South African constitution* (Pretoria, Governmental Printers).

1997. *The South African Schools Act* (Pretoria, Governmental Printers).

1997. *Curriculum 2005* (Pretoria, Department of Education).

1998. *Outcomes-based education in South Africa. Background information for educators* (Pretoria, Department of Education).

1998. *Report of the Ministerial Committee on RE* (Pretoria, Department of Education).

2000. *National statistics: Census* (Pretoria, National Department of Internal Affairs).

2001. *Manifesto on values, education and democracy* (Pretoria, Report of the Working Group on Values in Education, Department of Education).

2002. *Revised National Curriculum statement* (Pretoria, Department of Education).

2003. *National policy religion and education* (Pretoria, Department of Education).

2005. *National Curriculum Statement* [Life Orientation Subject Guidelines] (Pretoria, Department of Education).

Educating for hope, compassion and meaning in a divisive and intolerant world

Marian de Souza*

Introduction

The terms 'meaning', 'connectedness', 'moral and/or spiritual values' and 'resilience' have begun to appear at regular intervals, both in Australia and at the international level, in various reports on health and well-being, suicide prevention and on children and communities at risk.[1] However, while Britain and other western countries have incorporated, to varying extents, some understandings of spirituality into the educational context,[2] the secular character of Australian society creates a serious barrier to any recognition that spirituality may have a role in the educational process since, for many, spirituality and religion are seen as synonymous, or certainly, very closely intertwined. As such, Australian educational policies and documents tend to skirt

*Australian Catholic University, Aquinas Campus, 1200 Mair St, Ballarat 3350, Australia. Email: m.desouza@aquinas.acu.edu.au

around any language that may have spiritual connotations. Instead there has been some discussion of the place of resilience and values in education[3] without any acknowledgement that these elements may, indeed, be expressions of or outcomes linked to the spiritual dimension of the individual's life in terms of the layers of connectedness s/he may feel to the Other in their community, in the wider world and creation and, possibly, also to a Supreme Power/Being, that is the spiritual dimension (see de Souza, 2003b, 2004). Further, the need for these layers of connectedness to be nurtured and given expression in the contemporary world where few countries can live in isolation or ignorance of the global context has not been clearly articulated or recognized.

Therefore in this paper, I would like to explore three areas:

1. Australian society and education within a global context;
2. The concept that human spirituality may be described as a movement or journey towards Ultimate Unity, which is expressed as the connectedness that an individual experiences, and which should be nurtured and given expression in education;
3. A learning model that promotes resilience, connectedness, compassion and meaning.

The secular nature of Australian education

European settlement in Australia began at the height of the period referred to as the Enlightenment in Western history. One outcome was that social and political life was influenced by the Cartesian notion of duality—mind and body, religion and state, reason and faith—and this thinking impacted on the public education system. In other parts of the Western world, the separation of these entities was indeed a change from the more integrated society of earlier years when religion had been a fundamental part of the social and educational system. Thus, in recent years, when other Western countries have spoken of and incorporated elements related to spirituality in educational and learning programmes, it could be argued that they are revisiting and rediscovering what they once had and knew; the concept of an education system which incorporates all aspects of being: physical, mental, emotional, social and *spiritual*. However, given the period in European history that saw the beginnings of white settlement in Australia, dualism has been foundational to Australia's way of being—an inherent feature of the Australian social, educational and political system. Indeed, if we examine the nature of this duality we actually discover a third dimension: a triadic nature where little has been done to seek connections between mind, body and spirit; between mental, physical and spiritual aspects of the human world or between rational, emotional and spiritual thinking, particularly in education, where there has been a strong cognitive focus on different levels of thinking. This is clearly apparent in programmes that are based on Bloom's taxonomy or the Thinking Keys and De Bono's Six Thinking Hats, and so on.

It is only in very recent times that emotional learning has begun to receive attention in some Australian schools, and certainly, it has not been given the same emphasis as intellectual learning. Spiritual learning is usually ignored in the state education system and, with religion, is viewed as something separate, to be addressed elsewhere, for instance, in religious orientated schools. The constitutional right of Australians to religious freedom enables religious schools to offer religious education in an alternative education system, and in the past 30 years there has been some government funding for these schools. Given the secular context as described above, and the fact that for many Australians, spirituality is still seen as a by-product of religion, it is not surprising that there is a certain wariness among politicians and public servants who work in the field of education to discuss anything that reflects the spirituality of the human person in relation to education. This is despite ongoing research literature from several disciplines that recognizes spirituality as an essential human trait that can be identified through expressions of connectedness that an individual displays to Self, to the Social Other, the Physical Other and the Transcendent Other (e.g. de Souza, 2003a, 2003b, 2004). Instead, current curriculum reform documents are revisiting concepts and language about values in education.[4] The fact that most of the values listed are expressions of connectedness and, therefore, could be perceived as spiritual expressions of the human person is ignored.

This is the wider picture across the curriculum in primary and secondary education in many schools and, in the past several years, educational policy, as in other countries, has dictated the introduction of interventionist literacy and numeracy programmes as these are perceived to be the essential life skills that students need. However, the concept that perhaps an interventionist programme that is designed to give students the ability to access and nurture their inner lives, to develop their sense of self and to promote a feeling of connectedness to the Other in their community, world and beyond appears to be beyond the grasp of most decision-makers and politicians in contemporary educational circles. The fact that these elements may well be described as belonging to the spiritual dimension of education is not examined or discussed. Hence, knowledge and skills are taught in compartmentalized blocks and programmes focus on the achievement of particular kinds of knowledge that have been prioritized according to social, political and commercial perceptions of their usefulness, usually in terms of material gain. Accordingly, the gap between those who have and can do and those who haven't and cannot do continues to grow, thereby reflecting the bigger picture where, depending on their respective social, political and economic structures and attributes, countries are divided into those with power and wealth and those without.

At the educational level, these features contribute to creating an environment where competition, fragmentation and division are promoted, thus eroding most feelings of connectedness that students may experience, a connectedness which may help them to gain a sense of self and place within their world, thereby providing meaning and purpose in their everyday life, and perhaps preparing them to be purposeful and hope-filled citizens of the future. Since these aspects relate to the spiritual dimension in education, it means that this dimension is often not recognized or addressed appropriately.

It is this balance, or lack thereof, that I wish to address in the second half of this paper: the need to recognize that the human person is a thinking, feeling and intuiting being. These elements need to be addressed if we aim for education to be transformational, which promotes resilience, empathy, meaning and connectedness within the global context that frames the lives of most of our young people today.

Connectedness: an expression of spirituality

Elsewhere, I have discussed the findings of different research projects that have examined the spirituality of young people from varying backgrounds (de Souza, 2003a, 2003b, 2004; de Souza *et al.*, 2002) but those findings have relevance here. In general, we found, through the participants' responses, that they had an *intellectual* understanding of the relationships they spoke of and they *felt* a deep sense of connectedness and, in their perceptions, both these elements had influenced and shaped them to be the people they were. The other relevant finding was their appreciation and recognition of the role of their inner life on their learning and growth, and on their subsequent actions which echoed Merton's concept of the spirituality of education, where 'the activation and development of our inner capacity to understand and live fully as our real selves is the central concern' (Del Prete, 2002, p. 165). Thus, the participants identified the role of the intellect, emotions and inner lives as important to their learning and understanding as they progressed through life.

Drawing on these findings, spirituality was described as a movement through varying circles and layers of connectedness which gave young people a sense of self and place within their world, and which promoted a sense of resilience. Further, it provided them with a sense of meaning and purpose, so that they were able to gain some direction to their lives. The expressions of their spirituality were, then, expressions of connectedness to the Other. At one layer, this may have been reflected in their relationships to their families and friends in their more immediate circle, in other words, to those who were close and similar to them. At a wider circle, this may have been expressed in the feelings of empathy and compassion that they had to people who were different to themselves. It could be argued that when a person's growth reaches the wider circle, they enter another level of spiritual maturity, and their connectedness to the Other at this level helps them to understand another part of themselves, that is they may recognize a part of the Other as something that is a part of themselves. Thereby, the widening circle of connectedness to the Other brings a deepening knowledge of the inner Self; a deeper connectedness to Self. Thus, 'I must look for my identity not only in God but in other[s]' (Merton, cited in Del Prete, 2002, p. 165), where 'the process of inner transformation that leads to self-discovery is simultaneously a process of discovering our deep relatedness to others' (Del Prete, 2002, p. 165).

It is this concept of spirituality, as an expression of the relational dimension of being, or a 'relational consciousness' (Hay, 1998) that has implications for education, that is the need to develop learning programmes and environments that can promote connectedness and meaning. This point is discussed in the next section of this paper.

A learning model to promote meaning and connectedness

While the role of the intellect and the process of thinking has undoubtedly been the central focus of educational programmes over the past century, so that learning tasks have been generated by a concept of rational intelligence, it is only in recent years that theories of emotional intelligence (Salovey & Mayer, 1990; Goleman, 1995) and spiritual intelligence (Zohar & Marshall, 2000) have been clearly articulated and investigated. Mayer and Salovey (1997) proposed a model of emotional intelligence which had four levels, ranging from recognizing emotions and inputting information about the emotions to facilitating and managing emotions and using them in problem-solving, and Goleman (1995) claimed that the Emotional Quotient (EQ) contributes to intellectual performance and is perceived as 'operating across both the cognitive and emotional systems ... in a mostly unitary fashion.' (Mayer *et al.*, 2000, p. 107).

On another front, Zohar and Marshall (2000) proposed a theory for a spiritual quotient (SQ) in intelligence and argued that SQ is a tertiary process which relates to the sub-conscious mind, that is:

> based on the brain's third neural system, the synchronous neural oscillations that unify data across the whole brain. This process unifies, integrates and has the potential to transform material arising from the other two processes. It facilitates a dialogue between reason and emotion, between mind and body. It provides a fulcrum for growth and transformation. It provides the self with an active, unifying, meaning-giving centre. (p. 7)

Zohar and Marshall (2000) claim that both the Emotional Quotient (EQ) and the Spiritual Quotient (SQ) have some significance for the effective functioning of rational intelligence (Intellectual Quotient, IQ):

> Neither IQ nor EQ, separately or in combination, is enough to explain the full complexity of human intelligence nor the vast richness of the human soul and imagination ... We use SQ to wrestle with questions of good and evil and to envision unrealized possibilities—to dream, to aspire, to raise ourselves out of the mud. (p. 5)

While these theories have met with some criticism (for instance, Bar-On & Parker, 2000; Fontana, 2003), they have also been received with some interest, particularly by professionals who work with children and adolescents (for instance, there is a growing number of conferences and writings with themes relevant to this field). What is important is that these theories provide educators, in particular, with new ways of thinking and practising if their aim is to educate the whole person, so that both the outer and the inner lives of the individual may be engaged and nurtured. Further, if we subscribe to the theory that the human person is a thinking, feeling and intuiting being, the role of these elements in the learning process needs to be examined.

It is without doubt that the role of thinking and feeling in the learning process has been recognized in traditional educational programmes, although they have been given different emphases, and heavily weighted in favour of the former. Until recently, however, the role of intuition has, for the most part, been ignored in Western educational circles. Del Prete (2002) claims, that to activate and grow in our ability to understand the living dimensions of truth, we need to develop skills that lead to an intuitive way of knowing, something that has been largely ignored in Western society (p. 171). None the less, it is interesting to note that the subject, intuition, has begun to attract some attention in the corporate world in recent years where its role in more effective decision-making is being investigated (e.g. Breen, 2000). However, it is argued here that the role of intuitive learning plays an important part in the learning process and is not restricted to effective decision-making.

There is a growing body of research and writing into intuition as 'holistic interpretations of situations based on analogies drawn from a largely unconscious experiential database' (Claxton, 2000, p. 50). Certainly, Claxton's description appears to be influenced by Jung who offered the explanation that intuition was unconscious perception which

> tells us of future possibilities. It is the proverbial hunch and the function that informs us about the atmosphere that surrounds an experience or event' (O'Connor, 1985, pp.76–7)

Indeed, Jung's argument (O'Connor, 1985, 1988) that the process through which the individual engages with the world is foundational to the approach to learning proposed in this paper. Jung suggests that a person experiences phenomena through (O'Connor, 1985, p. 75):

1. Perceiving the facts; that is, taking them in through the senses consciously or unconsciously.
2. Thinking about them logically.
3. Developing feelings that produce value judgements.
4   Intuiting by looking beyond the facts to certain other possibilities.

Drawing on these views, intuitive learning would appear to operate at an unconscious level and result in the gaining of tacit knowledge (Polanyi, 1967), that is the knowledge that is absorbed unconsciously or implicitly such that individuals do not know they have it. It is this knowledge that springs from the inner recesses of our unconscious mind, in the shape of an intuition, when we are confronted by a situation or problem that bears some resemblance to other situations or problems that we have encountered before. The similarity may not be clear or obvious to the conscious mind but it may resonate at an unconscious level, thus prompting the 'Aha' moment that leads to a possible resolve or solution.

If we recognize the significance of tacit knowledge in prompting intuitive learning, and if we therefore acknowledge that intuiting may complement the thinking and feeling elements in the learning process, there is some indication that if learning is to be effective, it must be balanced between these three elements. I am further suggesting that it is reasonable to link these three elements—thinking, feeling and intuiting—to intellectual/rational, emotional and spiritual intelligences. While the links between thinking and intellectual intelligence have been recognized in traditional curriculum documents, more recently the role of the emotions and feelings have also been acknowledged (e.g. Palmer, 1998, when he discusses the integration of head and heart in teaching and learning). However, linking intuitive learning to spiritual intelligence is a relatively new concept (Sinetar, 2000; Zohar & Marshall, 2000), and it is important to acknowledge here that it is not the only expression of spiritual intelligence. Other expressions would include creativity, imagination, insights (sometimes linked to intuition), wisdom, and so on. The common element of these expressions is that they appear to spring not from without, but from deep within the individual, usually uninvited, but more often within an appropriate environment, and one that allows time and space for inner reflection, contemplation, beauty, stillness and silence.

Consequently, the learning model I propose here recognizes the complementarity of intellectual/rational, emotional and spiritual quotients and plans for the integration of five elements in the learning process: perceiving or sensing, thinking, feeling and intuiting, and it enables individuals to become familiar with both their inner and outer worlds. This is essential if learning is to become meaningful and transformational. Without integration, it is possible that learning may remain at a superficial level, perhaps laced with mis-information and mis-conceptions that lead to inaccurate knowledge. That is, the learning process may involve the head but not engage the heart and the soul, so that it remains disconnected to past learning and experience and lacks meaning.

This process begins with the conscious or unconscious perceptions that the students gain through their senses. The first response to this may be thinking (intellectual), based on past knowledge, or it may be a feeling (drawing on the emotions), based on past experiences. Either way, the thinking response is likely to elicit some feelings as the process moves on, or the feeling response is likely to colour all subsequent thinking on the subject. Either of these responses can lead to an integration of the two such that the intellect and the emotions work together to make connections and produce a higher and deeper level of knowledge and engagement.

However, the model also recognizes the role of unconscious perceptions so that as the integrated process of thinking and feeling continues, it may reach a depth level where conscious learning merges with unconscious learning prompting an intuitive response which cannot be explained, since it is drawn from knowledge that has previously been gained unconsciously. What is important is that, at this unconscious level, connections may be made such that relevance is perceived, which may lead to new insights. It is at this point that the learning process has the potential to become transformational since it has involved the head (thinking), heart (feelings) and soul (intuiting (unconscious) or inner reflecting (conscious), which may and should lead to outward expressions of changed thinking and behaviour, the ultimate goal of education. The motion then is generative, moving from initial conscious and unconscious perceptions at the surface through thoughts and feelings that merge with previous conscious and unconscious learning and instincts at deeper levels before returning to the surface in transformed expression.

To illustrate the above discussion, I would like to identify a topic for a lesson and explore various responses to it. For instance, if the topic of 'justice' is introduced, the word will immediately prompt a response from students. This response is influenced by previous perceptions, knowledge and experience. If, for instance, their previous perceptions, knowledge and experience have been at an impersonal level, their response will be very different to that of someone who has experienced injustice, whether the experience is their own or that of someone close to them. In the first case, the thinking is likely to be more dominant than the feelings. In the second case, the feelings will be supreme and will subsequently colour all thoughts that follow. In both cases, various levels and patterns of thoughts and feelings are going to surface, merge and translate into other levels and patterns. In an average classroom of 20 or more students, there are going to be many levels and patterns of thoughts and feelings which present a challenge for the teacher to bring together in some way, so that students become aware not just of the differences but also of the resonances, between their stories and experiences and the stories and experiences of the Other.

Accordingly, the learning activities need to be designed such that all students will have the opportunity to share/hear the thoughts and experience the feelings that are different to their own. Such learning and teaching should move thoughts and feelings through to yet deeper levels where unconscious relevant and previously gained knowledge may reside. This may include having unconsciously noticed the expression, body language or subsequent behaviour of a person experiencing injustice and knowing at a depth level that the person has been seriously hurt through the process, perhaps even traumatized. The merging of the new knowledge and the previous knowledge now raises the potential for the individual student to recognize what it means when someone is a victim of injustice, the wrongs of the situation and how the victim may feel. They may now be able to be sensitive to and empathize with the victim, and perhaps be stirred to compassion which may lead them to take a stand against unjust situations in the future—the transformation. In the current war against terrorism which is also aligned to a global world that is fast shrinking in size, the need for students to develop such learning and to be prompted to action for justice is undeniable, and a natural expression of a well-developed spirituality, that is a wide and deep level of connectedness to the Other.

In the planning of such a programme, learning outcomes need to be stated (this is necessary to fit with an outcomes-based educational model which is used in Australia and many other countries) for cognitive, affective and spiritual learning. This is essential if the integration of the three dimensions of learning and the four/five corresponding processes are to be achieved. Cognitive learning outcomes, as currently understood and practised, are expected to be demonstrated by the end of the lesson or unit of work and are assessable. However, measurement of affective and spiritual learning is not desirable. Indeed, this latter kind of learning may not be clearly demonstrated during the lesson and may only become evident in the near or distant future. Hence, it is articulated as a desired outcome rather than a demonstrated one. Acknowledgement is given here that such a statement more appropriately fits the concept of an educational objective rather than an outcome. Nevertheless, given the outcomes-based model that is in current practice, I would argue that it is simpler to restrict the terminology to outcome statements with a clear understanding of the above difference.

This model also challenges the teacher to find new ways to communicate the content in order to seriously engage their students. For instance, using an arts approach to teach a topic can raise the potential of connecting with the students since it can arouse in the learner different thoughts and feelings which may illuminate the students' perceptions of the familiar, or transform their vision of the world. Such an approach can create a sense of mystery, magic and wonder, and possibly a glimpse of something beyond. It may also promote a connection between students as they respond individually and collectively to the content of the lesson, which may lead to a deeper engagement with and understanding of the particular topic. In the learning and teaching situation that is attempting to address the emotional and spiritual dimensions of education, the arts provide an invaluable source and medium. They are an expression of the inner self/spirit and they provoke a response from the inner self/ spirit of the receiver, hence the arts may be viewed as the unconscious language of the inner self or the spiritual language of the human person.

Elsewhere, I have described other features that may promote the spiritual dimension of learning (de Souza, 2003a, 2003b, 2004). I briefly present them here:

- Promoting a sense of connectedness to develop tolerance, empathy and compassion.
- Valuing a shared story.
- Including silence and solitude.
- Creating avenues to assist in the search for wisdom, meaning and purpose.
- Offering experiences of awe and wonder.
- Encouraging a heightened awareness of moments of joy and delight.
- Discovering ways to rediscover creation.
- Exploring learning through the arts.
- Identifying moments of mystery and magic in the everyday.
- Recognizing opportunities for ritual, initiation and rites of passage.
- Becoming aware of and responding to a transcendent dimension in one's daily life.

To conclude, addressing the perceiving and sensing, thinking, feeling and intuiting processes in the learning situation is vital for a healthy classroom environment. Most importantly, teachers need to address this dimension in their own lives, so that they may become more reflective practitioners, thereby enhancing their own understanding of teaching as a spiritual practice. Finally, if we mean to provide our students with opportunities to become resilient, empathetic, compassionate, meaningful and hope-filled people who are more capable of responding to the perceived problems of the contemporary world and of contributing to the promotion of a fair and just global society, we must address the spiritual dimension in education.

Notes

1. A recent US report (September 2003) of the Commission on Children at Risk, *Hardwired to connect: the scientific case for authoritative communities*, has identified the rising rates of mental problems and emotional distress among US children and highlighted the need for spiritual and moral teachings and nurturing. Similarly, Mission Australia (2005) also noted the rising incidences of depression and other mental health problems for young people aged 14–17, and has identified the need for connectedness and resilience in this context. In addition, there has been a growing number of professionals in areas of mental health, youth and social work who have

begun exploring the notion of spirituality as a means to help young people find meaning and a sense of belonging; for instance, the topic for the 10th Annual Conference for Suicide Prevention (2003), in Australia, was 'Finding meaning to sustain life: the role of spirituality in suicide prevention'.

2. In Britain, the National Curriculum Council, in 1993, released a document entitled: *Spiritual and moral development: a discussion paper*, which described spiritual growth as a 'lifelong process of encounters in which people respond to and develop insight from experiences which are, by their very nature, hard to define'. Aspects of spiritual development were further discussed in a paper from the School Curriculum and Assessment Authority (SCAA, 1995). Also the Office for Standards in Education in Britain (OFSTED), in 1994, articulated spiritual development as relating to that aspect of inner life through which pupils acquire insights into their personal existence, which are of enduring worth. It is characterized by reflection, the attribution of meaning to experience, valuing a non-material dimension to life and intimations of an enduring reality. 'Spiritual' is not synonymous with 'religious'; all areas of the curriculum may contribute to pupils' 'spiritual development'. In the USA and Canada, various educators such as Moffett (1994), Miller (2000), Kessler (2000) and Palmer (1998) also have written extensively on the role of spirituality in education, in terms of promoting self-esteem, healthy relationships and improved learning.

3. See Fuller, A., Johnson, G., Bellhouse, B. & McGraw, K. (2003) *START: school transition and resilience training* (Victoria, Department of Education and Training).

4. A recent draft Consultation Paper (2004) which has been circulated by the Victorian Curriculum and Assessment Authority in Australia, Victorian curriculum reform 2004, proposes a new framework of 'essential learning' for all Victorian schools and identifies a relational dimension, that is the need to 'develop responsible individuals capable of relating with family, friends and colleagues'. It also refers generally and specifically to the teaching of values as foundational for the curriculum, and lists ten particular values. Finally, in one paragraph there is reference to moral and *spiritual* attributes and values.

Notes on contributor

Marian de Souza teaches in undergraduate and postgraduate education programmes at the Australian Catholic University, Ballarat Campus. Her main research interests are in spirituality and the implications for a holistic approach to education, an arts approach to teaching across the curriculum and the approach adopted by small ethnic communities to pass on their cultural and spiritual heritage to their younger members in a contemporary pluralist context.

References

Bar-On, R. & Parker, J. D. A. (Eds) (2000) *The handbook of emotional intelligence. Theory, development, assessment, and application at home, school and in the workplace* (San Francisco, CA, Jossey-Bass).

Breen, B. (2000) What's your intuition? *Fast Company*, 38, September, 290. Available online at: http://www.fastcompany.com/online/38/klein.html (accessed 12 May 2004).

Claxton, G. (2000) The anatomy of intuition, in: T. Atkinson & G. Claxton (Eds) *The intuitive practitioner: on the value of not always knowing what one is doing* (Buckingham and Philadelphia, PA, Open University Press).

Del Prete, T. (2002) Being what we are: Thomas Merton's spirituality in education, in: J. Miller, & Y. Nakagawa (Eds) *Nurturing our wholeness* (Rutland, VT, Foundation for Educational Renewal).

Fontana, D. (2003) *Psychology, religion and spirituality* (Malden, USA, BPS Blackwell).

Goleman, D. (1995) *Emotional intelligence: why it can matter more than IQ* (London, Bloomsbury).

Hay, D. with Nye, R. (1998) *The spirit of the child* (London, Fount).

Kessler, R. (2000) *The soul of education. Helping students find connection, compassion and character at school* (Alexandria, VA, Association for Supervision and Curriculum Development).

Mayer, J. D. & Salovey, P. (1997) What is emotional intelligence? in: P. Salovey & D. Sluyter (Eds) *Emotional development and emotional intelligence: implications for educators* (New York, Basic Books).

Mayer, J. D., Salovey, P. & Caruso, D. R. (2000) Emotional intelligence as *Zeitgeist*, as personality, and as a mental ability, in: R. Bar-On & J. D. A. Parker (Eds) *The handbook of emotional intelligence. Theory, development, assessment, and application at home, school and in the workplace* (San Francisco, CA, Jossey-Bass).

Moffett, J. (1994) *The universal schoolhouse* (San Francisco, Jossey Bass).

Miller, J. (2000) *Education and soul* (Albany, NY, State University of New York Press).

Mission Australia's National Youth Survey. (2005) Available online at: www.missionaustralia. com.au (accessed 8 December 2005).

O'Connor, P. (1985) *Understanding Jung* (Port Melbourne, Mandarin).

Palmer, P. (1998) *The courage to teach: exploring the inner landscape of a teacher's life* (San Francisco, CA, Jossey-Bass).

Polyanyis, M. (1967) *The tacit dimension* (New York, Anchor Books).

Salovey, P. & Mayer, J. D. (1990) Emotional intelligence, *Imagination, Cognition and Personality*, 9, 185–211.

School Curriculum and Assessment Authority (SCAA). (1995) *Discussion paper on spiritual and moral development* (UK, SCAA).

Sinetar, M. (2000) *Spiritual intelligence: what we can learn from the early awakening child* (Maryknoll, NY, Orbis Books).

de Souza, M. (2003a) *Identifying the elements that shape spiritual development and a sense of the sacred: tertiary students' perceptions of their spiritual journeys: implications for lifelong learning* (CD ROM of the proceedings of the *Lifelong Learning Conference: Reaching the unreached learner*) (Melbourne, Australian Catholic University).

de Souza, M. (2003b) Contemporary influences on the spirituality of young people: implications for education, *International Journal of Children's Spirituality*, 18(3), 269–279.

de Souza, M. (2004) The role of the school and educational programs in nurturing the spirituality of young people, in: J. Norman (Ed.) *At the heart of education: school chaplaincy and pastoral care* (Dublin, Veritas), 122–133.

de Souza, M., Cartwright, P. & McGilp, E. J. (2002) *An investigation into the perceptions of their spiritual well-being of 16–20 year-old young people in a regional centre in Victoria*. Unpublished report, Australian Catholic University, Ballarat.

Zohar, D. & Marshall, I. (2000) *SQ: spiritual intelligence: the ultimate intelligence* (London, Bloomsbury).

Creating an idyllic world for children's spiritual formation

Karen-Marie Yust*

Introduction

Christian camping ministries have been part of the American religious landscape since the late nineteenth century when philosophical enthusiasm for nature and the romantic belief in its positive formative effects on young men led several educators and ministers to design camping trips for their male students and adolescent parishioners as part of their general and religious education. Historians of Christian camping credit a congregational minister, the Reverend George Hinckley, with creating the first church-related camp in Maine in the 1880s. Camping ministries also developed as part of the work of the Young Men's Christian Association (YMCA), and eventually most Protestant denominations and the Catholic Church created camps for their constituent congregations (Venable & Joy, 1998). Contemporary Christian camping ministries include both denominationally run programmes that primarily attract children from member churches and independent evangelical campsites that seek to attract primarily 'unchurched' children as a form of evangelistic outreach in their communities.

*Union-PSCE, 3401 Brook Road, Richmond, VA 23227, USA. Email: kmyust@cts.edu

The 'conventional wisdom' among camp directors is that the experience of attending church camp is, for many people, one of the most significant factors in their overall spiritual formation as Christians. Residential camp settings, where campers come and stay for a period of time ranging from 48 hours (in the case of weekend retreats or introductory camping experiences for younger elementary children) to two weeks or longer (in the case of work camps and junior counsellor training experiences), are believed to be places where children and youth can experience a quality of life in a Christian community capable of shaping their spirituality in profound ways. Camping programmes claim to provide campers with important lessons in living, opportunities to develop new skills and talents, role models of who they can become, and friendships that often last a lifetime. Anecdotal accounts abound of young people who have attended church camps and returned home to leadership roles in their congregations or with a profession of a call to ministry. A study conducted in the late 1990s by the Auburn Center for the Study of Theological Education (cited in LEI, 2000) showed that more than half of new seminary students in the United States were involved in religiously related camping experiences as participants and leaders when they were younger. Informal admissions polling at my previous institution[1] suggests that as many as three-quarters of seminarians credit camping ministries with influencing their call to religious leadership. All these factors suggest that Christian camps merit closer scrutiny as formative influences in the spiritual lives of children and youth.

In April 2000, Lilly Endowment, Inc., a major American foundation active in funding research and experiments in American religious life, launched the Indiana Camp Ministries Enhancement Program (ICMEP) to explore the effects of Christian camping ministries on young people and encourage further development of effective spiritual formation programmes in camp settings. The Endowment invited camps in its home state of Indiana to submit grant proposals for facilities upgrades and programme development projects, with the understanding that the camps selected to participate in ICMEP would permit Endowment evaluators to visit their campsites and would attend six semi-annual peer learning and evaluation conferences throughout the three-year period of the programme. Twenty-one camping organizations representing 23 camps were selected to receive grants of up to $600,000 each for their projects. The Endowment also awarded Christian Theological Seminary a grant to oversee the research and evaluation components of the programme.

One of the key concerns guiding the research and evaluation process was the question of whether and how church camps are *distinctive* residential environments that are able to nurture children and youth spiritually, prepare them for Christian leadership, and encourage their commitment to lifelong vocations of ministry and service to others. As lead researcher, I posed the question: 'What are the key features of the educational and spiritual experiences upon which these camps rely?' I also asked: 'What are the goals and purposes of these experiences and how are camping organizations evaluating whether these goals and purposes are met?' I began visiting camps, interviewing camp ministries leaders, and reviewing ICMEP grant proposals and annual grantee reports with this concern and these questions in mind.

Defining the mission of camps ministries

As part of the application process, participants were asked to describe the mission of the camp, the various programmes with children and youth that make up their camp ministries, and the ways in which those programmes effectively advanced their mission, particularly with reference to the spiritual formation of campers. Most camps responded to this expectation by restating their organizational vision statement. These visions range from articulations of a general desire to provide 'children the opportunity to experience God'[2] to more programmatically descriptive statements, such as one camp's vision 'to provide a wholesome camping experience that will promote spiritual and personal growth, while having fun through creative activities, recreational sports, and thought-provoking breakout sessions, along with worship services'. As a general rule, more theologically main-stream-to-liberal camp ministries articulate generalized visions, such as the vision of a Presbyterian camp, which seeks 'to provide creative, joyful, formative opportunities for youth in the experiences of their Christian faith'. More theologically conservative camps tend to incorporate more specific theological expectations in their vision statements. A Salvation Army camp describes its vision as 'to offer a special venue in which to see the gospel of Jesus Christ as revealed in creation, to hear the gospel of Jesus Christ as explained, and to experience the gospel of Jesus Christ as lived through interaction with Christian leaders and mentors'.

What most of the camp discussions of mission have in common, regardless of the camp's theological orientation, is some reference to a 'set apart-ness' of the Christian camping experience. A second Presbyterian camp sees as part of its mission the provision of 'a place away from the busy world'. An independent evangelical camp emphasizes creating 'environments' and 'communities' that are different from the usual places and groups children and youth know. A United Methodist camp tries to create 'short-term Christian communities' for its campers. A United Church of Christ camp instructs its campers to divest themselves of 'electronic stimuli' before coming to camp, because 'this is to be a retreat from your daily life'. And, of course, there is the Salvation Army camp's reference to offering 'a special venue', noted earlier. Several other camps contrasted their 'natural setting' with the busy cityscapes that they assume to be their campers' usual environments. This propensity to assume a 'rural' versus 'city' contrast as part of a camp's distinctiveness is particularly interesting given the predominantly rural nature of Indiana, a Midwest farming state with only one large city and numerous counties sparsely populated by farm families. The use of a stereotypical industrial/natural binary seems more a feature of camping rhetoric—an unconscious assumption about the inherent natural power of the camp setting carried over from the nineteenth-century romanticizing of the country versus the city—than accurate portrayal of a difference offered by the Christian camping experience to the many Indiana campers who do not reside in the city for most of the year.

Comparing Christian and non-religious camps programmes

The reality of the Christian camp's 'set apart-ness' as a place of intentional spiritual formation is also challenged by the similarities between Christian camping programmes and those of non-religious organizations, such as university-sponsored sports camps, contemporary YMCA camps (which are non-sectarian), Audubon-sponsored retreats and scouting programmes. Observations during site visits suggest that much of the day at a church-related camp is structured like that of non-religious camps, in that campers spend most of their time in recreational activities with little explicit connection of these experiences to spirituality and the themes and practices of Christian community. Some camps have adopted the language of 'trust' and 'community-building' to highlight the value of rock-climbing walls and challenge courses, but this values-oriented language is not distinct from the language used for public school groups who also engage in such experiences for non-sectarian purposes. Training in the religious discourse that might accompany recreational and challenge activities is sparse. More theologically conservative camps are more likely to employ some religious language, but the majority of camps (mainstream or conservative) prefer a generic 'moral values' vocabulary over language that evokes the particularity of their denominational heritage and beliefs.

Christian camps are also modifying their programmatic themes in imitation of non-religious camp settings. While 'traditional' programmes emphasizing water play, arts and crafts, and other general outdoor activities are still offered for a few weeks during the summer, most camps have begun marketing camping programmes that offer 'extreme' sports (e.g. skateboarding, stunt cycling), sports skills (e.g. soccer or all-round team sports), music, drama, horseback riding, backpacking or rafting adventures, and other interest-based activities designed to compete with non-religious summer programmes in their regions. These 'special interest' camps include a morning devotional time or Bible study and may incorporate an evening worship or firelight vespers service, but are otherwise indistinguishable from similar camps in non-Christian settings.

An example of this approach is the 'ranch camp' programme being developed by a Methodist camp. The overarching goal of this camp is to become 'the premier' equestrian camp in the region. To accomplish this goal, they have hired a 'horsemanship programme director', whose expertise is horseback riding and who has no training or experience in spiritual formation, in lieu of a general programme director. The camp administrator explains that children and youth will know that they are at a Christian camp because of the caring counsellors and the opportunity to commune with horses and nature. He noted that they offer a morning devotional time before they start riding and an evening campfire vespers service to end the day. The rest of the day is spent on riding techniques, building rider confidence, learning proper care of one's mount, and swimming. A colleague whose daughter attends a local riding stable's equestrian day camp reports that this schedule, minus the morning and evening religious activities, is very similar to that of her daughter's camp. Spiritual formation is clearly a minor auxiliary concern compared to the camp's emphasis on equestrian training, and a non-Christian camper would likely feel 'at home' here. Indeed, the camp wants to attract public school groups during the off-season and is designing their curriculum so it will work interchangeably with both church and school groups.

Camp directors explain that diminishing enrolment in traditional camps has prompted the move into interest-based programmes. This might be construed as a responsive and responsible move to meet children and youth where they are, were it not for the intentional diminishment of overt references to and engagement in spiritual practices. Camp leaders assume that the fact of their identification as a Christian camp, the presumably inherent spiritual quality of the natural world, and the insertion of a few minutes of personal quiet time each day suffice to nurture the spiritual lives of participants. However, there is little evidence to reinforce this perception.

Camper perceptions

Interviews with campers during site visits have suggested that most focus not on spiritual formation, but on a sense of social community, as the part of camp they appreciate most, and they cite various social activities (a tug-of-war, a dance, a wiener roast, a talent show) as the cherished memories they will take home. Bible study, worship and personal devotional time are dubbed 'okay' but not memorable. Most campers would rather participate in dances, hang out at the commissary talking about the opposite sex, shoot one another with paintballs or dress up for a formal party than spend time talking about or intentionally practising the spiritual life. Some campers likened camp Bible studies to the boring stuff they do in Sunday School back home, except they liked the fact that they could sit on the dock dangling their feet in the water or dream about swimming and canoeing while they waited for the lesson to end. While every camp had campers who were attracted to the religious activities more than their peers, our observations suggest that even the counsellors wanted to get through the lessons as quickly as possible and move on to something else, for they often concluded lessons early and shifted the group into game-playing or informal conversations about sports, hobbies and other interests.

The reliable exception to campers' dismissal of religious activities as 'boring' is the closing evening 'mountaintop experience' with which many camps conclude their weekly sessions. Generally designed to appeal to camper emotions, which are already high because of the impending separation of new friends and loss of the close-knit camp community, these events create a context in which many campers make or renew spiritual commitments to ministry. Campers are told to expect something important to happen to them during the service; in fact, they often receive this message before they ever leave home from congregational leaders and friends who have previously attended camp. Camps may bring in a special speaker who is known for the ability to speak passionately about the need for young people to make a commitment to Christ and/or to the church. There is extended rhetoric about the short amount of time left in the camp experience and the need to carry the good feelings and community of camp back home in the form of a transformed self. Praise choruses abound, with their themes of Jesus' overwhelming love and call to discipleship. Counsellors and campers testify to how their week at camp has given them the strength to overcome some adversity or provided the love they do not get at home or among their 'secular' friends. The underlying message, sometimes stated explicitly, is that one must do *something* or be a fraud, someone who is just playing at being a Christian. Each year, scores of young people hear this message and choose to make a public profession of their genuine belief in themselves as good and faithful followers of Christ. Whether they do so because they have encountered a spiritual call to discipleship or ministry, or because they want to conform to the expectations of the adults and their peers and shore up their own insecure sense of identity, is an open question.

Camp directors readily admit that most of the spiritual commitments made at these services fade quickly. They also point out that regaining this personal and spiritual high is part of what brings campers back year after year and therefore the cultivation of such a high is necessary for the economic survival of camping ministries. However, a spiritual rhythm that depends on an annual mountaintop experience and coasts through the rest of the year is not a healthy spirituality. We might even argue that camp 'mountaintop experiences' do young people a spiritual disservice because they suggest the emotions and actions associated with such events are the norms for human spirituality, and thus that spirituality isn't really an attainable aspect of daily life, but an occasional overwhelming emotional experience in the presence of other spiritual people equally overwhelmed. Such experiences also suggest that spirituality is attached to emotion without reference to critical thinking, and that spirituality is about a mood or ambience rather than life practices. They imply that one must obtain spirituality from special places that have it, rather than seeking God wherever one is. Whatever genuine elements of encounter with God may be present in the typical camp 'mountaintop experience', the context can obscure the possibility of relating to God in the midst of ordinary activities and ordinary relationships.

Camp self-evaluations

Camping organizations do little to evaluate the effectiveness of their programmes, particularly with reference to the ways in which children and youth are being nurtured and challenged spiritually. Since most primarily use end-of-session camper surveys to gauge camper satisfaction, we know more about what campers think of the food and their feelings about their counsellors or specific activities than about how these camping experiences are shaping their spiritual lives and cultivating their leadership gifts. Many of these surveys do include a question that asks about a change in the camper's relationship with God, but the question is often phrased in ways that provide little insight into what campers mean. Asking campers to respond 'yes' or 'no' to the question: 'Have you grown closer to God this week?', tends to generate a high percentage of 'yes' answers, but this quantitative approach to data gathering doesn't help camps (or us) interpret the nature of the campers' relationships with God, nor determine which aspects of the camp experience contributed to this change. A few camps use more open-ended questions, which generate more helpful responses. Campers describe acquiring greater skill in studying the Bible, praying or leading worship.

The questionnaire (Wrigley, 2002) used in common by three Methodist camp grantees illustrates the problematic design and interpretative usefulness of camp programme evaluations. Provided to campers on the last day of camp, the survey posed seven primary questions and six sub-questions in two areas. Respondents were provided with Likert scales upon which to rate each item. Questions about how well the camper liked the food, the curriculum, the worship and camp programmes, and the overall experience of camp were judged in terms of 'very poor', 'poor', 'good' and 'very good'. Between 80% and 95% of all campers ranked these items as 'good' or 'very good', with the exception of older (junior/senior high) campers at one site, where 31% didn't like the food. Approximately 90% of all campers indicated (on a yes/no scale) that they intended to return to camp the next year.

One question asked campers to evaluate their 'family group counsellor(s)' in terms of how well those small group leaders contributed to the camper's spiritual formation. This section posed two statements according to which the respondent rated the counsellor: 'I have gained a greater understanding of the Bible' and 'I made a significant decision to follow Christ at camp'. Campers responded overwhelmingly (99% and 97%) that their counsellors had done a 'good' or 'very good' job of encouraging biblical literacy or a significant spiritual decision. Furthermore, in response to a set of four statements grouped under the question: 'How did your experience at camp effect your spiritual journey?', over 90% of junior and senior high school campers said (by marking 'agree' or 'strongly agree') that they had 'gained a greater understanding of the Bible', 'made a significant decision to follow Christ at camp' or 'renewed [their] commitment to Christ this week'. Sixty-five per cent said they 'feel called to some kind of Ministry'. Camp leaders, both at these Methodist camps and in other ministries that use similar evaluative tools, point to these kinds of questionnaire results as evidence of the effectiveness of their programmes in nurturing the spiritual lives of children and youth.

However, the timing of these assessments, which follow closely on the emotional and carefully scripted final camp gathering, as well as the campers' social knowledge that they are supposed to agree with the statements *and* to respond without offering any explanations or examples in relation to their answers, affects the reliability and interpretative usefulness of this data. The lukewarm reception campers give to formal Bible studies and personal devotional times, indicated by their withdrawn body posture and wandering attention, as well as the many counsellor promptings required to quiet their personal conversations and persuade them to participate in the conversation or work assigned, suggest that whatever gains campers have made in their understandings of the Bible were not highly sought-after achievements. Unstructured interviews with campers, as noted earlier, also demonstrate that religious programming is more tolerated than embraced. And the recently released findings from the American Camp Association's 'Directions' study, in which immediately reported increases in camper spirituality did not persist in six-month follow-up surveys, further underscores the difficulty camps face as institutions of spiritual transformation (ACA, 2005, p. 15).

Campers are more enthusiastic about worship and vesper services, especially in settings where PowerPoint, video clips, electronic instruments and other technical supports create a party or 'club' atmosphere. The focus in these services is on inspirational music and messages, and camp leaders deliberately set out to encourage high emotional investment in the dramatic testimonies of persons who have persevered through hardships, media clips of soap operatic adolescent groups in crisis, and/ or stories of hardship and sacrifice on the mission field. Many camps now import a 'praise band' or Christian rock group to perform and lead music, and campers are encouraged to behave as they would at a mainstream concert given by their favourite recording artist.

A new worship practice, generated by the recent acquisition of LCD projectors, laptop computers and digital cameras, is the daily creation of a camp video or slide show, which is then shown as part of the community's evening gathering. Witnessed and video taped observations of camp worship services suggest that most youth respond enthusiastically to seeing themselves projected bigger than life on screen and enter into the emotionally dramatic elements of the service with gusto. Less visually or emotionally dramatic elements, such as traditionally styled sermons or lectures, generate responses similar to those described in relation to Bible studies and devotional times. Campers whisper with persons next to them, doodle, nap, request permission to go to the restroom and generally convey with their body language that they are bored. It takes the reintroduction of singing or another multimedia moment to shake them from their lethargy.

Staff training in spiritual formation

While most camp leaders fervently believe in the power of Christian camps to change lives, few have much training in Christian education and spiritual formation, and many have little responsibility for the actual programmes that occur on their grounds. Several camps delegate program development responsibilities to a series of volunteer camp directors, each of whom creates a week's worth of activities and then leaves to make room for the next volunteer. Sometimes the judicatory or camp board selects a theme or provides a curricular resource, such as the ecumenical National Council of Christian Churches Outdoor Ministries Committee curriculum, produced annually. However, the implementation of this curriculum and others is generally left to the weekly camp directors, and site visit observations suggest many mainstream Protestant directors make little to moderate use of provided curricula, preferring instead to repeat a set of fun activities with little or no explicit spiritual content that they have carried with them from year to year.

Most camps are using a small group model of camping ministry, in which campers are divided into 'family' or 'cabin' groups who live together with a young adult counsellor and participate in most activities as a unit. The counsellors generally are responsible for devotional times and Bible study, and camp ministries count on counsellors to cultivate the intimacy and educational space necessary for quality small-group interactions and personal transformation. Only a few camps explicitly train their counsellors to articulate connections between overtly religious activities and other camp experiences. Counsellors also receive relatively little training in how to nurture and support spiritual formation, despite the degree to which camps rely on counsellor competence in this area for effective faith formation among campers.

The bulk of staff training at most camps focuses on camper management issues: safety, discipline, psychological support, developmental stages, etc. Some attention is given to leading camp devotions or Bible studies, but this training is usually in the guise of an orientation to the religious education curriculum purchased or created for the week/summer. An independent evangelical organization and an Episcopal camp have developed an extended training session that seeks to orient staff to a particular understanding of spiritual formation and cultivate staffers in the role of spiritual leaders, but this approach is unusual. Several camps report that they screen staff applicants for spiritual maturity prior to hiring them and then assume that their primary spiritual formation role in relation to campers is the testimony of their lives. While true in the sense that a lived witness is an important component of spiritual mentoring, this assumption overlooks the powerful roles that formal teaching and skilful small-group and 'teaching moment' facilitation can play in the spiritual formation of children and youth. It also contributes to the ongoing tendency to divide camp days into 'religious' sessions and 'fun' activities, implying that Bible study and worship are contrary to fun.

Camp contexts

In their second year programme reports, camps were asked to reflect on the following question: 'How are your building projects shaping your educational programmes in ways that nurture faith and encourage leadership development among campers and young adult staff?' The majority who responded to this question addressed it in terms of their buildings creating a more pleasant place to engage in activities than the spaces they replaced. Few leaders recognize the implications of adding air-conditioned buildings that encourage counsellors and campers to stay indoors on hot days rather than participate in the nature-based activities that are the hallmarks of camping ministries. Several times we observed family groups lounging in air-conditioned recreation halls or cabins playing board-games and cards or doing craft projects, much as they might at home or in an after-school programme. Nor did leaders realize that the addition of computers for Internet access, video editing and slide presentations—a move intended to help camps compete with non-Christian camps—further undercuts the 'set-apartness' they consider part of their identity as a spiritual environment.

Part of the difficulty is that camp leaders tend to accept without critical assessment the cultural assumption that something new is inherently better than something old. They contend that comments like: 'What a nice building!' and 'It was so clean and neat', constitute evaluative commentary on the ability of a space to nurture spirituality and encourage spiritual leadership because they assume a 'nice' and 'clean' room is inherently 'good' for the soul. Is there an echo of the long-standing moral claim that 'cleanliness is next to Godliness' operating here?

Certainly there is a middle-class economic standard of what constitutes a good and productive environment for spiritual formation at work, as well as some degree of dissonance with the camps' own articulation of a natural versus industrial paradigm. Modern buildings with all the conveniences of home set among fields and a grove of trees are little different from homes in well-developed suburbs or farmhouses among soon-to-ripen cornfields. In fact, several camp leaders indicated that their move to re-create spaces more like those children and youth know back home is based on their perception that young people are not willing to tolerate more rustic accommodations, nor do without the electronic gadgetry they use every other week of the year. Fear that camper enrolment will continue to decline if major changes in camp facilities do not address this perceived reluctance drove many of the building projects these camps undertook.

Camp ministries are also susceptible to the various activity 'fads' sweeping the larger American youth culture. Almost all of the grantees included in their projects the installation of climbing walls, high ropes courses, and/or water 'blogs'. These elements are popular items in sporting goods stores, public and independent school team-building programmes, public nature preserves and amusement parks. Camps leaders identify these items as investments in the spiritual formation of children and youth, although they admit that their presence at campsites is mostly to attract campers who might otherwise choose non-religious camp settings. All train their staff in use and safety procedures; only a few include training that encourages counsellors to link these recreational activities to the language of spirituality and spiritual formation. Several camps did employ a rhetoric of personal self-esteem and team-building in relation to these activities, although that rhetoric was more prominent among camp leaders than among the counsellors working with the campers.

In a camp that does specifically train its counsellors to use a high ropes course for spiritual formation, we observed a series of campers who were suspended swinging high in the air from a rope anchored by their family group and not allowed to descend until they could quote the Bible verse assigned for the day. Were it not for the prompting of teammates on the ground, most would still be hanging. Such an activity seems more about threat and coercion—all in good fun, of course—than spiritual formation. If we assess the implicit curriculum of this teaching practice, we can identify several themes related to spirituality imbedded in this exercise:

1.   it is dangerous not to know the right spiritual words to say when you've been told to learn them;
2.   certain spiritual words or formulae will get you out of danger;
3.   your spiritual community will test you to see if you are worthy;
4.   your spiritual community will help you when you are in trouble;
5.   you will have another chance to prove your spiritual merit if you fail the first time.

These themes are consistent with the theological perspective of the camp using the high ropes activity, and hence the activity represents an intentional implementation of this perspective. However, only some of the counsellors use this approach; others substitute singing silly songs or engaging in other funny actions before they will let the group lower their swinging friend.

Concluding reflections

My work with the ICMEP grantees suggests that it is much more difficult for Christian camp ministries to create a spiritually rich environment than the camps realize. Despite camp leaders' descriptions of their programmes as means by which campers are 'set apart' from their daily existence, camp settings are rarely the idyllic spiritual environments that we would like to imagine. Their 'difference' from the usual worlds of children and youth is more in the communal residential nature of the experience than in the distinctiveness of the activities, teaching orientations or physical environment of the camp setting. However, young people could have a similar experience in a non-Christian camp and might hardly notice the difference if their primary experience of a Christian camp occurred in one of the mainstream Protestant camps in Indiana. Those who attend a theologically conservative camp in that Midwestern state would notice a greater difference in the rhetoric employed during formal periods of religious instruction and might even hear spiritual commentary during their recreational activities.

But these campers would also experience camp primarily as an extension of their youth culture into another arena, where activities are comfortably similar to what one might do at school or home, but with a spiritual gloss. Christian camps have significant work to do in analysing the degree to which they are primarily purveyors of American cultural messages in a religious venue and also intentional communities of resistance against these messages. For many, successful engagement in this analytic task will first require them to question the conflation of Christian spirituality with American values and to confront their own fears regarding economic viability if they do not follow the lead of the youth market in shaping their programming. Given the reluctance of many denominations and congregations to do this work, it is not surprising that Christian camps in Indiana are, for the most part, reluctant to rock the American religious boat.

Notes on contributor

The Reverend Dr Karen-Marie Yust is the author of *Real kids, real faith* (Jossey-Bass, 2004) and co-editor of *Nurturing child and adolescent spirituality: perspectives from the world's religious traditions* (Rowman & Littlefield, 2006). She teaches Christian education and spirituality at Union Theological Seminary and Presbyterian School of Christian Education.

Notes

1. Reported by Mary Harris, Associate Dean for Student Services, Christian Theological Seminary, June 2004.

2. All quotations are taken from materials submitted by camp organizations participating in the ICMEP; camp names have been omitted to protect their privacy.

References

American Camp Association (2005) *Directions: youth development outcomes of the camp Experience* (Martinsville, IN, ACA).

Lilly Endowment Inc. (2000) *Request for proposals: Indiana camp ministries enhancement program* (Indianapolis, IN, LEI).

Venable, S. & Joy, D. (1998) *How to use camping experiences in religious education* (Birmingham, AL, Religious Education Press).

Wrigley, K. (2002) *South Indiana Conference Outdoor Ministries Summer Camp 2002. Report: compilation of questionnaire results* (unpublished document).

Conclusion

How we can enable and equip our children to meet and understand the social and economic pressures imposed on them?

The Lincoln, UK conference, which formed the backdrop to this Special Isuue, was an opportunity for interdisciplinary conversations and dialogue to determine and use the vocabulary of spiritual education to understand and challenge our divided world, communities and classrooms. This issue, with its variety of disciplines and interpretations, benefits from the ongoing dialogue in the community of those committed to visions of spiritual education, and thereby amplifies the challenge to us as educators, nurturers, parents or researchers, to confront and respond creatively and thoughtfully to our experiences and relationship with division and difference.

Specifically, we believe the nature of the challenge here is threefold. First, it exposes us to analysis of the context in which work with children and young people takes place. By doing so, it also cautions us about the power of the forces surrounding and compromising integral work: consumerism, violence, war, nationalism and covert moral agendas, to name just a few. These are powerful, perhaps indomitable factors. Finally, the challenge of this volume is that it cautions us about praxis. Spiritual education is still in its infancy, still struggles to make its voice heard in curriculum discourse and is still susceptible to shallow or opportunistic 'quick fixes'. For a spiritual education that faces the challenges, we need a praxis that seriously analyses its context with courage and honesty, and behaves accordingly. We need more penetration of analysis into practice.

A feature of the Lincoln conference was that all the keynotes, and many of the papers, were bringing the bad news: they focused solemnly on exposing the participants to analysis, and cautioning us on difficult circumstances and painful histories. They resisted any moral or pastoral temptation to make it easier and to frame solutions. Indeed, it may be that the managerialist language of solutions was deliberately eschewed, as part of the problem. The focus on bad news did not depress; the attention to praxis in difficult contexts was realistic and informed. There began a process of absorption of meanings and development of practical responses, which Bauman refers to as translation:

> 'translation' is woven into the texture of daily life and practised daily and hourly by us all. We are all translators; translation is the common feature in all forms of life ... Translation is present in every communicative encounter, every dialogue ... In the matrix of possible meanings ... the multitude of potential permutations, associations and divisions is for all practical purposes infinite, and there is no necessity for those permutations to overlap in

the case of their various users; on the contrary, there is a high probability that such an overlapping will never occur.

(Bauman, 1999, p. 200)

Overlapping suggests that, once again, relationality emerges as a key theme. The central importance of relationality (Hay with Nye, 1998) as the locus of spiritual education means that the visibility of relationality can be used as a measurement of the effectiveness of systems, since:

> relationality ... refers, in different ways, to the idea that the spiritual health of the modern world can only be recaptured and sustained if we understand and prioritise the importance of relationships.
>
> (Erricker *et al.*, 2001, p. 3)

But, at the same time, the political, economic and social analysis of a divided and dangerous world remains a radical challenge to contemporary values and approaches to living in a divided society:

> there is a concern with notions of spiritual well-being at an individual, societal and global level. The characterization of spirituality that pervades the observations and analyses of the researchers included is open, inclusive and accepting of diversity. It is not exclusive and doctrinaire. There is a clear concern with political and economic issues related to globalisation and corporatism ... There is evidence of real attempts to engage with and listen to young people's experiences and converse with them. There are signs of hope and conviction, even dissent ... Above all, spiritual education is beginning to find a voice and language with which to address the modern world and its education systems ... Spiritual education, we may say, is beginning to offer a radical challenge to our contemporary values.
>
> (Erricker *et al.*, 2001, p. 3)

Through this series, we are challenged; and, in return, we begin to articulate our challenge to contextualized educational values and practices. As this work continues, we will need to pay more attention to how our inter-disciplinary discourse operates, how our celebration of the subjective gains recognition and how our notions of freedom and responsibility may be impacting on our praxis. This latter point is of importance: not only has a freedom *from* the old, but still abiding religious constraints on spiritual education formed a central theme of our work to date, but freedom of manoeuvre *in* education systems has also been a persistent motif. And now, as the world watches a deepening confrontation between the Western and the Muslim worlds, models of freedom are very much in dispute. If children's spirits are to be freed from consumerism and violence, *for what* are they to be freed? In a context that includes the absolute freedoms of the suicide bomber and the compulsive consumer—mutually exclusive, yet strangely inter-dependent, and always equally dangerous—how will the child's spiritual subjectivity be both free and responsible, and what will be its ontological purpose? Much of our discourse here implies a need for solutions that *limit* someone's freedom (the advertiser; the teacher) in order to protect spirituality. If we have a rationale for how this should be achieved, it is, at the moment, ethical and pragmatic, in need of further examination.

Connections between human rights, democratic values and spiritual education will be the central theme of the next conference in the series (in July 2006), in Winchester,

UK. Following on from this, we will embrace a continuing international dialogue in Australia in January 2008.

The place and voice of spiritual education is to signal hope and challenge to our lives, relationships and education systems. Spiritual education offers, at the very least, a way to keep asking the questions and confronting the ambiguous, dangerous divisions in which we and our children live. A larger hope will be that the language of spirituality succeeds further in penetrating education and care systems, policy-making and economic and cultural activity, without being absorbed or compromised.

The Religious Studies scholar Marghanita Laski (1980) analysed religious communities by dividing them into three categories: the servants, the served and the enemy (the counter-elite). If education and the nurture of the young were also a religion—and in some ways, they can be understood as such—we could then wonder into which category we might place ourselves at this moment in the history of our work and the history of the world; and why, and whether, we wish to change.

References

Bauman, Z. (1999) *In search of politics* (London, Polity Press).

Erricker, J., Ota, C. & Erricker, C. (2001) *Spiritual education: cultural, religious and social differences* (Brighton, Sussex Academic Press).

Hay, D. with Nye, R. (1998) *The spirit of the child* (London, Zondervan).

Laski, M. (1980) *Everyday ecstasy* (London, Thames & Hudson).

Index